THIS MODERN POETRY

Books By

BABETTE DEUTSCH

Poetry

BANNERS
HONEY OUT OF THE ROCK
FIRE FOR THE NIGHT
EPISTLE TO PROMETHEUS

Novels

A BRITTLE HEAVEN
IN SUCH A NIGHT
MASK OF SILENUS

Criticism

POTABLE GOLD:
AN ESSAY ON POETRY
AND THIS AGE

THIS MODERN POETRY

By Babette Deutsch

NEW YORK

W · W · NORTON & CO · INC.

KRAUS REPRINT CO.
New York
1969

ACKNOWLEDGMENTS

Thanks are due to the individual poets and their publishers for permission to reprint poems and parts of poems from the works listed below.

Al Que Quiere by William Carlos Williams, Bruce Humphries, Inc.; Chelsea Rooming-House by Horace Gregory, and Chorus for Survival by Horace Gregory, both published by Covici-Friede, Inc.; High Falcon by Léonie Adams, John Day Co., Inc.; Counter-Attack by Siegfried Sassoon and Picture-Show by Siegfried Sassoon, both published by E. P. Dutton & Co., Inc.; Poems by Kenneth Fearing, Dynamo; A Draft of XXX Cantos by Ezra Pound, and Eleven New Cantos by Ezra Pound, both published by Farrar & Rinehart, Inc.; Poems 1909-1925 by T. S. Eliot, No Retreat by Horace Gregory, Poems and Sonnets by Ernest Walsh, Smoke and Steel by Carl Sandburg, all published by Harcourt, Brace & Co., Inc.; Collected Poems of Robert Frost, Last Poems by A. E. Housman, Collected Poems of Walter de la Mare, 2 v., The Veil by Walter de la Mare, all published by Henry Holt & Co., Inc.; the selections from the writings of Archibald MacLeish (Poems: 1924-1933) are used by permission of, and by special arrangement with, Houghton Mifflin Co.; Chills and Fever by John Crowe Ransom, Harmonium by Wallace Stevens, and Collected Poems of Elinor Wylie, all published by Alfred A. Knopf, Inc.; Machinery by MacKnight Black, copyrt. 1929, Collected Poems of Hart Crane, copyrt. 1933, Collected Poems of H. D., copyrt. 1925, New Spoon River Anthology by Edgar Lee Masters, copyrt. 1924, Personae by Ezra Pound, copyrt. 1926, all copyrighted by Liveright Publishing Corporation; Collected Poems by Thomas Hardy, Collected Poems of Vachel Lindsay, Collected Poems of John Masefield, Spoon River Anthology by Edgar Lee Masters, Collected Poems of Edwin Arlington Robinson, A Winter Diary by Mark Van Doren, Collected Poems of W. B. Yeats, all by permission of The Macmillan Co., publishers; Mr. Pope and other poems by Allen Tate, Minton, Balch & Co.; Collected Poems 1921-1931 by William Carlos Williams, Objectivist Press; Poems by Gerard Manley Hopkins, Oxford University Press (courtesy of Gerard Hopkins); Ash Wednesday by T. S. Eliot, G. P. Putnam's Sons; Poems by W. H. Auden, Collected Poems of C. Day Lewis, Give Your Heart To The Hawks by Robinson Jeffers, Roan Stallion by Robinson Jeffers, and Poems by Stephen Spender, all by permission of Random House, New York; Now With His Love by John Peale Bishop, Charles Scribner's Sons, Inc.; Collected Poems by D. H. Lawrence, Last Poems by D. H. Lawrence, copyrt. 1933, and Poems by Wilfred Owen, all published by The Viking Press, Inc.

For special courtesies the author wishes to express her appreciation to the following poets: Léonie Adams, Kenneth Fearing, Horace Gregory, T. S. Eliot, A. E. Housman, Edgar Lee Masters, Siegfried Sassoon, Mark Van Doren, and William Carlos Williams, and to the following publishers: Henry Holt & Co., Inc.; Bruce Humphries, Inc.; Liveright Publishing Corporation; Objectivist Press; G. P. Putnam's Sons; Minton, Balch & Co., and W. W. Norton & Co., Inc.

This book contains a few passages from critical articles by the author which appeared originally in *Books* (New York Herald-Tribune), *The Survey Graphic,* and *The Virginia Quarterly Review,* as well as in her essay, Potable Gold: Some Notes on Poetry and This Age, W. W. Norton & Co., Inc.

6

TABLE OF CONTENTS

FOREWORD

MODERN POETRY addresses itself to the modern mind. To enjoy it fully, the reader needs more than acquaintance with the verse of the past or with the shifts in literary fashions. He must be acclimated to his time: to the ideas about the psyche, about the physical universe, about the social order, which that poetry breathes. He must be prepared to adopt an unaccustomed attitude in order to perceive unfamiliar forms. He must be willing to learn the language with which the poet creates awareness of a changed world.

This book is an effort to trace the development of the verse of the past two decades, to take some account of the forces which have shaped it, and so to suggest ways of understanding it. No one could be more acutely conscious than the author of the difficulties of the task and the inadequacy of the result. It is too early to place contemporary writers in historic perspective. Nor has it been possible to treat in any detail more than a few of the outstanding figures. Of these, some merit a more careful study than space permitted. Moreover, the personalities of those considered are so distinct, their private lives so dissimilar, the social and intellectual forces of their period have affected them so differently, the literary influences that have fed their work are so various, as to forbid satisfactory grouping. In trying to single out the main trends, there-

9

fore, certain poets have been examined from several standpoints. Thus, William Butler Yeats may be seen as an heir to the symbolists, as filiated with the metaphysical school, and again as a metaphysical in the larger sense—one constrained to answer the Great Questioner, one bravely shouldering "the burden of the mystery." Where a number of poets are writing on similar themes or employing similar techniques, it has seemed best to examine the performance of one or two representative men, to the neglect of equally competent, possibly of even abler, writers. A few nineteenth-century men no longer living, such as Gerard Manley Hopkins and Thomas Hardy, have been included in the discussion because their work is modern in temper and has had a bearing upon current verse. Some attention has been given to poets working in the tradition, whose performance has noticeably influenced their juniors. Certain traditionalists have been set apart for separate consideration, when their work illustrates particular tendencies. The emphasis has been upon Americans, chiefly because so many of the significant poets writing in English are Americans. The author holds no brief for current poetry as opposed to the poetry of the past. The value of poetry lies in elements apart from its contemporaneity. But a poet who has something to say, and who knows how to say it, is apt to speak the language of his own time. Neither man nor nature has changed profoundly since Chaucer's day: the company who traveled to Canterbury on horseback some five centuries ago could find their counterparts on any ocean liner or transcontinental train; the same stars shine on the same passions; flood and drought, earthquake, plague, and war undo the labor of generations of men. But the poet who shares Chaucer's interest in character is guided by theories concerning men's impulses and behavior that alter his approach. And if we have no one equal to Shakespeare, surely a modern Shakespeare would outdistance his great ancestor by as much as the mentality and the sensibility of the twentieth century are richer than the mentality and the sensibility of the sixteenth. It is insofar as the poetry of today

10

FOREWORD

differs from that of yesterday that it helps to give a new shape to the experience of tomorrow.

This is, then, not so much an attempt to evaluate the men of our own day: we are too near them to do that with any assurance—it is rather an effort to clarify their intentions, their methods, and their meaning. Poetry is important. No less than science, it seeks a hold upon reality, and the closeness of its approach is the test of its success. It has its roots in our savage past and so speaks to the oldest instincts of man. But also it communicates the experience of those whose imaginative faculty makes them the sensitive antennae of the race.

11

THIS MODERN POETRY

CHAPTER I

INTRODUCTORY: BACKGROUNDS AND FORERUNNERS

> For out of olde feldes, as men seith,
> Cometh al this newe corn for yeer to yere;
> And out of olde bokes, in good feith,
> Cometh al this newe science that men lere.
>
> *Chaucer.*

MODERN POETRY, like contemporary America, was fathered by a revolution and seems preparing to beget another. Whether or not this revolt of the younger generation means progress, in more senses than one it means revival. The tradition of English poetry runs back some five hundred years, and the more adventurous men today tend to imitate the performance of their remote forebears. History never repeats itself exactly, yet in verse, as elsewhere, the past is part of the future, and in every change of direction it is possible to detect a swing of the pendulum, back and forth, a perpetual action and reaction; so that one is reminded of those barometers—the delight of our childhood—in the shape of a little house with two doors: when it was wet the gentleman came out and the lady stayed in; when it was fine, the gentleman retired and the lady came out. So, as emotion came in, reason went out, and vice versa. So, as authority and discipline and elegance went out with classicism, willfulness and strangeness and wonder came in with romanticism. The shift, of course, is never so abrupt or

15

so simple, and is only clear from a distance which obliterates important distinctions.

The poet, though he may choose not to trim his sails to them, is more sensitive than most men to the way the winds of doctrine are blowing. So that poetry, which has been contemned as an enervating influence, an escape from the demands of practical life, a mere jingling of silver bells; dismissed as a civilized amusement; praised as an emotional release, and exalted as the finer breath and spirit of all knowledge, may also be conceived as an index to the genius of the age. Through its poets one may learn the language of the *Zeitgeist*, that no statistician speaks, and which finds only partial interpreters in the spatial art of painting and the temporal art of music.

Thus the verse of the eighteenth century, with its metallic shine, its clocklike regularity, its elegant simplicity, has rightly been regarded as reflecting the eighteenth-century notions of the universe as a mechanism, easily explained by the mathematicians and the astronomers, and running like a well-wound clock. Thus, at the close of the century, the revolutions in France and in America breaking down the established machinery of government, one finds the poets revolting against the mechanistic view of nature and writing about liberty, equality, and fraternity in free forms that are anathema to the conservatives. The romantics revolted against the tight, closed little scheme which flattered their predecessors with the belief that all was for the best in the best of all possible worlds. They rejoiced with Byron in "the eternal spirit of the chainless mind." They applauded the triumphant song of Shelley's Chorus of Spirits:

> We come from the mind
> Of human kind,
> Which was late so dusk, and obscene, and blind.
> Now 'tis an ocean
> Of clear emotion,
> A heaven of serene and mighty motion.

16

Introductory

They felt, with Wordsworth,

> a sense sublime
> Of something far more deeply interfused,
> Whose dwelling is the light of setting suns,
> And the round ocean and the living air,
> And the blue sky, and in the mind of man.

But towards the middle of the century there was a shift toward the mechanistic view again. This time it was not the physicists who were responsible for it, but the biologists, and, to some degree, the technologists. The machines which were to have liberated men from the curse of Adam and to have created a new heaven on a new earth had only succeeded in creating more machines and greater inequalities of wealth. The theory of the survival of the fittest had substituted for the mysterious workings of Providence a process which looked more like the survival of the survivors. Matthew Arnold was crying out with desperate anxiety against

> this strange disease of modern life,
> With its sick hurry, its divided aims,

while Tennyson, less troubled by the fever of an industrial civilization than by the Darwinian hypothesis, stretched "vain hands of faith," and groped, while

> Nature, red in tooth and claw
> With ravine, shriek'd against his creed.

Poets ceased to write rhapsodies glorifying an abstract Liberty. They began to attend more closely to the concrete realities of their world and to paint them in sharp lines and clear colors, or, disappointed and disgusted by what they saw, turned to the imaginary beauties of the chivalric age of Arthur and to a tapestried medievalism.

Meanwhile, in barbarous America, where the practical tasks of pioneering, a puritan distrust of the arts, a snobbish provincialism, and unfortunate copyright laws combined to crush

17

poetry, "a Bostonian" (so he signed his first book of lyrics), educated in Richmond, dying in Baltimore, had left a legacy of verse and critical theory which was to swell the capital fund of the French symbolists. Edgar Allen Poe has been called "a poet without a neighborhood." This not only helps to explain the private nature of his verse, but also why his influence had to travel to France, there to be absorbed by Baudelaire and transmitted to Mallarmé and Verlaine and Jules Laforgue, before, through the offices of T. S. Eliot, it began to affect the poetry of his own compatriots nearly seventy years after his death. What Poe sought was something very different from the concerns of the English poets of his time. He was not engaged in exact description, either of gallant knights riding down to Camelot in the bright blue weather, or of Bishop Blougram's soul as it unraveled itself over the nuts and wine. He did not share Tennyson's will-to-believe in

> one far-off divine event
> Toward which the whole Creation moves,

or Browning's faith that

> it is the glory and the good of Art
> That Art remains the one way possible
> Of speaking truth.

Poe defined poetry as "the rhythmical creation of Beauty," adding: "Unless incidentally, it has no concern whatever either with Duty or with Truth." Elsewhere, quoting Coleridge without acknowledging his source, he described it as "music, combined with a pleasurable idea." His own verse is lacking in ideas and calculated to afford pleasure of a singularly morbid nature, but his desire to suggest, by a stream of dissolving images and with a care for verbal melody, the poet's personal emotion, his subtle and transient states of mind, is significant for its relation to symbolist theory and practice. Not his dull *tours de force*, *The Raven* and *The Bells*, nor yet his by now exhausted lines *To Helen*, but such lyrical fantasias as *Israfel*,

18

and *The City By The Sea,* where Death has reared himself a throne, are the tokens of his power and its influence. Such lines as those on "the long night-time of that town," and the "light from out the lurid sea," that streams up the turrets and the spires,

> Up shadowy long-forgotten bowers
> Of sculptured ivy and stone flowers,
> Up many and many a marvellous shrine
> Where wreathèd friezes intertwine
> The viol, the violet, and the vine,

have a suggestiveness that is as much a part of their verbal texture as of the associations which cling to the words.

At the very period when Poe, ill in body and mind, was experiencing torments as exquisite as any that he ever imagined, another American poet was exploring himself and his country with unexampled vigor and enthusiasm. There are few contrasts in literary history as sharp as that between the melancholy subjectivity of Poe's melodic fantasias and the robustious efforts of Walt Whitman to identify himself as comprehensively as possible with his place, his time, and his people. He knew these States as it was given to few men to know them: the highways and byways, the bustling East, the placid South, the generous West. Himself an offshoot of old Dutch and English pioneer stock, with revolutionary memories (had not Lafayette kissed the cheek of the child in a pinafore?), and with faith in the solid virtues of the farmers and artisans from whom he sprang, he was physically strong enough to survive every evil but the moral and corporal suffering known at first hand during the Civil War, and he was spiritually strong enough to survive even that. In middle life, stricken with paralysis as a result of an infection received in an army hospital, left lonely by the death of his mother and by the defection of his friends, tricked out of his small savings by a Barabbas of a publisher, with apparently nothing to hope for, he could still write: "I am feeling decidedly better these last twenty-four hours. Guess

19

I shall come out in the spring with the frogs and the lilacs." It was out of this richness of vitality, and a breadth of experience which included both well-being and sickness, success and defeat, comradeship and isolation, peace, war, and the bleak period of reconstruction, as well as the city and the sea, the peaks and the plains—it was out of all this that he drew power to celebrate life with such ardor and inclusiveness, and in the end he consented to death as only those can who live fully.

Whitman was in every respect the contrary of Poe. Far from being "without a neighborhood," he had a strong feeling for America, for that *genius loci* which most major poets discover. Poe was a maladjusted orphan, unable to achieve a satisfactory relation with any of the women who attracted him. Whitman was a devoted son, a lover able to reconcile affection with liberty, and a proud if not too responsible father. Instead of delighting in whatever was aristocratic, private and exclusive, Whitman could not sufficiently exalt the democratic ideal that he had taken from Jefferson, along with other bequests of the French enlightenment. Instead of fearing and hating science, which Poe apostrophized as a "Vulture, whose wings are dull realities," he insisted that "the true use of the imaginative faculty of modern times is to give ultimate vivification to facts, to science, and to common lives," and in his *Song of Myself* he shouted:

Hurrah for positive science! long live exact demonstration!

Instead of regarding poetry as a means of communicating pleasure, and interesting himself in technical nuances, he looked upon it as having a function akin to religion, and made nature his supreme arbiter.

His delight in the divine average had the unfortunate effect of leading him to ignore those finer perceptions which are not open to the common man. His belief that the basic necessities of food, clothing, and shelter were available to every American, and "the morbid facts of American politics and society" that

20

he could not avoid seeing were but "passing incidents," blinded
him to the way in which a growing industrialism was aggran-
dizing the few at the expense of the many. For some time after
his death, however, it was still possible to accept the mixture
of romantic and evolutionary optimism which had fired him.
It was not alone the rise of a predatory group of industrialists
and investment bankers that came to discredit his cheerful faith
in American democracy. The War and the Russian Revolution
shook the eager young reformers who preached his gospel as
profoundly as the French Revolution and the Napoleonic Wars
had shaken the young romantics of a previous century. But this
reaction was not immediately registered in their work. Indeed,
it was not until long after the Armistice that the poets to any
degree found reason to question his advice to one of his most
devoted disciples: "Be radical—be radical, be not too damned
radical."

When Emily Dickinson was asked if she knew of Whitman,
she replied that she had not read his book, but had been told
that it was disgraceful. One fancies that, had she plunged into
it, she would have agreed with Gerard Manley Hopkins, the
Jesuit poet who found, to his distress, Whitman's mind nearer
to his own than that of any of his Victorian contemporaries.
Emily Dickinson pastured on Keats, the Brownings, Sir Thomas
Browne, and Revelations. She also mentions Ruskin, but his influence is happily missing from her verse. Her letters are as
revealing as her poems, which, like Hopkins's, often seem to be
letters, too:

> ... cries like dead letters sent
> To dearest him that lives alas! away.

In one written when she was a girl of sixteen she confided to
a friend that while she had perfect confidence in God and His
promises, she felt, she did not know why, that the world held
the predominant place in her affections. "Give me the world
if Thou wilt," goes the familiar plea, "but grant me an asylum
for my affections." The world afforded her, in fact, no asylum.

21

She lived a recluse, companioned by the single hound of her own identity. But she joined a rich delight in the things of the senses to spiritual insight, and this, equally with her quick intelligence and ironic wit, made her at once kindred to the moderns and the natural heir of the metaphysicals of the seventeenth century. These lyricists, most happily represented by John Donne, had been sharply aware of the complexity of their environment and had possessed the peculiar faculty of analyzing their passions and feeling their ideas. They had reacted to experience as she did, with the whole soul, with body and intellect at once.

Her poetry abounds in vivid expressions of physical pressure, physical energy. She had, too, a feeling for tone-color which allowed her to convey sensations by means of sound, although her capacity for loading words with meaning is more remarkable than her sense of verbal texture. Moreover, she was no stranger to the commonplaces of law and banking, and was as ready to use their terminology and to draw her imagery from their processes as Donne had been to make the business and the science of his time do duty in the metaphor of a theological poem. Not the least index to the modern sensibility of this nineteenth-century New England spinster was the fact that she was as quick to perceive the beauty of a locomotive as that of a butterfly, and to communicate her feeling for it. In this, as in her responses to the details of her outwardly ordinary existence, she resembled Whitman. But she differed from him in two important particulars.

Her devotion to that proud rigorous man, her father, was so extreme, and his attitude toward her so possessive—a fact which must have excited her admiration of Elizabeth Barrett Browning—as to exclude her from the greatest satisfactions that a woman of her time and circumstances could expect. She was a bride, she was a wife, in spirit, never in fact. And her shyness, fostered by the stupidity of her cleverest intimates, made it impossible for her to say with Yeats, when she had come close on forty-nine, that she had no child, she had nothing but—she had, at least, a book. This meagerness of experience, for however deep ran the current of her spiritual life, her work shows definitely the limitations of her world, creates a gulf between her and Whitman. What further separates these two is that while he was perpetually celebrating the "average identity," Emily Dickinson never ceased to ask herself, as she asked a friend in an early letter, what it is that makes a few people (she included herself and her correspondent) so different from others. He delighted in the universal, she in the unique. He was the poet of the general, she of the particular, the rare. He relished variety, she valued distinction.

It is not until the close of the first quarter of the twentieth century that one finds the influences of these two poets fusing in the work of another American: Hart Crane. Significantly enough, Poe was also tributary to this stream, for Crane not only addresses Poe as an intimate, but uses the technique of Rimbaud, himself a student of Poe and a devotee of Poe's French admirer and translator, Charles Baudelaire.

One of the distinguishing elements in contemporary verse is the eclecticism that Crane exhibits. The modern poet moves from the style of one period or of one predecessor to that of another with unexampled freedom. The Elizabethan merchant adventurer knew triumphs that the explorer to-day, with his expert knowledge and technological resources, cannot equal. The Elizabethan poet, to whom the language was a relatively untried instrument, made discoveries that we cannot match. But the modern poet, like the modern traveler, if he does not conquer a new world, explores a known one more thoroughly and rapidly than ever before. The interest of current work is to no small degree the result of this easy purchase of materials once violently struggled for or laboriously achieved, this free passage from one region to another. It is not merely that if Shakespeare could not turn Pope's practice to his own uses, Pope might translate Shakespeare into eighteenth-century verse, while the modern can draw upon both. He can also cross frontiers and continents to find new means of communicating his experience. The points of reference for modern poetry lie not alone in England and America, with their debt to Greece and Rome, but in France as well, and to some extent in China and Japan.

In technical matters the pendulum swing of taste cannot, of course, be ignored. In a period when gardens were combed and pruned and clipped to look like elegant drawing-rooms, when ladies' head-dresses were made to look like formal gardens, poetry, too, was put into corsets and laced until it could scarcely breathe. Men wrote verses in which the rhythm of the words as spoken was identical with the metrical stresses. One gentleman felt so outraged by the freedom of Shakespeare's handling of iambic pentameter in Hamlet's soliloquy that he rewrote it thus:

> My anxious soul is tore with doubtful strife,
> And hangs suspended betwixt death and life;
> Life! Death! dread objects of mankind's debate;
> Whether superior to the shocks of Fate,
> To bear its fiercest ills with steadfast mind,
> To nature's order piously resigned,
> Or with magnanimous and brave disdain,
> Return her back th' injurious gift again.

It was in rebellion against such dull conformity that Wordsworth began to question the use of metre at all. It was in rebellion against the elaborations of metrical verse from Wordsworth's day to Swinburne's that the vers librists introduced the notion of cadence, building their verse on the musical phrase instead of on regularly stressed, precisely numbered syllables. And it was in disgust with the tedious repetition of speech cadences in this loosened form that the moderns eventually returned to the strictly patterned stanza, with its neat end-rhymes and its pleasing contrast between the exact beat of the underlying metre and the rhythm of natural utterance. The contemporary has inherited the legacy of these several techniques, along with the grindstones of critical theory suitable for the sharpening of his different tools. To an understanding of quantitative verse, as exemplified by the ancients, of metrical verse as exemplified by the English poets from Chaucer on, of free verse, as exemplified variously by Coverdale, Blake, and Whitman, to mention only the honorable dead, he has added an appreciation of the discipline and the freedom of "sprung rhythm": the practice of Langland, of Mother Goose, of Skelton, and of Hopkins.

In any good poem the diction, like the rhythm, is inseparable from the subject-matter, and even where the poet is writing on a theme as old as love or death, he will be affected by the speech that is current on the streets through which he walks, at the shop or office where he works, and in the rooms in which he meets his friends. Wordsworth held that the common language of common men was best suited to express the passions which find vent in poetry. Coleridge pointed out that Wordsworth's best work failed to illustrate his theory. The contemporary, agreeing with Wordsworth that rhetoric is a bad thing, agrees with Flaubert that exact speech is a good thing, and seeks to effect a compromise between simplicity and precision. He realizes, too, that the vocabulary suitable to an eighteenth-century peasant is useless for expressing the sensibility of a twentieth-century intellectual.

The quarrel of the public with the modern poet is very different from the quarrel Wordsworth's public had with him. Where they condemned the bard for using vulgar diction, even the sympathetic audience to-day finds its poets too idiosyncratic, and declaring that it cannot follow their flights into the intense inane, exalts, as audiences have ever done, the comprehensible lyricists of yesteryear. No charge is so frequently brought against current verse as its obscurity. Even those poets not moving, as many do, in the privacy of a dream-world, and using language governed by emotional rather than logical sequence, offer problems not readily solved. Sometimes it is a matter of vocabulary, sometimes of sentence structure, often of both.

It is perhaps inevitable that the vocabulary of the modern poet should need elucidation. With the increasing specialization of knowledge, he is apt to use the idiom of his special field of interest: astronomy, scholasticism, geology, physics—an idiom which an audience unfamiliar with it may regard as mere pedantry. If he uses words not only for their symbolical connotations, but for the multiple meanings provided by the pun, he erects so many more hurdles for the reader to leap. Before education became popular, the poet wrote for his intellectual equals. Today, aware that the circle of those who will understand all his references is limited, he is apt to offend the general by addressing his peers in the key-phrases, the elliptical diction that we all use in commerce with our intimates, and of salting his verse with private jokes. His readiness to try every rhythmic invention is matched by his interest in all the resources of language, including specific jargons and dialects, and neologisms of his own making.

The poets who initiated the renaissance which dates roughly from 1914 were not so difficult. The anemia from which English verse had been suffering for years was cured by a blood-transfusion from the veins of the common people, so that it was no great wonder that the regenerated art delighted the common reader. At long last there was an answer to Whitman's summons:

Poets to come! orators, singers, musicians to come!
Not to-day is to justify me and answer what I am for,
But you, a new brood, native, athletic, continental, greater
    than before known,
Arouse! for you must justify me...

I am a man who, sauntering along without fully stopping, turns
    a casual look upon you and then averts his face,
Leaving it to you to prove and define it,
Expecting the main things from you.

This new and native brood had further stimulus from the straightforward verse narratives of John Masefield and his precursors, Kipling and Hardy. But the poetry of the Americans had an indigenous flavor which made it fresher than the somewhat literary naturalism of Masefield, and their work satisfied the public as much because of the homeliness of its diction as because of the commonplaceness of its subject-matter.

The period from this revival to the present saw at least three phases of apprehension and expression, while to-day one finds yet another outlook shaping the poet's world. The lines cannot, of course, be too sharply drawn. There is always a residue of attitudes inherited from the past, and the authority of a few powerful men lingers beyond the time of their apogee. But though the traveler may have no reason to observe that he has crossed a frontier, he may nevertheless find pleasure and convenience in a map, and so, as we survey briefly the poetry of the last two decades, we may draw certain boundary lines and note certain distinctions.

The men who excited an interest in poetry just before the War shared Wordsworth's interest in the run-of-the-mill experiences of ordinary men and women. Their first concern was not manner, but matter, and while they introduced the jargon of the street, the shop, and the shanty into their verse, they were readier to accept customary forms, such as blank verse, or the familiar rhymed stanza, than to adopt the free rhythms of common speech.

During the War and immediately after it the poets ceased to examine the local scene with an objective eye and turned with renewed concern and unexampled acuity to the world within. Their forefather was Browning, with his passion for psychological speculation, and his packed conversational style, but they were even more nearly related to the metaphysicals. New developments in psychology and philosophy were compelling them to search their inner selves in a fashion more sympathetic to the sensibility of a Poe, a Baudelaire, and a Donne than to that of a Wordsworth or a Whitman. The psycho-analyst's novel version of original sin and predestination shocked and pained men as the Darwinian hypothesis had shocked and pained their grandfathers, and fascinated them

27

as the psychological doctrines current in his day had fascinated and stimulated Coleridge. This emphasis on the nature and power of the subconscious, together with Bergson's theory of the *élan vital,* and more particularly his idea of duration, of the past persisting in the present, of the irresistible, irreversible stream of memories which form the substance of life, gave men a different picture of themselves than that which had formerly satisfied them.

The fact that the moderns employed the symbolists' method was perhaps due no less to the influence of Bergson and Freud than to a growing interest in the technical experiments of the French, and was a further index to their alliance with the metaphysical school. However vague a poet's stream of thought may be, he has to be thinking about something. However bound up with his private experiences his emotion may be, it will be aroused—unless he lives in a madman's universe—by something outside himself. The things on which the thoughts and feelings of the moderns centered were part and parcel of their irrational, unstable universe. They were living in a war-torn world, in a society disorganized by abuse of the machine, and disturbed by intellectual revolutions in physics and psychology no less terrifying because they were half understood. The desperate—and the poets despaired—not finding refuge in fantasy, must shell the enemy with a play of blinding irony. With the economic framework toppling, with religious sanctions fallen away and science not yet happy in supplanting them, the poet had not merely to respond to and interpret his world, he had practically to create it. The symbolists had telescoped images to convey the rapid passage of sensations and emotions. The metaphysicals had played in a like fashion with ideas. Both delighted in paradox. The cinema, and ultimately the radio, made such telescopy congenial to the modern poet, as the grotesqueness of his environment made paradox inevitable for him.

The disruptions of the War and its aftermath delayed the reaction against poetry which smelled of the wasteland. The exploration of the deserts and underground caverns of the psyche had helped to prepare the way for the violent irrationalism of the Dadaists and the revolutionary abandon of the surréalistes. The poets writing in English did not go to the lengths of their French confrères, but they were not without sympathy for an extremism they could not fully imitate. Only by distorting language, by wrenching diction out of its customary procedures, by collapsing one absurd fantasy, one monstrous image into another, was it possible to hold the mirror up to the comic nightmare in which they were living. But eventually reason protested against her long exile, and the classicism that at least one pre-War critic had preached and more than one post-War poet had made a pretense of practicing appears now to be gradually re-asserting itself. Even those who are not up in arms against the time-minded romantics are inclined to agree that

> These times require a tongue that naked goes,
> Without more fuss than Dryden's or Defoe's.

It is true that the younger generation, the group which has succeeded the poets of the post-War period, speaks with a good deal more fuss than Dryden or Defoe. As one of their number has pointed out, these young men, for all their revulsion from the cynicism and defeatism of their immediate predecessors, have not entirely abandoned their methods. Influenced, if only at second-hand, by the War psychology and by the philosophies current during the War, with their emphasis on emotion and the subconscious, aware of the limited audience to which an intelligent man can safely appeal, finding satire the natural weapon against a world hostile to their dream of the great society, they speak to their intimates in the private language of friends and lovers. But they do this from necessity rather than choice, and they take the view of their beloved master, Gerard Manley Hopkins, that, with a little patience, they will be understood by a gradually growing public.

29

They differ from their seniors in being more aggressive because they are more hopeful. Where the men of twenty years ago were primarily concerned with subject-matter or technique, and the men of ten years ago with the problem of how to find words for a world that had ceased to have a meaning, the younger group to-day takes the immediate scene for granted, and uses as many tools as convenient to carve out an image of its desire. The question they ask is not what they shall write about, or how, but to what end. They share the post-War poets' disgust for institutionalized religion and for a facile idealism; they recognize, too, that rationalization often goes disguised as reason; but they go armed with faith in the mind of man and in the greatness of the human spirit.

They do resemble Dryden in the gaiety of their satire, if not in the simplicity of their diction, and concerning their kinship with him, they might, with some qualifications, quote his own lines:

> For sure our souls were near allied, and thine
> Cast in the same poetic mold as mine.
> One common note on either lyre did strike,
> And knaves and fools we both abhorr'd alike.

But the object of their abhorrence is not so much the fool and the knave as a system which empowers knavery and folly, and in this respect they are close to a poet of quite a different temper. Their certainty that this iron age will provide metal from which a new social order may be cast echoes Shelley's assurance that

> The world's great age begins anew,
>   The golden years return . . .

> Another Athens shall arise,
>   And to remoter time
> Bequeathe, like sunset to the skies,
>   The splendour of its prime;
> And leave, if naught so bright may live,
> All earth can take or Heaven can give.

30

They are more sharply aware than Shelley of the agony and
waste that is inevitable before such a happy consummation can
be even roughly approximated, and their obscurity—so different from his—is not a little due to the fact that they are as
quick to recognize and to quarrel with the enemy in their own
breasts as with the forces of evil in their environment. They
are as savage as another revolutionary visionary who wrote:
"Drive your cart and your plow over the bones of the dead."
Their favorite "ancestor," however, is Hopkins, from whom
they have taken some technical devices, such as assonance and
alliteration, therewith tapping an old and neglected vein of
English verse, but whom they prize no less as a man than as a
technician. Hopkins responded hotly to Whitman's pantheistic
sensuousness even while he feared it, and he shared Emily
Dickinson's feeling for individuality, though he was ignorant
of her expression of it. Perhaps the young moderns love him
most, however, because this mid-Victorian religious was, as he
confessed, "in a manner a Communist," convinced that communism offered the noblest—the only just—secular ideal. The
letter in which he says this contains a passage expressive of the
attitude which animates some of the most notable contemporary
work. "... it is a dreadful thing for the greatest and most
necessary part of a very rich nation to live a hard life without
dignity, knowledge, comforts, delight, or hopes in the midst
of plenty—which plenty they make. They profess they do not
care what they wreck or burn, the old civilization and order
must be destroyed. This is a dreadful look out but what has
the old civilization done for them? As it at present stands in
England it is itself in great measure founded on wrecking. But
they got none of the spoils, they came in for nothing but harm
from it then and thereafter. England has grown hugely wealthy
but this wealth has not reached the working classes; I expect
it has made their condition worse. Besides this iniquitous order
the old civilization embodies another order, mostly old, and
what is new in direct entail from the old, the old religion,
learning, law, art, etc and all the history that is preserved

in standing monuments. But as the working classes have not been educated they know next to nothing of all this and cannot be expected to care if they destroy it. The more I look the more black and deservedly black the future looks . . ."

Those young men who draw upon Hopkins and Shelley, upon Blake, and to ever so slight a degree upon Langland, look backward only to turn and face the future with a steadier gaze. There are, among the moderns as among their predecessors, a few whose power and integrity allows them to stand alone, making every influence tributary to the force of their peculiar genius. Of these unique personalities, William Butler Yeats is the unaging, the outstanding example. But aside from such an isolated instance, and in spite of the special gifts which characterize each individual, one may find in the work of the period under review certain general trends which are not without interest. There is observable a shift from realism to symbolism, from concern with the outer world to concern with the inner, from interest in matter to interest in manner, and, after a period of technical triumphs and spiritual disaster, a recrudescence of energy and conviction creating a different kind of verse. Like the best of the old, it is fed by subterranean springs though it flows into strange channels. The purpose of the pages which follow is to examine these changes in more detail, in the hope of showing not only how modern poetry differs from the poetry of the past, but in what ways the contemporary expresses every poet's delight in all that the senses offer and all that the spirit promises.

CHAPTER II

RETURNING TO REALISM

I have a commonplace book for facts and another for poetry, but I find it difficult always to preserve the vague distinction which I had in mind, for the most interesting and beautiful facts are so much the more poetry and that is their success . . . I see that if my facts were sufficiently vital and significant—perhaps transmuted more into the substance of the human mind—I should need but one book of poetry to contain them all.

Thoreau.

THE REBIRTH of poetry some twenty years ago was due both to the poets' keener awareness of themselves in the setting of their own time, and to a new insight into the past. Like a greater renaissance, it naturally did not mean a complete break with the previous age, but a fresh impulse, which was felt even by those whose work was essentially traditional. Already in the early nineties a young Irishman, writing on Irish letters for a Boston paper, was describing the typical poet of his day as "an Alastor tired of his woods and longing for beer and skittles." By 1914 this hunger was no longer so pressing, so that the same man, recalling the struggle of the writers of his youth, and their effort to rid their work of every artificiality, could complain humorously: "We rebelled against rhetoric, and now there is a group of younger men who dare to call us rhetorical."

Looking back upon the poetry of this period, one recognizes that it startled the public not because it was new, but because it was of a kind that had grown unfamiliar. Those whose work was hailed as the signal of a renaissance were merely trying to bring their art back to its source. Not a few of them were irritated, as Wordsworth had been irritated more than a century earlier, by what he called "the gaudiness and inane phraseology of many modern writers"—a gaudiness, an inanity which defeated the poet's purpose. They were largely sympathetic with what he had proposed to do in his preface to the *Lyrical Ballads:* to relate, in the language commonly used by men, the events of common experience. The history of poetry is marked by such recurrent revolutions, led by men whose feeling for words is acute and profound, against the use of a vocabulary which is too literary to give a sense of life. Shakespeare was a revolutionary of this stripe:

> Taffeta phrases, silken terms precise,
>   Three-piled hyperboles, spruce affectation,
> Figures pedantical; these summer flies
>   Have blown me full of maggot ostentation:
> I do foreswear them; and I here protest,
>   By this white glove—how white the hand, God knows!—
> Henceforth my wooing mind shall be express'd
>   In russet yeas, and honest kersey noes.

The speech of Biron in which the playwright thus mocks his own early manner might have served these moderns as a motto.

The impulse toward this honest kersey style seems to have come from Ireland, where it was fostered by an increasingly fierce nationalism. John Millington Synge, although best known as a dramatist, was among the first to indicate the direction which poetry was to take. In the preface to his one thin book of lyrics, almost half of which is given over to racy translations, he showed what was wrong with most of the verse then current. He set the poetry of exaltation above any other, "but when men lose their poetic feeling for ordinary life, and cannot write poetry of ordinary things," he said, "their exalted poetry is likely to lose its strength . . ." He insisted that poetry needed the strong things of life, to prove that what is noble or tender is not the product of weakness, and he added that "before verse can be human again it must learn to be brutal." These words, written in December, 1908, borne out to some degree by Synge's slight output and by the work of his compatriots and contemporaries, were largely prophetic. Synge wrote with a terrible simplicity of his own broken life; Padraic Colum was sensitively setting down the commonplaces of suffering endured and small pleasures relished by the Irish peasantry in their smoky cabins and on their boggy roads; and Yeats, though scarcely the poet of ordinary things, was soon to turn from the proud high-flown style of his first poems to the proud severe style of his middle period and to recall in his own verse, as sharply as James Stephens in his translations, the savagery of Raftery. These men set the tone, but it remained for John Masefield to produce a narrative poem abounding in brutality, and withal emulous of tenderness and exaltation, *The Everlasting Mercy*, and its companion piece, *The Widow in the Bye Street*.

Both poems deal with the crasser aspects of life, both are realistic not only in their frank recital of unpleasant facts but also in their freedom from any moral lesson. The everlasting mercy is extended to Saul Kane, drunkard, bruiser, fornicator, through no virtue of his. The widow lives to see her son hanged for murder—" 'Crime passionel' in Agricultural Districts," the lawyers list it—to have her heart broken, through no fault of hers. Although these poetic narratives are inept and sentimental in their lyrical passages, the dialogue is a candid presentation of the language of the prize-ring and the public house. The drunken hired man's threat to the farmer in the famous couplet:

> "I'll bloody him a bloody fix,
> I'll bloody burn his bloody ricks,"

35

is a use of common language in a common situation which
would have lifted the hair from Wordsworth's head in horror,
but which would also have assured him that poets were beginning to have the courage of his convictions.

It is noteworthy that the young Masefield knew Synge, that
he read Kipling's soldier songs with pleasure, and that his
great admiration among the traditional English poets was
Chaucer. All of these influences worked in him to stimulate an
interest in character-drawing and that care for liveliness and
exactness in description which he professes to be his chief
ends. He was impatient of technical perfection. He wanted to
write the sort of verse which would appeal not to a small group
of comfortably-situated connoisseurs, but to the general, and
he felt that this could best be accomplished by poets who,
violent and crude though they might seem, cared more for life
than for artifice. In the prefatory remarks to his collected
poems he observes, somewhat wistfully, of himself and his
fellows: "however harshly the next school may treat them,
that school must be a little livelier for their efforts." Not for
nothing do the words "lively" and "harsh" recur in the two
short pages of this introduction. To look at life closely, as
Masefield tried to do in the beginning, was to see it as harsh—
for the large majority of mankind squalid in its circumstances,
cruel in its processes, meaningless in its conclusion. Let others,
he roundly asserted, sing

> of the wine and the wealth and the mirth,
> The portly presence of potentates goodly in girth;—
> Mine be the dirt and the dross, the dust and scum of the
> earth!

There is some food for irony in the fact that the man who was
to become laureate of England should have opened his career
with a poem consecrating his songs not to the ruler, not to the
be-medaled commander, but to "the men with the broken heads
and the blood running into their eyes." If he has achieved a
place not generally accorded those who choose such unsavory

subjects, it is because for all his knowledge of and sympathy with the common man, his attitude from the first was not one of rebellion but of simple tenderness and pity. He has been as uncritical of the established political order as he has of the traditional forms in poetry. There are some biting lines in *The Everlasting Mercy* in which Saul Kane tells the parson that he is teaching his flock that the greed of the squire is the law of God, and berates him in terms which recall the irreverence of I. W. W. balladry. But the poet seems to agree with the parson's quiet reply to the effect that Rome wasn't built in a day, and that whatever is, since it seems to work, is better than something new, however fine, which might not.

It remains for poets with keener eyes and ears, quicker minds, wilder blood, to write the short and ugly annals of the poor in a more thoroughly realistic fashion. But within his limitations Masefield did what he could to make his readers enter more fully into the daily life of the sailor, the agricultural laborer, the village seamstress. It meant noting such concrete details as the "stink of bad cigars and heavy drink" in the public house, "the fag-ends, spit and saw-dust" on the floor, the "filthy hut . . . without a drain" where mangy chickens with sore necks search the room for crumbs, the gale at sea in which the sails are "whirled like dirty birds." It meant dealing with raw lust, savage stupidity, brutish work, futile deaths.

The naturalism which had informed the novels of the latter half of the nineteenth century was thus beginning to find tardy expression in the verse of the twentieth. The poets were asking, as the Goncourt brothers had asked themselves half a hundred years earlier, whether, in a democratic age, there were people too mean, misfortunes too low, dramas too foul-mouthed, terrors too ignoble to find a place in literature. They were no longer unnerved by our industrial civilization and aghast at the theory of the survival of the fittest. This later generation of poets, to whom neither the factory system nor the Darwinian hypothesis was news, could attend more closely to current realities and, free of panic, if not of disgust, describe them in clear, sharp, homely words.

There were plenty of precedents in English verse for such candor and objectivity. The tavern scene in *Piers Plowman*, with butcher and cobbler, tinker and fiddler, priest and rat-catcher, drinking, singing, bargaining, quarreling, and drinking again, is just such a plainly phrased picture of plain folk as Masefield delighted to paint. Sir Glutton, dim-eyed, staggering back and forth like a blind gleeman's bitch, stumbles on the threshold, and Clement the cobbler catches him by the middle—

> But Glutton, that great churl, was grievous to lift,
> And coughed up a caudle in Clement's lap;
> So hungry no hound is in Hertfordshire lane
> As would lap up the leavings, unlovely of scent.
>
> With all woe in the world his wife and his wench
> Bore him home to his bed, and brought him therein.
> And after this surfeit he slept in his sloth,
> All Saturday and Sunday, till sunset had come.
> Then woke he in wonder, and wiped both his eyes;
> The word he first uttered was—"Where is the bowl?"

Chaucer, whether he spoke through the mouth of the jolly Wife of Bath or told dirty stories with the summoner, or in his own person wrote pointed lines to his purse, was given to forthright speech on such events as do not transpire in any ivory tower. The *Canterbury Tales* abound not only in an antique and healthy coarseness, but in such precise descriptions of ordinary things as this, of the miller's nose:

> Up-on the cop right of his nose he hade
> A werte, and ther-on stood a tuft of heres
> Reed as the bristles of a sowes eres;
> His nose-thirles blake were and wyde.

That wart with its bristling red hairs and those wide black nostrils bring the man before us as the "aungellyk natyf beautee" of Cressida cannot quite bring her. In an age nearer our own, George Crabbe wrote of the parish workhouse, an ugly commonplace of the eighteenth century, in simple words which made a poet feel, two hundred years later, that "his hard human pulse is throbbing still"; and Burns could sing with equal verve of a rural drinking-bout or a venturesome louse. Browning is generally considered to have held the happy conviction of his Pippa that all's right with the world, but he painted many portraits of men and women for whom all was wrong. His poem on the Paris morgue, for all the brash optimism of its close, contains as objective and straightforward a statement as any realist could ask:

> Money gets women, cards and dice
> Get money, and ill-luck gets just
> The copper couch and one clear nice
> Cool squirt of water o'er your bust,
> The right thing to extinguish lust!

The moralizing and sentimentalizing verse of the mid-century, the nostalgic Satanism cultivated by the men of the nineties who rebelled against the stodgier Victorians, and the productions of a locust-swarm of academic mediocrities, had combined to make people forget this way of writing, so that a return to it came with all the force of a fresh attack.

Curiously enough, it was a group of Americans who made this kind of poetry popular, although Masefield, like Kipling and Hardy before him, wrote about ordinary things with a frankness that approached brutality, and Wilfrid Wilson Gibson's verse, for all its mawkishness, showed a clear vein of realism. Carl Sandburg, Nicholas Vachel Lindsay, Robert Frost, Edgar Lee Masters, even *la Byron de nos jours*, Edna Millay, then a mere girl, were exploring the native scene and observing their near neighbors with objectivity and candor. They found their subject-matter not in a romanticized past, but in the harsh exciting present: the farms and the slums, the factory-hand and the hobo, the shop-girl and the boarding-

39

house keeper—here was material to displace the isles of Greece and Helen's tiresome classic lineaments. They captured the attention of a wider public than poets had enjoyed for generations by the close view and the plain statement of the commonplace. How difficult such a task is one may discover from the failures of genius to accomplish it. Wordsworth tried repeatedly to obey his own dictates, to write simply of usual matters, and too often he merely wrote dully, sentimentally, or with unconscious humor, of trivialities. Whitman was continually celebrating the ordinary, the everyday, "the divine average." And though sometimes the poem was a superb evocation of the glory that lurks in the commonplace, repeatedly Whitman only drew up an inventory of things which he failed to turn to the uses of poetry. The response to these later comers was not entirely, however, a tribute to their excellence, which was sometimes questionable. It was also an index to the public's eagerness for a more democratic, intelligible kind of poetry, not art for sentiment's sake, nor yet art for art's sake, but an exploring of the immediate scene that would represent art for life's sake.

Perhaps because such British poets as Hardy, Kipling, and Masefield had paved the way, perhaps because these States had not yet shaken off their provincialism, the welcome was first extended from England. It came to Robert Frost with the publication of his first thin book of lyrics, *A Boy's Will.* It is strange to remember the warm reception accorded this book, for it is not lacking in easy rhetoric and weak echoes. But it showed, if tentatively, the road Frost would take, in a sober couplet here, a sharp phrase there, in a few isolated lyrics like *The Tuft of Flowers, Now Close the Windows,* and always in the slight elucidating line that accompanied the poem's title. The voluntary self-dependence, the devotion to nature, especially in her more domestic aspects, the care for clarity and simplicity, the not unfriendly reticence, grow more apparent in his later verse, and all of these qualities work together to make Frost the honest, homely poet that he is. It may be that he was

40

readily accepted because he dealt with the rural rather than the urban scene, but his view of it was fresh in being as disillusioned as Crabbe's, as sincere as John Clare's.

The author of *North of Boston* did not become acquainted with that part of the country until he was ten years old: he was born in California. But eight generations of his family had lived in New England, and it seems as if, when the Frosts moved back to their native soil, the boy felt the journey to be a homecoming. Much of his poetry is expressive of the sights and sounds and smells, the way of looking at life, that we accept as the rural New Englander's experience, the rural New Englander's viewpoint. The people he writes about are generally of New England stock, folk who cultivate their rocky acres with stubborn courage, and bear, until they break, the drudgery and isolation of their lot. His subjects are the commonplaces of the countryside: a runaway colt, the sleep of an old man alone in an old farmhouse, the cleaning of the pasture spring. His speech is simple, colloquial, frugal. Frost never uses a rich word where a plain one will do, and it is these laconic, seemingly casual phrases which his first audience found more precious than any piling up of poetic ornament. He has inadvertently described his own verse in a passage from an early lyric where he says of a reticent woodland creature,

> The bird would cease and be as other birds
> But that he knows in singing not to sing,

and again in a more recent poem about a maker of ax-helves:

> Baptiste knew how to make a short job long
> For love of it, and yet not waste time either.

In speaking of the places and people which have touched his imagination, Frost shows the lingering tenderness of Baptiste, together with his workmanlike character.

Possibly because during the greater part of his life Frost has made his living from the soil, he has the farmer's taciturn habit

41

and shrewd dispassionate outlook. In one of his early poems he writes: "The fact is the sweetest dream that labor knows." Was not this Thoreau's thought, too? When "a New York alec" insists that the poet choose between being "a prude, or puke," he tries to get out of the dilemma as that more solemn hermit might, by declaring: "Me for the hills where I don't have to choose," but being cornered, he admits: "I wouldn't be a prude afraid of nature." He never ceases to feel that the central fact in nature for himself and his kind is human nature, and although he is fond of observing such impersonal things as storms and stars, he relates his observations to some insight into humanity. Mankind has consecrated the earth for him, both as a poet and as a tiller of the soil:

> Nothing not built with hands of course is sacred.

Mending Wall, which opposes the farmer who feels that good fences make good neighbors, to his neighbor, who doesn't love a wall, is a famous example of the transmutation of a fact into the substance of the human mind. That central fact is simple enough, yet the poet manages, in bare concrete language, with a few images, and an insistence on the plain heap of separating stones, to suggest fundamental human differences in viewing eternal things. As the one farmer works with the other, and sees him grasp a stone in either hand "like an old-stone savage armed," the object takes on the character of a symbol without losing its physical actuality. Frost has a kinship with the recluse of Walden, in spite of his keener interest in the human drama: the vested interest of a man who has accepted the customary social pattern. He shares Thoreau's knowledge of the bases of existence which the city dweller can ignore, Thoreau's loverly patience with and delight in the natural scene.

The poet's senses are awake, not to the imagined delights of silken Samarcand and cedar'd Lebanon, but to the seasonal commonplaces of rural experience: the lumps, "like uncut jewels, dull and rough," of the scented spruce gum which

comes to market golden-brown;
But turns to pink between the teeth;

the dry brook

That shouted in the mist a month ago
Like ghost of sleigh-bells in a ghost of snow,

though, June being gone,

Its bed is left a faded paper sheet
Of dead leaves stuck together by the heat—
A brook to none but who remember long.

His poetry dwells not only on the fact seen with the eyes and heard with the ears which any alert passerby might record, but on the fact registered in the workers' nerves and muscles. After apple-picking, his

instep-arch not only keeps the ache
It keeps the pressure of a ladder round.

And in the midst of his labors, with the gentleness Burns showed for a frightened field-mouse, a daisy cut down by the plow, he pauses to care for a nest exposed by the cutter bar, to enjoy a tuft of flowers which another mower has allowed to stand. He has not Burns's tunefulness, and lacking the homely idiom and the delicate word-endings of the Scots tongue, he cannot make as tender a song. But, though he is given to aphorisms, he is less inclined to make a mouse's panic the occasion for moralizing on the best-laid schemes of men. There is humor as well as lovely intimacy in his dialogue between man and wife, spoken amid the bang and clatter of moving-men in the dark clutter of the farm-house where they are belatedly taking up a new life, as in the poem about the hired man who has come "home" to die. The two definitions with which the farm couple meet the return of the shiftless incompetent are as casual as they are final. The one:

"Home is the place where, when you have to go there,
They have to take you in."

The other:

"I should have called it
Something you somehow haven't to deserve."

In the many instances where he allows some rural figure
to speak for himself, Frost uses the language of common
speech with a complete freedom from the self-consciousness
which spoiled most of Wordsworth's experiments in genre
poetry. With the dramatist's faithfulness to the diction of his
characters, he conveys the tragedy of the woman who must see
her baby's grave every time she looks out of the farm-house
window; of the kitchen drudge whose mad uncle was housed
in a home-made cage in the barn, and who feels his fate
creeping toward her; of the man who, while he tills his thin
acres, watches his wife sicken of loneliness until her mind
goes—tragedies enacted amidst the heavy routine of caring for
crops and animals, instead of with the pomp and circumstance
that surround kings.

These grim scenes are relieved by glimpses of such features
of the farmer's day as cast a spell, for the poet at any rate,
over his limited and burdensome life: the reward of watching
the seedling "shouldering its way and shedding the earth-
crumbs"; the jeweled vision of blueberries in rain-wet leaves;
the madness of the cow in apple-time; the noise of trees; the
whirl of snow in which the city withdraws into itself and
leaves "at last the country to the country." Frost has about as
much to say of happy wooings and matings, of friendly encounters and generous neighborliness, as of the bleaker aspects of
the farmer's experience. His love for the unsophisticated pleasures of the countryside, his simple diction, ally him with the
Georgians. But one cannot confuse this twinkling American,
who talks of "the trial by market everything must come to,"
with such men as William Davies, standing and staring happily

at sheep and cows, or Rupert Brooke, longing for honey with his tea on a lawn at Grantchester. He does not see the country with the eyes of the carefree vagabond or the city-sick romantic, who finds it as charming and refreshing as a new mistress. He has for it rather the understanding, slightly quizzical look a man gives the wife of his bosom. He is learned in the ways of the land as no amateur of roads or gardens can ever be, and, for all his unworldliness, has a knowledge of men which permits him to salt his verse with humorous observation. Some of Mark Van Doren's early lyrics, and more notably, his happy eclogue, *A Winter Diary,* offer insights that indicate something of Frost's temper.

For the general run of people, life is not a mountain chain of crises, nor is it an electric bath of romantic excitements, nor is it lived upon a plane where ideas matter supremely. It is of the general run that Frost writes. Such poetry, taking for its material the substance of ordinary living and dying, cannot, even by throwing over it "a certain colouring of imagination" or by tracing in it "the primary laws of our nature," excite us as do poems of passion and of vision. Even the introspective lyrics of the poet's riper years have the shrewd sober character, the slow pulse, of his early work. The virtue of his performance is that it makes us more aware of the quality of ordinary experiences, however small, fragmentary, sordid, or painful these may be, and so alters and refines our responses to the common hours.

While Frost, in England, was writing about the rural life of New England, another American poet was tramping from his home town of Springfield, across Illinois, Missouri, and Kansas, into Colorado and down to New Mexico, preaching his "Gospel of Beauty" to the farmers of the wide West. This was not the first pilgrimage of the sort to be made by Vachel Lindsay, but since he published a record of his adventures by the way, it became the most famous. He carried neither baggage nor money, only an oilcloth-covered bundle of thin-leaved pamphlets entitled *Rhymes To Be Traded For Bread.* He was

45

resolved to keep away from railroads and cities and to pay for his food and lodging by reciting poetry—chiefly his own verses—to his hosts. He preached "the love of beauty and the love of God" and a "new localism" which should seek to develop the art of the community in the spirit of the Declaration of Independence and the Gettysburg Address.

Lindsay, who had been both an art student and a settlement worker, and who had never come out from the benign shadow of the Lincoln Memorial in which he grew up, was too fond in his patriotism and too naïve in his ethics to be as much of a realist as Frost. He had, moreover, an ear for rhythm and for verbal melody which is frequently associated with the romantic impulse and which may have inclined him to give freer play to his fantasy. He was to develop this along with his music. His later work, though exhibiting a bold use of the vernacular and a simplicity to which no less an artist than Yeats paid tribute, was not without bombast. He had too strong a nostalgia for the confident America of his youth, with its Rogers group in the parlor, its iron deer on the lawn, its torchlight processions in the street—he had too facile a faith in the democratic tradition, to see clearly which way the country was going. But if his verse reflected, in a sentimental fashion, the dreams of a disappointed Populist, it also carried a feeling for the vernacular, a sensitiveness to the tunes and cadences of popular song.

When he bragged and ranted about Bryan, Bryan, Bryan, in martial rhythms and brazen rhymes, he evoked the glitter that the promise of free silver held for the farmers, along with the excitement that the campaign oratory roused in a lyrical boy. In *John L. Sullivan, The Strong Boy of Boston,* he introduced, along with the mocking-bird singing in the lane, the shrill voices of the pavements chanting "East side, west side, all around the town," "Ring-around a-rosie," and "London Bridge is falling down," with the smashing effect of one of John L.'s punches. His *Congo* is scarcely "a study of the Negro race in its basic savagery"; but the resonant syllables of its opening,

the childlike simplicity of the phrasing, the sound as of pound-
ing drums in the refrain, and the shadowy quality of the long
"a-s" and "o-s" with which the lines are filled, all convey a
sense of something primitive and dark, of a wild dancing, fearful or exultant, which is richer and more alive than the pious
idea hovering around it.

> Fat black bucks in a wine-barrel room,
> Barrel-house kings, with feet unstable,
> Sagged and reeled and pounded on the table,   *A deep*
> Pounded on the table,   *rolling bass*
> Beat an empty barrel with the handle of a broom,
> Hard as they were able,
> Boom, boom, Boom,
> With a silk umbrella and the handle of a broom,
> Boomlay, boomlay, boomlay, Boom.

General William Booth Enters Into Heaven, which is written
"to be sung to the tune of The Blood of the Lamb with indicated instruments," is another processional poem, which should
move to the thrumming of banjos, the crying of flutes, the
jingling of tamborines, and the hard pulse of drum-beats.
Here and elsewhere Lindsay seems unwittingly trying to recall
the glamour of the bonfires and the brasses and the singing of
the political parades of his boyhood, and the vision of democracy which floated like a banner above them for the dreamy
eyes of a boy. In his efforts to produce a kind of communal
poetry, using words snatched from the street, using chants in
which his audience might freely join, he was working more
consciously to retrieve that lost glory.

It was Lindsay's strong democratic sentiment which allowed
him to recognize the hard actualities of American life. He
revered not only the orthodox representatives of the native
tradition, but also the forgotten eagle, John P. Altgeld, who
had dared to reopen the Haymarket case by pardoning the
three remaining victims of that notorious affair. Lindsay was
not fully aware of the complexities of the economic pattern.
He was apt to identify the evils of our civilization with the

brute machine, and to some degree with the Republican party. Yet he knew enough of poverty to abhor those who helped to create it, and with an absence of rhetoric the more striking because it was rare with him, he spilled his indignation upon a world which crushed the idealism of youth and sapped the manhood of the poor. He resented that they starved so dreamlessly more than the fact of starvation. He hated their dying like sheep more than he hated death. And in at least one short poem he showed a fidelity to fact which turned lyricism to the uses of irony:

> Factory windows are always broken—
> Somebody's always throwing bricks,
> Somebody's always heaving cinders,
> Playing ugly Yahoo tricks.
>
> Factory windows are always broken,
> Other windows are let alone.
> No one throws through the chapel window
> The ugly snarling derisive stone.
>
> Factory windows are always broken—
> Something or other is going wrong.
> Something is rotten—I think in Denmark.
> End of the Factory-window song.

Lindsay was hampered by his ethical bias from exploiting his technical resources to the full. At his best, he is more of a symbolist than a realist. But he was unique in his generation for having frequently chosen his symbols from the American background (even his *Chinese Nightingale* poem features a weary Chinese laundryman), and in employing the language of the plain man, the movements of familiar hymn-tunes, and the vulgar jazzed rhythm of "blues," which, years later, was to lend poignancy to the mordant lyrics of Langston Hughes.

At this period even some poets who preferred lyrical flights into the realms of romance were showing for the nonce a bald directness of approach, an adherence to the harsh stubborn fact, which gave their work the effect of prose. One reason for

48

the success of Edgar Lee Master's *Spoon River Anthology* was that it had the fascination of a series of compact candid biographies. Taking his readers into the cemetery of a small community in the neighborhood of Chicago, he let them listen to what the frank dead had to say of themselves. These unfulfilled women, these self-righteous predatory men, these narrow, misshapen souls of both sexes, speaking of the vain love, the abortive ambition, the sardonic injustice that had plagued them in life, present the substance of nearly two hundred novels, each compressed into some twenty lines.

The germ of the book, its author has said, was the idea of telling the story of an American country town in such a fashion as to make it the story of the world. His own boyhood, spent in a town five miles from Spoon River, furnished him with memories of such a microcosm, while his career as a Chicago lawyer gave him a clearer insight into the forces which shape both the large and the little community. All manner of people are represented in this book, and practically every occupation save that of the miller, the cobbler, the barber, the tailor, and the garage mechanic. The work has, too, some coloring of autobiography, and celebrates American idealism as the young Masters had learned it from the lore of his Virginian and New England forebears.

Technically, the book has its prototype in the *Greek Anthology*, that vast collection of lyrics, ranging from the period of the Persian Wars down to the eleventh century of our era, and giving us the quality of Greek life much as the Tanagra figurines which were the ornament of countless anonymous households lead us back to the hearths, the fountains, the markets of that tenacious people. Among the epitaphs included in the classic *Anthology* some are acrid enough:

Dion of Tarsus, here I lie, who sixty years have seen.
I was not ever wed, and would my father had not been.

Some, like the following, have a faint Rabelaisian tinge:

49

This rudely sculptured porter-pot
Denotes where sleeps a female sot;
Who passed her life, good easy soul,
In sweetly chirping o'er her bowl.
Not for her friends or children dear
She mourns, but only for her beer.
E'en in the very grave, they say,
She thirsts for drink to wet her clay;
And, faith, she thinks it very wrong
This jug should stand unfilled so long.

But Masters's performance lacks the detachment of his models. It is characterized by the savage candor of Daumier's political cartoons.

The book opens with a lyric echoing the cry that haunts the centuries. Villon murmured it (*Mais où sont les neiges d'antan?*), remembering the lovely ladies gone to dust, the brave knights perished. William Dunbar rang the changes on it in his *Lament for the Makers*. And centuries earlier the Persian tent-maker had sung the same strain to a different instrument:

They say the Lion and the Lizard keep
The Courts where Jamshyd gloried and drank deep:
    And Bahram, that great Hunter—the Wild Ass
Stamps o'er his Head, but cannot break his Sleep.

Masters's prelude lacks the music of these older elegies, although his reiterated,

All, all, are sleeping on the hill,

has a mournful cadence in sharp contrast to the prosaic phrases in which he relates the histories of those sleepers. But what sets his poem apart from the others is that instead of remembering Heloise and Jeanne d'Arc, King Arthur and Charlemagne, the brave masters of balladry, or the Sassanian sovereign, it recalls Ella, Kate and Mag, Bert, Tom and Charley, men who were burned to death in a mine or "killed in a brawl," women who "died in shameful child-birth," or "of a thwarted love," or "at the hands of a brute in a brothel." And the poet's emotion, as it reveals itself in the epitaphs, is not pity for those whose worldly hope,

> Like Snow upon the Desert's dusty Face,
> Lighting a little hour or two—is gone,

but indignation at the greed, the bigotry, the malice of men.

The memory of the Haymarket riots and their cruel consequences burns in him as it burned in Lindsay. Though not as much of a democrat and an individualist as Lindsay, he is yet somewhat reluctant to grant that these people were disabled by forces outside themselves. Take, for example, the case of Adam Weirauch, who lost many friends fighting for Altgeld, and lost his slaughter-house with the rise of the house of Armour. Weirauch entered politics and was elected to the legislature, but he sold his vote on a street-car franchise, and was caught. He ends up asking whether it was Armour, Altgeld or himself that ruined him. The book has none of Lindsay's easy optimism. On the contrary, Masters appears to suck a bitter pleasure from the contemplation of those ugly, petty, sordid dramas which made up, for the most part, the life of Spoon River. Mrs. Kessler, who supported her family by taking in washing, learned people's secrets from their curtains, bedspreads, and shirts. These epitaphs do not hide any of the stains, the running colors, the rents and patches. Editor Whedon, who is in miniature the representative of those gentlemen upon whom Ezra Pound pours the vomit of his Fourteenth and Fifteenth Cantos, lies in death

> close by the river over the place
> Where the sewage flows from the village,
> And the empty cans and garbage are dumped,
> And abortions are hidden.

The epitaphs make no attempt to conceal the sewage, the empty cans, the garbage, or the abortions. Not the shames of Spoon

River alone, but the shames of a nation are exposed here. The facts of the Spanish-American War as the soldiers in the swamps knew them are related by a boy who went to uphold "the honor of the flag." Near him lies a veteran of the Revolution, who endured the heartbreaking struggle of the frontier and whose last word is: if the soldier who fought the Filipinos is to have his grave decorated with a flag, "Take it from mine!"

Yet Masters is careful to show that not all the inhabitants of the cemetery had lived meanly, thwarted by the prudishness of their neighbors, by the viciousness of the profit system, or by the weakness of their own souls and bodies. There is Lucinda Matlock, who lived together with her husband for seventy years, raising twelve children, and who cries out on the "degenerate sons and daughters" of the younger generation,

> "Life is too strong for you—
> It takes life to love life."

And there is Fiddler Jones who

> ended up with forty acres;
> .... ended up with a broken fiddle—
> And a broken laugh, and a thousand memories,
> And not a single regret.

There are William and Emily, who die together and content, as they had lived. There are the three or four men who rejoice in one another's comradeship, bearing the burden of the mystery, worshiping heaven more heartily because they also worship earth. The *Spoon River Anthology* is good realism because, while acknowledging all the ugliness of life in a small American town of the industrial age, it admits the beauties which may also flourish there. In later works, notably in his long narrative poem on contemporary life, *Domesday Book*, Masters attempted to handle a similar theme in a more ambitious fashion, but without the same success.

Most of the inhabitants of Spoon River were native Americans. But the population of the small towns of the mid-West,

the workers in the wheat-fields, in the factories, in the stock-
yards, on the railroads, are Swedes and Dagoes and Hunkies,
and it was these less articulate men and their women whom
the author of *Chicago Poems* put into his verse. Some seventy-
five years ago Emerson wrote: "Our log-rolling, our stumps
and their politics, our fisheries, our Negroes and Indians, our
boasts and our reputations, the wealth of rogues and the pusil-
lanimity of honest men, the Northern trade, the Southern planting, the Western clearing, Oregon and Texas are yet unsung."
That summons was partially answered by Whitman. But Carl
Sandburg could answer it in a more intimate fashion, partly
because he had Whitman to lean upon, to depart from, partly
because he knew the songs sung by rogues—and some honest
men, too—from the Erie Canal to Macon, from the Great
Lakes to the Gulf of Mexico, from the Atlantic to the Pacific
coast. He knew that the voice of the land is to be heard in the
homely tunes and lyrics of its half-literate people, in bawdy
songs and sailor chanteys and sentimental ditties, wherever
there are pick and shovel gangs at work, or dances in lonely
hill cabins, or gatherings around prairie fires, or sailors at a
keg party. He had listened to them from a fellow coal-shoveler
in Omaha, from a Mexican negro in a Texas saloon, from a
private who fought beside him in the rain and mud of Porto
Rico, from an old fiddler turned milkman with whom he
washed delivery cans, from railroad workers sitting in box-car
bunk houses, from switchmen and Wobblies, jailbirds and cow-
boys. Sandburg's verse has the peculiar tang of this native
balladry, flavored as it is with half a dozen foreign traditions.
His work is sensual, tender, slightly sentimental, and alive with
the idiom of the plain people.

As Frost is open to what the New England landscape and
the New England character have to offer, Sandburg celebrates
chiefly the spaciousness of the mid-West, the hospitable soil.
"the gold of a ripe oat-straw, gold of a south-west moon," the
outlook of people who live on the land and who are used to
permanencies like earth and stars, things that last longer than

skyscrapers and empires. City people build a skyscraper twenty stories high and then tear it down and build another eighty stories high; but no man put the Dipper and the North Star where they are, and no man will tear them down to put up a bigger and better Dipper and North Star. That is what Sandburg's poems say rather often. He has written a paean to Chicago. But for the most part his poems about cities are written with some resentment and some pity. The huddle and the dirt and the foolish mechanical routine of city life make him sick and sorry. Yet he knows a good deal about the loneliness of life on a farm or in a small town where nothing seems to happen but the shooting by of the express. Much of his verse is as wistful as the sound of a ukulele on an unpainted back porch of a soft summer night, and some of his verse is hot with anger at the ways of a world where millions of people are starving behind a plow or starving behind a counter.

He has the feeling Whitman had crossing on the Brooklyn ferry, wanting to look into the lives of the other passengers, wanting to know what they felt, looking at the sunset and the river and the tall buildings. But Sandburg, like the elder poet, while he cares about people and is full of pity for their griefs and pleasure in their joys, does not search their minds deeply. The men and women in his poems are like moving-picture actors seen on the screen before the days of the talkies. They register sorrow and love and amusement and rebellion, but they do not do much questioning or explaining. They lack the depth, the solidity, the intimacy of living actors on the legitimate stage. It is as part of the picture, the endlessly moving, endlessly fascinating picture, that they appeal to him.

Like Whitman, he is equally interested in a beautiful woman and in a rooming-house slut, or perhaps more deeply interested in the slut. And he has Whitman's way of marveling at the history of the universe as he looks at a blade of grass and marveling at the history of mankind as he looks at the miracle of his own body. But Whitman, for all his frankness, did not write about the railroad worker who sat on a bench in the

54

sun beside the poor-house as a "swarthy, swaggering son-of-a-gun"; nor, with all his feeling for places, of shanties hanging "by an eye-lash to the hill slants back around Omaha." Nor, remembering the body and the soul of John Brown, would he have celebrated him in words like these:

> They hauled him into jail.
> They sneered at him and spit on him,
> And he wrecked their jails,
> Singing, "God damn your jails,"
> And when he was most in jail
> Crummy among the crazy in the dark
> Then he was most of all out of jail
> Shambling, dark, and strong,
> Always asking: Where did that blood come **from?**
> They laid hands on him
> And the fool killers had a laugh
> And the necktie party was a go, by God.

> They laid hands on him and he was a goner.
> They hammered him to pieces and he stood up.
> They buried him and he walked out of the grave, **by God,**
> Asking again: Where did that blood come from?

John Brown has become part of the American legend. Every schoolboy knows Mrs. Howe's anthem well enough to parody it—the ultimate test of fame. Stephen Vincent Benét's narrative poem, *John Brown's Body*, was a best-seller, partly because it was written in lively, unpretentious verse, largely because of its subject-matter. Sandburg's tribute—one of several by the same hand—carries a weight beyond Mrs. Howe's rhetoric and Stephen Benét's competence by reason of its vivid use of the vernacular and the hammer-stroke of rhythms which yet have an almost conversational quality.

Sandburg has, along with some of Whitman's virtues, some of his faults. He is apt to be verbose. He often sentimentalizes. But his delight in colloquial language, his feeling for slang as poetic diction of a fresh sort, his sense of the values in the cadences of common speech, were a distinct contribution to

55

American poetry. Unlike Frost, he has had few imitators. A
poem or two by Ernest Walsh shows his direct influence, especially the lines in a piece addressed to Sandburg:

You for the day
                    when moons visit summer fields
Flushed to copper fever,
                    fields with wounds
From skeleton fingers after one bronze potato,
                    one petrified ear of corn,
                    one cow-skull,
                    one onyx egg.

The proletarian poets of this generation, being remote from
him politically, tend to distrust his technique. Yet he might
say with Masefield that however harshly the next school may
treat him, that school must be a little livelier for his efforts.

As one moves closer to the present, the passing moment, one
sees the poets making different responses to the changing life
about them. The scene shifts, the emotion is qualified by events
and ideas that the verse of two decades back could not take into
account. But the desire to come to closer grips with actuality,
however tawdry or terrible, to express it in words that are as
much of the moment as the feeling which stirs beneath them,
is permanent in poetry. It is a quickening element in the work
of the men touched upon here, and it is chiefly for their regard
for the actual that they appealed as strongly as they did to their
own generation and to some later comers.

CHAPTER III

THE IMAGISTS AND THEIR BEQUEST

The shadowe in the roome fromme open dore
The tyght harde beate quikke loudde hittinge the ribbes.
Ernest Walsh.

THE TERM "imagisme"—it was anglicized later on—was invented by Ezra Pound, but the man responsible for a good deal of the theory, as well as for the first specimens of imagist poetry, was T. E. Hulme. For some time before he went to the front, to be killed in 1917, this English thinker was the center of a small group of poets who were working toward a new method. The mass of elliptical notes and unfinished essays bearing upon their discussions that Hulme left at his death were edited by Herbert Read and published under the title *Speculations.* Hulme argues there for "a new technique, a new convention," supported by a belief in order, an adherence to ethical and political discipline. He opposes this new art to that of the immediate past by reason of its acknowledgment of human limitations, and the clarity and precision of its style. He opposes it to the art of the remote past because it will express that "change of sensibility" which has been effected by the machine age. Hulme is worth reading for his packed original aggressive style. He is significant for having preached what his contemporaries were to practice—for, among other things, his neo-classicism.

57

It is risky to use words like classicism and romanticism, because they have been worn smooth by too much handling. One thinks of Keats, for example, as a romantic poet. Yet Hulme, fighting romanticism, demanding "verse strictly confined to the earthly and the definite," adduces, by way of illustration, the work of Keats. Such writing as he praises may be found in the sonnets and in the odes, in *Sleep and Poetry:*

> A pigeon tumbling in clear summer air;
> A laughing schoolboy, without grief or care,
> Riding the springy branches of an elm;

in *Hyperion:*

> ... the sickening east-wind
> Shifts sudden to the south, the small warm rain
> Melts out the frozen incense from all flowers;

even in so pure a piece of fantasy as *La Belle Dame Sans Merci:*

> The sedge is withered from the lake,
> And no birds sing.

What classicism meant to Hulme and his circle is not as clearly exemplified in the compact witty verse of a Dryden or a Pope. For all his emphasis upon the beauty that there is in "small, dry things," for all his insistence that "in the classic it is always the light of ordinary day, never the light that never was on land or sea," Hulme did not forget that emotion is the matrix of poetry. In his discussion of its proper themes, he restated Wordsworth's dictum by declaring that it was useless to work up an emotion about motor-cars on the theory that motor-cars are beautiful: the emotion must precede the poem. Attacking the matter from the other side, he argued that the work of those minor men who traffic in the jewels of the past suffers from "a lost poetic content."

Strength of feeling, clear perception of the object, accurate description of it, implied for him the accomplished use of imagery. The emotion, he contended, cannot be conveyed except by illuminating metaphor. For himself, he saw each word with an image attached to it. He wanted no decoration, no ornament. If he argued against the use of plain speech, it was because he held that plain speech is not accurate; that new metaphors, that fancy, make for precision. The five brief lyrics which form the complete poetical works of T. E. Hulme and which were printed under that title in an appendix to a book of Pound's, are an excellent illustration of his esthetic, as witness even so slight a thing as

The Embankment

The fantasia of a fallen gentleman on a cold, bitter night

Once, in finesse of fiddles found I ecstasy,
In the flash of gold heels on the hard pavement.
Now see I
That warmth's the very stuff of poesy.
Oh, God, make small
The old, star-eaten blanket of the sky,
That I may fold it round me and in comfort lie.

Hulme happened to have, along with the distrust of logic that belongs to a Bergsonian, a visual imagination. Hence his emphasis on the pictorial character of poetry. He started from the premise that a poem is the record of an emotion. To be precise, such a record must have the immediacy of the feeling itself. The brief concentrated image was his accepted instrument. In thus choosing and sharpening their tools, Hulme, Pound, and their circle turned naturally to France, whose writers have been more analytical in theory and more factional in practice than their fellows in other western countries. In the careful prose of Flaubert, in the criticism of Rémy de Gourmont, and, paradoxically enough, in the poetry of the symbolists, they found the justification and the stimulus that they needed. Flaubert, searching for *"le mot juste,"* had pursued his art in the spirit of Dante, on a panther-quest for the exact evocative word. De Gourmont, following Huysmans, had

59

said that the one excuse for writing was that a man should write himself down, and that the essence of style was to feel, to see, and to think. The imagists wanted to escape from the steaming bath of sentiment in which English poetry had lolled for too long. They wanted to give, unmistakably, the very sting of the experience, endured and known. Hence their emphasis on the concrete detail—the object seen, heard, smelt, tasted, and touched, on the metaphor that carries the quality of physical sensation.

The complete imagist would seem to be at the opposite pole from such a poet as Mallarmé, who sought, by phrases as vague as the music toward which they tended, by metaphors as private as the ritual of an illicit religion, to suggest his emotional and intellectual response to the world of "appearances." He would be, rather, close to Gautier, "a man for whom the visible world exists." And yet so notable an exponent of symbolism as de Gourmont saw in imagism a natural development of the symbolist movement. It was, if you please, a kind of inverted symbolism. Instead of suggesting to the mind of the reader, by a cumulation of tremulous images, merging into one another, the poet's emotion, which always carried as an overtone a sense of mystery, the imagist roused a sufficient feeling of wonder by presenting the naked impact of the object upon the senses in a concentrated metaphor. Both welcomed the evidence of the developing science of psychology that the image, the symbol, floating up from the depths of the mind, was the most faithful ambassador of the psyche.

The nucleus of the imagist group appears to have been formed in 1912 by Ezra Pound, H. D. (Hilda Doolittle), and Richard Aldington. Pound has stated the principles upon which they were agreed: "1. Direct treatment of the 'thing,' whether subjective or objective. 2. To use absolutely no word that does not contribute to the presentation. 3. As regarding rhythm: to compose in the sequence of the musical phrase, not in the sequence of the metronome." The first anthology of imagist poetry, which appeared two years later, bore the title,

IMAGISTS AND THEIR BEQUEST

Des Imagistes, as though to stress the debt of the contributors to France. The volume included poems by Pound, H. D., Aldington, Skipwith Cannell, John Cournos, Ford Madox Hueffer (now Ford), F. S. Flint, Amy Lowell, James Joyce, Allen Upward and William Carlos Williams. The majority of these poets, together with two later comers, put forth the *Imagist Anthology* published sixteen years later. Of those who appeared in both the first assembly and what is presumably the last, H. D. and William Carlos Williams have been the most faithful to the imagist tenets. Pound reëxamined and restated them in his *Few Don'ts by an Imagiste*. His principal articles of dogma were utter concision, the stripping away of every superfluous word; the use of concrete detail, and abhorrence of abstractions; strict attention to verse technique, involving an expert understanding of cadence. The models he suggested were Sappho, Catullus, Villon, Heine, Gautier and Chaucer.

It is apparent—though when the battle was being fought there was some doubt of the matter—that the imagists were literally revolutionists, in that they were adopting a way of writing that had fallen into disuse. Even a translation into English prose suggests the bare simplicity of such a fragment from Sappho as this: "The moon has set, and the Pleiades; it is midnight, the time is going by, and I sleep alone." Thanks to Pound and Eliot, the strict line of Gautier has become part of the tradition of English verse. But no rendering gives quite the biting quality of Catullus's meager-worded passion, the mordant tenderness of Heine, or the vigor of the terse testaments of Villon, whose lips have scarcely uttered their *"Aeternam requiem dona"* than he pictures himself drily:

> Hair, eyebrows, beard all fallen away,
> Like a peeled turnip...

Rebelling against the ruminant attitude, the stale, adjective-ridden verse of their predecessors, these writers found support in such various practitioners of their art as the classical poets, the symbolists, and the lyricists of ancient China and Japan.

To read a Chinese poem—or, for that matter, a piece of Chinese prose—in the original hieroglyphics is to see a series of pictures. The language, as Professor Fenollosa has pointed out, is much more metaphorical than one cumbered, like our own, by medieval logic and rendered anaemic by abstractions. Moreover, it is built more obviously upon the verb, so that the eye is constantly confronted by action, process, development. In Fenollosa's essay on *The Chinese Written Character as a Medium for Poetry*, which Pound edited and published ten years after it was written, he offered a new approach to these essentials of the art: the picture which metaphor makes an intimation of the unpicturable, the verb which vibrates with life beyond the power of adjective or noun.

The period of the T'ang Dynasty, when the Chinese emperors were poets, and the writing of poetry a required part of the training of every scholar and public official, saw the development of regulations which made for extreme concentration. Some of the rules would apply only to poems written in a language made of individual hierographic characters, each of which is a monosyllable having its fixed tone. But though it is impossible to produce an English lyric according to the complex laws governing the so-called "ruled" Chinese poems, a study of the pattern, and the reading of such of them as exist in translation, may point the way to a greater concision of style and subtlety of effect. Even in translation these poems offer glimpses of a civilization which appears to have joined a rural simplicity to an urbane intelligence. The Japanese *tanka*, a five-line lyric of thirty-one syllables, and the briefer *hokku*, afforded further lessons in brevity. In the poetry of both peoples there is a telling concreteness of imagery which finely evokes the court or the philosopher's mountain retreat, the lasting grief or the moment of communion, imagery more often than not carrying a weight of allusion which, for the instructed, deepens the poem's significance.

The extreme compression of the best imagist poetry was a fault in the eyes of a public accustomed to the leisurely pace, the vague phraseology, and the cosmic ambitions of academic verse. Even more shocking was their departure from the accepted norm in the matter of rhythm. Yet, as its exponents repeatedly stated, the use of free verse, once so startling and later so tedious, was the use of nothing more novel than the rhythms of Whitman, bidding his followers come

... by stealth in some wood for trial,
Or back of a rock in the open air,
(For in any roof'd room of a house I emerge not, nor in
    company,
And in libraries I lie as one dumb, a gawk, or unborn, or
    dead) ...

the rhythms of Blake:

Where goest thou, O thought? to what remote land is thy
    flight?
If thou returnest to the present moment of affliction
Wilt thou bring comforts on thy wings, and dews and honey
    and balm,
Or poison from the desart wilds, from the eyes of the envier?

the rhythms of such portions of the Bible as the twelfth chapter of Ecclesiastes, David's lament over Jonathan, the song of Deborah and Barak.

If Pound was the first poet of the period to rouse his fellows to a sense of technical problems, the chief publicist for imagism in this country was Amy Lowell. Pound was scarcely the man to shelter under her arrogant maternal wing, and by the time she began agitating for the principles he had formulated, he had twitched his mantle, and gone to meet tomorrow in fresh woods and pastures new. Miss Lowell, an indefatigable creator of costume dramas, assembled three anthologies of imagist poetry, the first of which contained a preface in which she set forth her version of the theory. It was practically a restatement of the ideas of Pound and Hulme, except for her insistence on the use of the language of common speech. This was a new principle, which consorted neither with her demand for the exact word nor with the practice of the members of the group, as when Miss Lowell herself wrote of a woman bathing as another Venus, sea-borne, "Cinctured by bright winds." What she meant was probably not the language, but the locutions of common speech: the avoidance of inversions, acceptable enough in inflected languages like Latin or German, where a change in word-order means a change of emphasis, but, unless a deliberate technical device, fantastic and confusing in English. Pound was conspicuous by his absence from these anthologies. The poets represented, in addition to the compiler, were Aldington, H.D., F. S. Flint, and two newcomers, neither of whom could be fairly described as an imagist: John Gould Fletcher and D. H. Lawrence.

The shift in the membership of the group, the wide variety in the kinds of poetry they produced, make it clear that here was not a school, in the French sense, but rather a set of people drawn together by a common interest in technical experiment. Those most eager to be received by a doubting public peered into the dark backward and abysm of time to discover poets whose work exemplified their own seemingly novel theories. Had they looked about them they might have found contemporaries who, without making any special plea for it, were also producing imagist poetry. One thinks of Emanuel Carnevali, whose slight output is characterized by an audacity, a sensitiveness, above all, a definiteness of imagery, recalling his compatriots of an earlier century and his contemporaries in America. One thinks of Lola Ridge, whose first book presented in clear, memorable pictures the green-walled tenements, the flare-lit huddle of traffic, the pressure of stricken, indomitable life in the ghetto, as she had come intimately to know it. Her most ambitious piece, the long Christ poem, *Firehead*, may almost be regarded as an extended, an amplified image. She is not so sensitive a craftsman as H.D., nor so dry a commentator as Dr. Williams. Sometimes her emotion—as though in revenge on a body too frail to contain it—destroys the poem into which it is poured. But if an eye for exact detail, a visual

64

imagination, a sense of rhythm uninhibited by metrical rule of thumb, combine to make an imagist, then this passionate speaker for the disinherited belonged with these insurgents from the first.

A later comer, possessed of more detachment, and gifted with the discerning eye and the discriminating vocabulary demanded by imagism, is Marianne Moore. For emotion, Miss Moore substitutes observation, sensation, and reflection. She is particularly good at catching animals in movement: the plumet basilisk, "a nervous naked sword on little feet," the pelican gliding or quivering about "as charred paper behaves." She has Miss Lowell's pleasure in choosing the proper colors with which to paint creatures, fruits, and jewels. Her technique, which is nothing if not studied, is elegant enough, but has the defect of elegance: an obtrusive sophistication which deprives her work of intensity. Her end-rhymes tend to make her rhythms jerky and persistently obtrude upon the prose-sense of her verse instead of assisting it. Her predatory mind impels her to stud her verse, not always effectively, with quotations from miscellaneous and unlikely sources. Her wit allies her with the heirs of the metaphysicals. But her astuteness helps her to apt description, and when she is concerned with visual representation she is peculiarly happy.

Of a younger generation there is of course Archibald MacLeish and, more obviously, Ernest Walsh. Walsh died young, with little work done, and some of it too plainly modeled on that of his seniors. But in his poems he keeps his promise to warm, to urge, the living, in words as keen as cognac, as fresh as an April wind.

A reasoned account even of those few who claimed the name of Pound's invention would require as many chapters as there are poets. Accepting, then, the tenet of concentration, we may concentrate upon the poetry of H. D., generally accepted as the purest imagist of them all. Her effort, from the beginning, has been to summon for us again the clear light that was Greece. Travelers, some twenty-five centuries ago, might stop at a

town in Rhodes to examine such treasures of antiquity as
Teucer's bow and Helen's bracelet. Those relics are long since
lost to us, and the Hellas that widened its eyes or bit its lips at
them is almost equally past recovery. The researches of a Jane
Harrison or an Alfred Zimmern bring us no more than scraps
and snatches of the reality. What survives, altering a little with
the mind of each age, is the ideal Greece. One of the values of
H.D.'s poetry is that it clarifies and reburnishes that ideal for
this generation. Scholars delight in the scrupulous precision of
her renderings. Poets, more alive to the temptations she has
resisted, admire the chastity of her work. One may measure
this by contrasting the bareness of her translations from
Euripides with Sir Gilbert Murray's melodious but all too
lush and Swinburnian treatment of the same choruses. Even
in her most highly personal lyrics H.D. seldom loses sight of
those Hellenic originals which have been the source of her art.

She cannot cross the barrier into her own time. It may be
an index to her feeling for the ancient world that, like the
Greek poets, she tends to forget that among them there lived
slaves as well as freemen, and men felt the sweat of labor as
well as the dews of love. Some theme of Sappho's is nearer to
her than the problems of women caught in the complexities
and derangements of our civilization. What some might call
a poverty of inspiration, is, however, in more than one sense
a means of orienting the reader. The flowers that grow sparsely
on those rocky headlands, the waves that beat at their base,
the gleam of gray marble, the haunting presences of gods and
those too well loved or too well hated of the gods, recur again
and again, until the whole body of her poetry shines and
trembles with the sea-light of the archipelago, the billow of the
island winds. Whether H.D. speaks for herself or for some
woman out of Greek story, the point from which she speaks
is the same, so that in her invocation to Athena, Artemis, or
Aphrodite, there is nothing awkward or strange, but the beauty
of complete sincerity. Her awareness of her peculiar situation
is expressed in *Epitaph*, where she speaks of one who, like her-

self, solicits the fervor, follows the measure of the ancient world.

Though her best verse is polished until it has the hard luminous surface of alabaster, it is not cold. Even where the poem has an intellectual content, it is quick with passion, pointed with concrete images. If there is anything unGreek about her work, it is just her care for the minute detail, the sharpness with which she outlines flower and fruit, the iris, painted blue,

> painted like a fresh prow
> stained among the salt weeds,

the "cyclamen-purple, cyclamen-red" of the last grapes, the crisp line, the hot color of a petal, the texture of hill-grass, the feel of stone to be carved, of an oar to be lifted and pulled. A French critic, describing her gift for the brief incisive image, has paraphrased Verlaine: *"Voir, tout le reste est littérature."* This is a witty appraisal, but when he goes on to say that her work has little verbalism and no music, he is mistaken.

The famous lyric about heat, called *Garden*, shows her sensitiveness to tone-color, with the heavy effect of the "p-s" and "t-s" and "d-s" and "b-s" in the lines:

> fruit cannot fall into heat
> that presses up and blunts
> the points of pears
> and rounds the grapes.

And what could vary liquid vowel-sounds with whispering consonants more happily than this passage from *Sea-Gods:*

> We bring hyacinth-violet,
> sweet, bare, chill to the touch—
> and violets whiter than the in-rush
> of your own white surf.

The changing vowels in "sweet, bare, chill," suggest the various colors of the violets named in this part of the poem, and

67

the repeated "i" in "hyacinth-violet," "violets," "whiter," "white," give the lightness of the flowers themselves, while the "in-rush of . . . surf" carries the sibilance of foamy waters. In the beginning H.D. seldom employed rhyme, and she is not always successful with it now, although she retains a mastery of assonance. It is where she does not follow the imagist rules strictly, either because of an obtrusive rhyme, or because of the use of a conventional stanzaic form, or because of the undue lengthening of a poem by embroidery on a simple theme, that the results are questionable.

In her cadences, no less than in her clear-cut pictures, she finely illustrates imagist theory. When the *vers libre* controversy was at its height, T. S. Eliot observed that "the ghost of some simple metre should lurk behind the arras in even the 'freest' verse, to advance menacingly as we doze, and withdraw as we rouse." Eliot is a poet who welcomes ghosts, and who knows both how to entertain and how, courteously, to dismiss them. The imagists, however, hostile to such visitations, denied that there was a skeleton in the family closet. H.D., one of the few members of the group who has allowed her work to speak for itself, produced poetry that justified their denial. Her rhythms are almost the rhythms of speech, but speech when it is most passionate, at once charged with and restrained by the emotion that weights it. Her lines are short and heavy with emphasis, the tension of them heightened by the skillful use of spondees. Her poems are seldom metrical, but for all their irregularity, the recurrence of certain phrases, the parallelism of others, give the effect of symmetry. An instance in this passage from *Orion Dead,* spoken by Artemis, savage with grief:

> Arise,
> lest I bend an ash-tree
> into a taut bow,
> and slay—and tear
> all the roots from the earth.

The cornel-wood blazes
and strikes through the barley-sprays
but I have lost heart for this.

I break a staff.
I break the tough branch.
I know no light in the woods.
I have lost pace with the winds.

It is in her longer poems and in her attempt at poetic drama that this method fails, the parallelism becomes obvious, and the repetition tiresome.

With these means: the definite, clear image, the brief halting cadence, she builds a moment's monument. Her themes are few and simple: the breathless hurt of natural beauty, the toll of a rigorous art, the agony of physical passion. Edith Sitwell, whose admiration for the eighteenth century would scarcely incline her to sympathy with the imagists, mentions, in the introduction to her book on Pope, "a school of American-Greek posturants, resembling not so much marble statues as a white-tiled bathroom," who "exuded a thin stream of carefully chosen, watery words." With no naming of names, the reference is plain enough. Yet this barb from the Sitwellian quiver cannot undo H.D.'s achievement. If her scope has always been narrow, her intensity remains unchallenged.

William Carlos Williams represents the other face of imagism—its more severe, more contemporary aspect. Today he might more properly be called an objectivist. Certainly for him the objective world exists. That is plain even in so early and relatively ornamental a poem as *Sub Terra,* where he cries for companions to go with him,

Poking into Negro houses
with their gloom and smell!
In among children
Leaping around a dead dog!
Mimicking
Onto the laws of the rich
You!

69

To go with me a-tip-toe
Head down under heaven,
Nostrils lipping the wind!

Much of that early work shows the influence of Pound: the sense of brightness on the air, of cool winds and clear waters, that marked Pound's first lyrics; the desire for comrades: a desire different from loneliness in its impatient vigor; something faintly reminiscential, here in vocabulary, there in cadence, and with it all, an unexpected tenderness, a dryness not Gallic, but—for all Carlos Williams's foreign antecedents—essentially native. He has moved toward an increasingly bare style, so that an admirer in the opposite camp, Wallace Stevens, can rightly call him "a kind of Diogenes of contemporary poetry." Accepting this analogy, one may say that the anti-poetic is the tub in which Williams takes refuge, and that not only rhyme and metre, but all ornament and elaboration, myth and metaphor, have become an imperial interference between him and the sun. His later poems especially make no overtures. They do not seek to flatter, to cajole, to enchant the reader. They may repel him by their unexampled nakedness. For Williams the object seen, the clear line, the pure color, is enough. Or the mangy line, the dirty color, if he is looking, as he often must, at the uglier realities of city street or suburban alley. One must come to his work with his own rapid response to the sensual world—the five-and-ten, the quick-lunch-room, the aquarium—in its concrete immediacy. He has not the mind or the emotions of a child, but he has the child's innocency of the eye. This is as evident in the meditation addressed to a servant girl as in his own favorite bit: *The Red Wheelbarrow*, or the clear simple scene, *Nantucket*:

Flowers through the window
lavender and yellow

changed by white curtains—
Smell of cleanliness—

Sunshine of late afternoon—
On the glass tray

a glass pitcher, the tumbler
turned down, by which

a key is lying— And the
immaculate white bed

He has the abrupt manner that often goes with frankness, and
also with sentiment. He exhibits, too, the swift contrast, the
pleasure in the grotesque, which one associates with Laforgue
and with Eliot, but he is free of their bitterness. With most
unlikely means he conjures back for us

Unworldly love
that has no hope
of the world

and that
cannot change the world
to its delight—

He is not a particularly skillful melodist. He can make a nota-
tion about a cat on the jam closet which is interesting for the
repeated "p-s" and "f-s" and "t-s" suggestive of the tentative
planting of her careful paws, and his early work often has
loveliness of accent and phrasing, but it is the object, it is the
image, which chiefly matters. This reliance on the eye, this
singling out of the brief moment, however keen, is a limitation.
These poems cannot offer the exaltation that comes of the
myth-making power. The narrowness of attention which makes
for concentration may make also for a certain meagreness.
One feels this in Williams's work, as in that of H.D. But one
recognizes further that, unlike her, and unlike most of his
fellow imagists, Williams is aware of America as something
more than a place from which to escape. He presents with
fidelity the suburban slum, the apple orchard, the city sky-
signs at night, the men and women moving across his line of

vision as he passes through the slum on the errands of a physician, or halts beside the orchard, or, in the metropolis, looks away from the white lights to the faces they shine upon. In the midst of the commonplace he finds exhilaration. Of the many whom Whitman called, William Carlos Williams is, oddly, one of the chosen. The younger poet might have addressed the elder as Pound did:

> It was you that broke the new wood,
> Now is a time for carving.

What Williams carves is a corner of the American scene as it strikes an alert eye. It is a small corner, but it is his own.

What Pound carves is unique, and singularly unAmerican. The details that he introduces into his larger designs are almost all of foreign origin, and when he speaks of the States it is the voice of an exile speaking. He has ranged more widely, and his poetry has altered with his movements. In his primer for readers he takes his former comrades to task for having made propaganda for imagism in so careless a fashion that people came to think of the image as stationary. "If you can't think of imagism or phanapoeia," he writes, "as including the moving image, you will have to make a really needless division of fixed image and praxis or action." If you do not make this division, it is still possible to discuss Ezra Pound as an imagist.

Through all the turns of his career, this protean poet has held with uncommon faithfulness to the principles he enunciated in 1912: direct treatment of his subject, be that subject a personal mood or a fragment of legend; suppression of every superfluous word; fidelity to the musical phrase. This last was easy for a man who has steeped himself in Provençal song, and learned to make his own relatively harsh language the vehicle of any wandering air. So practiced is Pound in the subtlest devices of metrics, so apt at marrying the meaning and the melody, that the student of his work is apt to neglect his other gifts for his gift of phrasing. How fine his sense of cadence is can only be realized by examining, one after another, such various poems as his *Night Litany*, his rendering of the Anglo-Saxon *Sea-Farer*, his use of sapphics in *Apparuit*, the smashing force of the dactyls in the *Game of Chess*. If one analyzes the movement of these poems, filling in the beats with nonsense syllables, so as to make them poems in a foreign language, his versatile musicianship will be apparent. The fact that in each instance the words do throw a clear "image on the mind's retina," an image which corresponds visually to the audible pattern, is a further testament to his mastery.

Pound began with an admiration for Browning, "Old Hippety-hop o' the accents," and an intimate knowledge of the romance literatures. His debt to Browning has never been sufficiently remarked, partly because of the almost instinctive sneer which contemporary critics have for the Victorians, partly because Pound turned in later years to more admired masters. But he is fairly suffused with the Browningesque. He has the same talent for the conversational style in poetry, sharpened considerably by his study of Laforgue, Corbière, and Tailhade. He has the same delight in recovering and reworking

> pure crude fact
> Secreted from man's life when hearts beat hard,
> And brains, high-blooded, ticked two centuries since.

Two centuries and more, for it is less renaissance Italy than medieval France that rides and sings and climbs fighting through his poetry. But if the period changes, if the approach alters somewhat, the essential interest remains the same. At twenty, Pound was employing his *Wanderjahre* tramping up and down the roads of Spain, Italy, and Southern France. The life that once filled the medieval countryside, the game of mating, fighting, "barter, lands and houses, Provençe knew," crowds his *Cantos* only to a lesser degree than it does his early lyrics. He has always been at war with those whose idea of the tradition is confined to less than half a dozen centuries and one continent, but his own work is built upon a cornerstone of

medieval story. One wonders whether his enthusiasm for
Fascismo may not be in part an outgrowth of his overweening
sense of the past. He might nod to Whitman briefly, but from
the beginning of his self-imposed exile he has been more aware
of Europe and Asia than of the land he left behind him. He
has never been a democrat. It is not that he loves the common
man less, but that he hates the mob more. His close contact
with Yeats must have fostered his aristocratic temper. It
opened to him, too, the world of Celtic legend and Celtic
melody, and, for a little space,

> the subtler music, the clear light
> Where time burns back about th' eternal embers

and

> Nature's herself turned metaphysical.

It is difficult to determine how profoundly these two poets,
alike only in their energy and in their hatred of mediocrity,
have influenced one another. One suspects that Yeats, seeking a
more austere athletic style, drew support from Pound's interest in the naked image, while Pound, tireless in his metamorphoses, rejoiced in the new modes offered by Yeats's knowledge
of symbolism, Celtic myth, and Hindu philosophy. It is at any
rate worth noting that his poem *The Return*, which he has himself described as "an objective reality" having "a complicated
significance," answers almost equally to the prescriptions of
the imagists and the symbolists. It is as definite as a picture by
Hokusai, its cadences are as pure as an air by Debussy, and
withal, if it is not allusive as the poetry of Mallarmé and so
much of the poetry of Yeats is allusive, it suggests more than
it expresses, and so echoes and reëchoes in the mind.

Pound has frequently made the distinction between the kind
of poetry that addresses itself primarily to the eye and the
kind that addresses itself primarily to the ear, and again
between each of these and the kind of poetry that speaks to
the intellect. In his epigrammatic verse, although one hears

his individual voice, and although certain pictures—the glistening Chestertonian cheek, Celestine painfully reëntering her slippers—stick in the mind, it is the acerb wit which counts chiefly. Since he stretched the term "imagism" to cover Masters's Spoon River epitaphs, one might possibly stretch it to cover his own brief comments on this serene adulteress, that reserved fornicator, and the other passionate cuckold, not to mention the numerous gentlemen and ladies whom defects of person or of breeding, a dull regard for the conventions or a distorting family setting, have reduced to follies and rascalities.

The poems included in *Lustra*, wherein he ranged his tiny vials of acid, comprise one of the most complete collections he has given us. There one may find almost all the elements which go to make this complex and vigorous poet. The liquid rhyming, the forthright diction of the Provençal singers is in his version of de Born's "Dompna Pois De Me No'us Cal." The mesmerizing passes learned from Browning evoke *Provincia Deserta* and *Near Perigord:*

> End fact. Try fiction. Let us say we see
> En Bertrans, a tower-room at Hautefort,
> Sunset, the ribbon-like road lies, in red cross-light,
> Southward toward Montaignac, and he bends at a table
> Scribbling, swearing between his teeth; by his left hand
> Lie little strips of parchment covered over,
> Scratched and erased with *al* and *ochaisos.*
> Testing his list of rhymes, a lean man? Bilious?
> With a red straggling beard?
> And the green cat's-eye lifts toward Montaignac.

The lines addressed directly to Whitman are scarcely needed, when his signature is writ large on the first *Salutation* which makes mock of "the thoroughly smug and thoroughly uncomfortable," and on *Commission*, bidding his songs

> go against all forms of oppression,
> Go like a blight against the dulness of the world;
> Bring confidence upon the algae and the tentacles of the soul.
> Go in a friendly manner,
> Go with an open speech.

There is a scattering of simple images, of which *Alba* and *In a Station of the Metro* are the most succinct, and *Dance Figure* appropriately the most graceful. The kinship with Yeats is not obvious, though one guesses it in some of the early work, but the quiet intensity of the few Chinese fragments and the suggestive mystery in some of the remoter images belong to the elder poet as to his junior. Here too are tokens of a new, more astringent influence. Witness *Les Millwin, The Bellaires*—with an epigraph from Heine for a reminder that not all ironists were born in France—and the savage lines *To a Friend Writing on Cabaret Dancers*, with its frank reminiscences of both Gautier and Tailhade. Contact with the French, and with another scholarly American Francophile, must have contributed to *Pompes Funèbres*, which has its parallel in T. S. Eliot's almost forgotten *Aunt Helen*. The voice of Propertius is unheard, but there is homage to others among his countrymen. Pound's superb renderings of Chinese poetry are relegated to *Cathay*, but if *Lustra* contains nothing equal to the *Song of the Bowmen of Shu*, the *Lament of the Frontier Guard*, or the incomparable *Exile's Letter*, there are hints and portents in several slight lyrics.

Here they are, then, the multifarious cultures, Provençal, and English, American and Italian, Celtic and Roman and French and Chinese, most of which are built into the *Cantos;* here is the ranging up and down the centuries, across the continents; here is the pressing sense of the past which makes his major work "our Sargasso sea," tossing in its depths "strange spars of knowledge and dimmed wares of price." But in that work, which attempts to merge all times, he fails, whereas in his evocations of individual poets, single periods, he wonderfully succeeds.

The poems in *Cathay* are as fine as anything Pound has produced, possibly because the spirit of Chinese poetry is so congenial to his own. There is now a large body of Chinese poetry in English, done by several careful hands. Yet one returns repeatedly to Pound's versions, not necessarily because they are closer to the original—only a Chinese scholar-poet with a knowledge of English could vouch for that—but because he came to these records of old griefs and rejoicings, love, exile, battle, meetings and partings, with so strong a feeling for the pictorial character of words, for the physical being which seeks to communicate itself thereby. *Cathay* is remarkable because it is at once exotic and immediately real. The properties are unfamiliar: pine-trees, willows and waterfalls for the scenery of the Lake country or the American prairie; the mountain temple for the country churchyard; the chattering of monkeys, the music of mouth-organs and drums for the song of the lark, the cry of the jay, and the sound of viol and flute. The drama is different, too: warfare is seen with the eyes of the common soldier rather than with those of the crusading knight or the gay cavalier; love is less often passion than the tender strength of friendship. But the strangeness never draws one away from the poem to itself.

One reason for Pound's victory over this alien material is that he has so sensitive an ear. His wisdom in slowing up a line with hard consonants for dignity:

Red jade cups, food well set on a blue jewelled table,

or for difficulty:

> ...I won't say
> it wasn't hard going
> Over roads twisted like sheep's guts...

in smoothing a line for gentle gaiety:

With ripples like dragon-scales, going grass green on the
    water—

his favorite cadence, the dying fall of the end of a hexameter, all serve to make more meaningful these grim laments and biting reminiscences. The conversational tone, the frequency with which a sentence commences with "And...", a trick

Pound's pupils have learned too well, quickens the intimacy. One may tire of Provençe, its brutalities, its intrigues. Cathay, being more civilized, is, though more foreign, somehow less remote.

> What is the use of talking, and there is no end of talking,
> There is no end of things in the heart.

To turn from these poems to *Hugh Selwyn Mauberley* is to turn from the lucid serious beauty of a Chinese painting to the oblique caustic line of a sophisticated French drawing. It is not surprising that Eliot prefers these ironic comments to the rest of Pound's work, for they show clearly, in substance, tone, and technique, the influence of poets admired by the creator of Sweeney. Yet *Mauberley,* though possibly better known than some of Pound's finer work, is so distinctly apart from it that it must be considered in another connection.

The *Cantos,* an attempt to obliterate the personal, are Pound *ipsissimus.* He poses here as the historian to whom Odysseus descending into Hades to have speech of Elpenor dead is as close as Hulme and Gaudier-Bzreska walking "eye-deep in hell" in 1914; the historian to whom the shrewdness and power of Kublai Khan are as important—no more, no less—as the shrewdness and power which built the house of Morgan. The *Cantos* are also an attempt to make poetry do the work, in a more profound way than usual, of music and of painting.

The two main themes, in the musical sense of the term, are Odysseus in Hades, as given in Andreas Divus's sixteenth-century version of Homer, and the myth, retailed for English readers in Golding's translation of Ovid's *Metamorphoses,* concerning the sailors who would have carried Bacchus off to be sold for a slave, and who were transformed into dolphins playing about a vine-wreathed ship. These themes, which recur as in a fugue, are interwoven with others taken from Greek legend, medieval story, modern history, and the items which fill the day's newspaper.

Imagists and Their Bequest

Seen as a picture, the *Cantos* are a fresco covering two panels, on the one Odysseus, on the other Bacchus, these enormous figures wreathed with crowding images from every age and country: Malatesta, Confucius, Frank Robert Iriquois of Oklahoma City, Thomas Lamont, Cabestan's lady before whom was set the heart of her lover in a dish, Thomas Jefferson, Major Douglas; and among bankers, gangsters, ecclesiastics, munitions-makers, art patrons, politicians, sages, and profiteering publishers are insets in the shape of scenes from the conflicts of the Italian tyrants and those of the American robber barons, elaborating, enhancing, enriching the main design. The reader who looks for narrative sequence, who seeks if not plot then something by way of argument, will find himself at a loss. He must learn to accept the *Cantos* as thematic in the musical sense, as design in the painter's sense.

If they presented no other difficulty, they would not be the magnificent failure that they are. But Pound has been betrayed by his attachment to a neglected corner of the past, as also by his blind rage against the mediocre, the provincial, the prurient, and the panders of the press, in whom he sees the chief enemies of civilization. He exalts a trivial incident which his special scholarship has made important to him above matters of larger significance. He pours his blistering wrath equally upon the yellow journalists, the academic bats, the Fabians, and the profiteers. His worst fault, however, is neither the privacy of some passages nor the mistaken violence of others, but the extreme dullness of those in which he approaches matters of contemporary interest. He is writing about people who excite only anger and disgust, and he transfers the objects described, in all their lifelessness and putrescence, to the printed page. Cantos XXXI to XLI, with the exception of Canto XXXVI, are amazing not as poetry but as a too-perfect reproduction of

> The slough of unamiable liars
> bog of stupidities,

79

mentioned in the passage on the modern Inferno. It is the realism of the photograph-studio rather than of the artist.

His treatment of his main themes is the work of a master. One reads and rereads those Cantos in which he moves with Odysseus, goes down to the ship, sails, through the mist, through the dark, makes sacrifice, holds speech with the dead; those, even more, in which he relives the legend of Bacchus:

> God-sleight then, god-sleight:
>   Ship stuck fast in sea-swirl,
> Ivy upon the oars, King Pentheus,
>   grapes with no seed but sea-foam,
> Ivy in scupper-hole.
> Aye, I, Acoetes, stood there,
>   and the god stood by me,
> Water cutting under the keel,
> Sea-break from stern forrards,
>   wake running off from the bow,
> And where was gunwale, there now was vine-trunk,
> And tenthril where cordage had been,
>   grape-leaves on the rowlocks,
> Heavy vine on the oarshafts,
> And, out of nothing, a breathing,
>   hot breath on my ankles,
> Beasts like shadows in glass,
>   a furred tail upon nothingness.
> Lynx-purr, and heathery smell of beasts,
>   where tar smell had been,
> Sniff and pad-foot of beasts,
>   fur brushing my knee-skin,
> Rustle of airy sheaths,
>   dry forms in the *aether*.
> And the ship like a keel in ship-yard,
>   slung like an ox in smith's sling,
> Ribs stuck fast in the ways,
>   grape-cluster over pin-rack,
>   void air taking pelt.

One returns, for other reasons, to the terrible Cantos XIV and XV, the blasting stench, the gagging sight of hell, unthinkable, unforgettable:

80

Above the hell-rot
the great arse-hole,
        broken with piles,
hanging stalactites,
        greasy as sky over Westminster,
the invisible, many English,
        the place lacking in interest,
less squalor, utter decrepitude,
the vice-crusaders fahrting through silk,
        waving the Christian symbols,
        ... frigging a tin penny whistle,
Flies carrying news, harpies dripping sh-t through the air.

One returns to Canto XXXI, both for its technical interest, the halting movement of its cadences, which seem almost to wait upon strings and flutes, the irregular chiming of the rhymes, and for its quiet exalting speech of that

                affect, wild often
        That is so proud he hath Love for a name.

But for all the splendor, the horror, the grace of the finest passages, for all that they show the poet capable of the most fastidious lyricism and the most furious invective, the *Cantos* are ineffective as an entity. Pound has stretched his theory of the co-existence of many times too far. He does not move back and forth in history and mythology with the bewildering speed of Joyce in his *Work in Progress*, but too often he seems to be walking forward with his eyes turned in the other direction. Moreover, he is so outraged by what he sees around him that he must hark back, only to breathe, only to wash his eyes clean, to Homer and Ovid and to Bertrans de Born, and the present is a blurred palimpsest. There is indeed only one real time in the *Cantos*: the past.

What Pound has achieved in the best of them and in those superb lyrics which lack the faults of his more ambitious performance is to recreate lost worlds. He has beyond any contemporary the Pygmalion touch. The poets who have learned most from him, Archibald MacLeish, who not seldom may be thought of as a modern Odysseus invoking another Elpenor, William Carlos Williams, Basil Bunting, Ernest Walsh, for all their differences, are alike in an intensity that demands accuracy of expression, in the gift for discriminating and conveying atmosphere:

> Butte no cigar wude taste gude inn the sam room
> With a bowl of gold-fish...

for that clarity which is the logic of the emotions rather than of the intellect. *Conquistador* might not have been written, certainly it would not speak so eloquently with the mouth of a dead man, if Pound's *Personae* had not spoken first.

Because imagism came to denote a small circle of people experimenting with modes of writing that are no longer new, the term has fallen into disrepute. Moreover, by this time it is clear that some of the demands of the group are answered by an art which can scarcely be called imagist. Certain of their requirements sound, after twenty years, somewhat quaint. A growing body of poets insists that content is of supreme importance, that too close attention to the form of expression betrays an absence of something to express. MacLeish jeers:

> He that goes naked goes farther at last than another
> Wrap the bard in a flag or a school and they'll jimmy his
> Door down and be thick in his bed—for a month:
>
> (Who recalls the address now of the Imagists?)
> But the naked man has always his own nakedness:
> People remember forever his live limbs.

It is precisely these lines which show his indebtedness to the derided group. They follow, rhythmically, the sequence of the musical phrase, for though they approach a precise pattern, they delight with more disappointments and surprises than a metrical scheme generally allows. Moreover, they are hard, clear, definite: they present, and vividly, an image. They are free of the taint of sentimentalism and of rhetoric. Indeed, one might describe the imagists as advocates of nudism in poetry. Not all of them have made poetry their major pursuit, and the fewest of them were content to stay stripped. But people have remembered their live limbs.

CHAPTER IV

BEARERS OF TRADITION

> And ye, red-lipped and smooth-browed; list,
>   Gentlemen;
> Much is there waits you we have missed;
> Much lore we leave you worth the knowing,
> Much, much has lain outside our ken:
> Nay, rush not: time serves: we are going,
>   Gentlemen.
>
> *Hardy.*

WHILE POUND and his circle in England were exploring their technical resources in the light of French experiments and the refinements of classical Chinese and Japanese verse, and, on this side of the water, such men as Frost, Sandburg, and Lindsay were coming closer to American folk-speech and folk-song, the breath of a new spirit was whistling in the ears of even the more insular British poets. Harold Monro prefaced his first anthology of Georgian verse, published in December, 1912, with the statement that the volume was issued "in the belief that English poetry is now once again putting on a new strength and beauty." Among the men whose names figured there, in addition to the editor, were Lascelles Abercrombie, Rupert Brooke, William H. Davies, Walter de la Mare, James Elroy Flecker, Wilfrid Wilson Gibson, D. H. Lawrence, John Masefield, T. Sturge Moore, James Stephens. In spite of their salute to newness, for the most part they harked back to the simple, sensuous verse of an earlier period.

84

It is strange to find Lawrence in this company, and it is somewhat illuminating. Lawrence was a carrier of the romantic tradition in English poetry: a passionate individualist, in revolt against the machine and the mass, against those forces in the modern world which seemed to him to hamper the free personality. He shared with such Georgians as Masefield and Gibson a first-hand knowledge of the ugliness of lower-class life in England, and some of his early poems record it unflinchingly in his native idiom. He shared with others a need to liberate himself from the pressure of the actual world, which for him meant the conflicts bred by difficulties in social and sexual adjustment. He could not pass into fairyland with de la Mare or into a beglamoured antiquity with Flecker, nor could he retire with Davies into a rural beatitude, yet much of his work betrays a desire to escape, no less urgent because it was thwarted by a healthier impulse. Although, being more badgered, he was more savage than any of them, and although he was saved by his essential candor, insofar as he was in flight, he was of their company.

Literally, Georgian verse should include all the poetry written by Englishmen since the beginning of the reign of George V. Actually, the term has come to connote the work of some forty poets (the academic number seems significant), work which, where it does not offer retreat into a dream-world, is apt to be characterized by a tender-minded quietism, and which generally exhibits a reluctance to abandon traditional forms and traditional matter. If it eschews the themes upon which the Victorians anxiously meditated and those with which the men of the nineties sought to *épater le bourgeois,* and if its diction has the charm of simplicity, for the most part it ignores the major features of our industrial and urban age: the factory, the city, and the slum, as it ignores the less obvious problems which confront the contemporary mind.

The finest technician of them all, Walter de la Mare, exemplifies strikingly the excellences and, to a lesser degree, the faults of his fellows. Although he dwells upon real and re-

85

membered beauties—the obscure exquisite lady of the West Country, the shy titmouse, quick to flit away, his poetry is itself a flitting, be it to far Arabia, to the mountains' "untroubled snows," or to

> the quiet steeps of dreamland,
> The waters of no-more-pain.

His verse is peopled with such vague allegorical figures as Time and Fate, Idleness and Hope, Fear and Pity, and, chiefly, Death, along with ghosts and elves, witches and mermaidens, while more rarely Pan or Endymion glide softly through the dreamlike place. The air is strange: there is a breath of roses and, at once, a breath of snow, and always a long shadow waiting. Nothing is vivid, nothing sharp, save when the poet summons, skillfully if somewhat gratuitously, characters out of Shakespeare, or evokes such a homely figure as Miss Loo, with

> Her tabby cat, her cage of birds,
> Her nose, her hair, her muffled words.

He is at his happiest when he sings *Songs of Childhood* in which faint echoes of the nonsense verse of Edward Lear and James Whitcomb Riley play hide-and-seek with tunes from *The Tempest,* or when his subtle music weaves in and out of the question by which he is perpetually haunted: the problem of personal identity.

It is not merely because he has turned his back upon the city and the thoughts bred by the city that he calls us away from this present. Those lyrics in which he deals with the harsh realities of old age and death show him as remote from us as do his sojourns in the country of Nod. One has but to contrast de la Mare's nostalgic melodies with the strong poem that D. H. Lawrence made, bidding the world farewell, to feel that the living poet is further from life than the dead one was even in dying. Lawrence did not welcome the end, but he launched out upon the waters of oblivion, "in the fragile ship of courage, the ark of faith," his heart "filling with peace." For all his blind hate of a machine-made civilization, for all his invalid's petulance against the mob and the snob, he was knit to life too closely to distrust that aspect of it which is death. A sense of recurrent renewal, which went hand in hand with a distinct sense of loss, bound Lawrence to an age that is clamorous with dreadful birth-pangs. It is de la Mare's aching insistence upon loss: the grief of aging, the stab of personal extinction, the sacrifice which fancy lays on the altar of knowledge—which marks him a stranger to his time. This, though in at least one lyric he admits that poetry, looking into the eyes of that old beast, science, encounters her own eyes.

His is a kind of twilight land, where birds call, with little curious cries that he carefully notes, and seas complain, in almost human moans, where flowers bloom and fall to dust with an equally tender grace, where the tread of time is never soft enough, and the empty eyes of the skeleton peer ever behind one's shoulder. He likes to insist that imagination is of the essence of the real. Certainly decay and death are realities in both the imaginative and the phenomenal world. How is it, then, that he leaves us clutching at a ghost's garment, at a handful of air? It is not merely because, like others among the Georgians, his regret over death is more eloquent than his passion for life. It is also because that regret dons the vocabulary and moves in the measures of an elder day. "Despair becowled in lead" might have stepped out of a Rossetti picture. "The cresset fire of noon" suggests less the blaze of midday than a worn piece of stage property. "The flames Hell has kindled for unassoiled sin" could singe only those who walk in the limbo of the nineties. If the metre needs another syllable, de la Mare supplies it by means of an archaic accent: "Remote, unnamèd stars," and he does not hesitate to employ inversion for the sake of verbal texture where the sense does not call for it: "This sprite ... plume will his wing in dappling light." Both the mood and the manner of his lyrics take us into a region of fairies and phantoms which now wears the guise of a rural solitude, now of some country of the moon. The marvel is that, not unwillingly, we follow. For though much of the time we are invited to walk in graveyards and to commune with shadows, we walk, we commune, to melody.

De la Mare has an extraordinarily delicate ear, a fine sense of tone-color, and the symbolist's delight in the associations which cling to his words. He conveys the feeling of slow, lumbering progress by the heaviness of his consonants and the solemnity of his vowels, as in the line:

Plodded the fetlocked horses. Glum and mum,

where the last two adjectives, though referring to the coachman who is introduced in the next line, seem to carry backward to the movement of the coach-horses. In the quatrain below, "cold" applies both to the poet's scornful observer and, by transfer of reference, to the fabulous land of *La Belle Dame Sans Merci:*

Still eyes look coldly upon me,
Cold voices whisper and say—
"He is crazed with the spell of far Arabia,
They have stolen his wits away."

One hears not only the obvious rhymes, but such echoing assonances as "still" and "spell," "coldly" and "stolen," "whisper" and "Arabia." De la Mare has the skill of an Ariel in evoking a sweet air which is no sooner gone than it begins again. This is partly thanks to his manipulation of pure sound, partly to the irregularities he skillfully introduces into his traditional metres. His syllables ring upon the ear like a bell of glass. It is not only to a haunt of ghosts, it is to music's blessed island that these poems carry us. And the monitory final stanza of *Fare Well* is one of the keynotes of this music:

Look thy last on all things lovely,
Every hour. Let no night
Seal thy sense in deathly slumber
Till to delight
Thou have paid thy utmost blessing;

Since that all things thou wouldst praise
Beauty took from those who loved them
In other days.

Too often, however, the verse of the Georgians, and de la Mare is not exempt, leaves the reader with the conviction that the author has been caught in a backwater—one giving on a charming view, and not without pleasant rural sounds, but having also the less agreeable elements of a place fed by no fresh springs. With few exceptions, notably that handful whom the horrors of the trenches shocked into life, these men remained out of step with their time. So many critics pointed this out that when, a dozen years ago, Mr. Monro published a fifth anthology, he was at pains to deny their charges and initiate a counter-attack. "Much admired modern work," he wrote, "seems to me, in its lack of inspiration and its disregard of form, like gravy imitating lava. Its upholders may retort that much of the work which I prefer seems to them, in its lack of inspiration and its comparative finish, like tapioca imitating pearls." The metaphors hold good respectively for the sloppiest free verse and the most insipid performances by the Georgians, if they cannot be applied to the successes in either group. At the same time Mr. Monro gave himself away in his final statement: "I have tried to choose no verse but such as in Wordsworth's phrase,

'The high and tender Muses shall accept
With gracious smile, deliberately pleased.' "

The reference to Wordsworth, the mention of the Muses, no less than the quaintness of the adjectives applied to them, and the nature of the pleasure they are supposed to receive, indicate the peculiarly literary character of much of this verse.

The difficulty with it is not that the poets have sought to perfect their technique by study of the masters, as every craftsman must, but that instead of using what they have learned to give form and color to their own experiences, they have taken over the very attitudes of an elder generation. There is testimony to this weakness in a remark by Rupert Brooke, a representative Georgian and in every way a figure of romance. In extenuation of the harsh realism which intrudes upon some of his lyrics: the nausea of the lover at sea, the hideous close-up of Helen in her old age, he pleaded: "There are common or sordid things—situations or details—that may suddenly bring all tragedy, or at least the brutality of actual emotions, to you; I rather grasp relievedly at them, after I have beaten vain hands in the rosy mists of other poets' experiences." Too many of his fellows too often beat vain hands in the rosy mists of other poets' experiences.

Actual, as opposed to literary, emotions savagely broke in upon a nostalgic lyricism when some of the younger men were caught in the wheels of the war machine. Robert Graves and Siegfried Sassoon wrote out of the horror, the disgust, and the terrible pity which filled them, poems that refused to look away from the man-flesh hanging on barbed wire or gone to filth in the bloodied wood. A good deal of Graves's war-verse is devoted to happy fantasies about "golden-houred 'Après-la-guerre,'" but he too has set down sharp and certain cures for lust of blood. Sassoon is tenderer, more obsessed by the waste and agony, the physical and spiritual wreckage. He will not let us forget, as he cannot forget, the survivors:

> These boys with old, scared faces, learning to walk . . .
> Children, with eyes that hate you, broken and mad.

the rear-guard, "with sweat of horror in his hair," climbing

> through darkness to the twilight air,
> Unloading hell behind him step by step;

the soldier on the convoy at night:

> We are going home. The troopship, in a thrill
> Of fiery-chamber'd anguish, throbs and rolls.
> We are going home . . . victims . . . three thousand souls.

Three sensitive-minded young poets, Wilfred Owen, Isaac

90

BEARERS OF TRADITION

Rosenberg, and Edward Thomas, were killed in the fighting. Owen's *Anthem for Doomed Youth*, with the grim onomatopoeia of its opening lines, has been widely anthologized:

> What passing bells for these who died as cattle?
> Only the monstrous anger of the guns.
> Only the stuttering rifle's rapid rattle...

But less familiar and more telling is the bitterness of his *Apologia Pro Poemate Meo*, in which he speaks of the laughter which springs up in the midst of war's hell, and, addressing those who have not endured this hell, concludes:

> You shall not hear their mirth:
> You shall not come to think them well content
> By any jest of mine. These men are worth
> Your tears; you are not worth their merriment.

The validity of one of his finest poems, alas, incomplete: *Strange Meeting*—a subtle painful dream of an encounter between two soldiers from opposing lines, took less than a decade to become brutally apparent.

> It seemed that out of battle I escaped
> Down some profound dull tunnel, long since scooped
> Through granites which titanic wars had groined.
> Yet also there encumbered sleepers groaned,
> Too fast in thought or death to be bestirred.
> Then, as I probed them, one sprang up, and stared
> With piteous recognition in fixed eyes,
> Lifting distressful eyes as if to bless.
> And by his smile, I knew that sullen hall,
> By his dead smile I knew we stood in Hell.
> With a thousand pains that vision's face was grained;
> Yet no blood reached there from the upper ground,
> And no guns thumped, or down the flues made moan.
> "Strange friend," I said, "here is no cause to mourn."
> "None," said the other, "save the undone years,
> The hopelessness. Whatever hope is yours,
> Was my life also; I went hunting wild
> After the wildest beauty in the world,
> Which lies not calm in eyes, or braided hair,

91

But mocks the steady running of the hour,
And if it grieves, grieves richlier than here.
For by my glee might many men have laughed,
And of my weeping something had been left,
Which must die now. I mean the truth untold,
The pity of war, the pity war distilled.
Now men will go content with what we spoiled.
Or discontent, boil bloody, and be spilled.
They will be swift with swiftness of the tigress,
None will break ranks, though nations trek from progress.
Courage was mine, and I had mystery,
Wisdom was mine, and I had mastery;
To miss the march of this retreating world
Into vain citadels that are not walled.
Then, when much blood had clogged their chariot-wheels
I would go up and wash them from sweet wells,
Even with truths that lie too deep for taint.
I would have poured my spirit without stint
But not through wounds; not on the cess of war.
Foreheads of men have bled where no wounds were.
I am the enemy you killed, my friend.
I knew you in this dark; for so you frowned
Yesterday through me as you jabbed and killed.
I parried; but my hands were loath and cold.
Let us sleep now. . . .

Owen is only now coming into his own, but it is his technical achievement as much as the vehement pity for which it was the vehicle which is influencing his more belligerent successors. This is the more curious since Owen had the sensuous quality of Keats, and his technique, though experimental and fascinating, was not always suited to his material. The Georgians were not given to violence. In the midst of horrors, most of them inclined to a grim resignation.

That is the attitude of a singer whose work has some kinship with theirs, though he belongs to an older generation, A. E. Housman. The distinguished classical scholar who is best known as the author of *A Shropshire Lad*, holds to a plain quaint diction and a stoic philosophy which are now alike unfashionable. He prefers the ancient themes:

BEARERS OF TRADITION

What is this world? What asketh men to have?
Now with his love, now in the colde grave,
Allone, withouten any compaignye.

He employs common metres, does not disdain inversion, and
his vocabulary, though not without russet yeas and honest kersey noes, recalls the Elizabethans, while his tunes might well
have pleased such melodists as John Fletcher and Robert Her-
rick. There is an old-fashioned grace to the lyric beginning:

> With rue my heart is laden
> For golden friends I had,

and to this:

> 'Tis spring; come out to ramble
> The hilly brakes around,
> For under thorn and bramble
> About the hollow ground
> The primroses are found.
>
> And there's the windflower chilly
> With all the winds at play,
> And there's the Lenten lily
> That has not long to stay
> And dies on Easter day.
>
> And since till girls go maying
> You find the primrose still,
> And find the windflower playing
> With every wind at will,
> But not the daffodil,
>
> Bring baskets now, and sally
> Upon the spring's array,
> And bear from hill and valley
> The daffodil away
> That dies on Easter day.

But it is less the familiar melodies and the easy speech than
the underlying thought which made Housman acceptable to
an audience which found the younger realists too sordid and
the imagists too free. If he speaks of the demiurge as "What-

93

ever brute and blackguard made the world," a phrase suggesting post-Darwinian rather than post-Copernican disillusion,
on the whole his temper shows the ironic fortitude of those
Englishmen who were tutored by Seneca. The more experimental poets dislike his willingness to use the lyrical forms
of an elder day. The more radical thinkers hate his counsels
of despair:

Be still, my soul, be still; the arms you bear are brittle,
  Earth and high heaven are fixt of old and founded strong.
Think rather—call to thought, if now you grieve a little,
  The days when we had rest, O soul, for they were long.

Men loved unkindness then, but lightless in the quarry
  I slept and saw not; tears fell down, I did not mourn;
Sweat ran and blood sprang out and I was never sorry:
  Then it was well with me, in days ere I was born.

Now, and I muse for why and never find the reason,
  I pace the earth, and drink the air, and feel the sun.
Be still, be still, my soul; it is but for a season:
  Let us endure an hour and see injustice done.

Ay, look: high heaven and earth ail from the prime foundation;
  All thoughts to rive the heart are here, and all are vain:
Horror and scorn and hate and fear and indignation—
  Oh why did I awake? when shall I sleep again?

One of Pound's telling satires is aimed directly at the *Shropshire Lad*:

> Some lads get hung and some get shot
> Woeful is this human lot.
> *Woe, woe, etcetera.*

But Housman has not left it to others to mock his seriousness.
"But oh, good Lord," he echoes the familiar complaint,

> the verse you make,
> It gives a chap the belly-ache,

offering, however, the pointed answer:

94

Why, if 'tis dancing you would be,
There's brisker pipes than poetry.
Say, for what were hop-yards meant,
Or why was Burton built on Trent?
Oh, many a peer of England brews
Livelier liquor than the Muse,
And malt does more than Milton can
To justify God's ways to man ...

'Tis true, the stuff I bring for sale
Is not so brisk a brew as ale:
Out of a stem that scored the hand
I wrung it in a weary land.
But take it: if the smack is sour,
The better for the embittered hour;
It should do good to heart and head
When your soul is in my soul's stead;
And I will friend you, if I may,
In the dark and cloudy day.

One returns to Housman partly because of a technique which, if it does not surprise with its novelty, charms with its skill: like Heine, he has written scarcely a lyric that fails to sing; he is extremely felicitous in his management of tone-color: the nice balancing of light and heavy consonants, of closed and open vowels; and he has a way with alliteration which forbids monotony. But beyond that, while he may not express the sensibility of a twentieth-century mind—a sensibility which of recent years is apt to seek relief from its complex burden in the simplicities of either the Catholic or the communist faith—Housman expresses an attitude sufficiently common in every age to be important to our own.

On Wenlock Edge the wood's in trouble;
  His forest fleece the Wrekin heaves;
The gale it plies the saplings double,
  And thick on Severn snow the leaves.

'Twould blow like this through holt and hanger
  When Uricon the city stood:
'Tis the old wind in the old anger,
  But then it threshed another wood.

Then, 'twas before my time, the Roman
    At yonder heaving hill would stare:
The blood that warms an English yeoman,
    The thoughts that hurt him, they were there.

There, like the wind through woods in riot,
    Through him the gale of life blew high;
The tree of man was never quiet:
    Then 'twas the Roman, now 'tis I.

The gale, it plies the saplings double,
    It blows so hard, 'twill soon be gone:
Today the Roman and his trouble
    Are ashes under Uricon.

He may dwell upon the endless road which shows nothing but the night; he may even commend the luckless suicide and, more rarely, envy the dead. Yet chiefly he reminds us that

to look at things in bloom
Fifty springs are little room,

and, in more desperate moments, that if

The troubles of our proud and angry dust
Are from eternity, and shall not fail.
Bear them we can, and if we can we must.

It is not a doctrine that serves men in righting intolerable wrongs, but is one that helps them to bear inevitable griefs. His slight output—he has published in a quarter of a century not more than one hundred and four short lyrics—has influenced, not always happily, many younger poets, and, when the tumult and the shouting of this day die, should again receive their tribute of praise.

Two American lyricists, Lizette Woodworth Reese, who is of Housman's generation, and that more vocal and versatile later comer, Edna St. Vincent Millay, bear an interesting resemblance to him. The homely rural imagery and clear little melodies of Miss Reese are as frankly traditional as his. Yet her work, because of a greater delicacy of timbre, as well as because of its references to a faith he cannot share, is less an echo of his than its feminine counterpart. Her praise of the thorn tree in flower repeats, less soberly, his warning to gather rosebuds while we may. Her apostrophe to the dust treats one of his frequent themes only a shade less musically and less grimly than he treats it. Miss Millay's filiation with the Shropshire lyricist is not so obvious, owing to her wider range and emphatically romantic approach, but it should not be gainsaid.

What Housman says, over and over again, is that life is short and cruel, that lovers are fickle, and that brief recompense for the harshness of man's lot comes with a glimpse of natural beauty or the solace of song. Miss Millay says, over and over again, that death comes in a day or two, that love goes over, but that there is still the blue-flag in the bog, the balm of music and great verse. The sense of the injustice which attends most of man's waking hours and brings them to so swift a terminus is more present to the elder poet. Miss Millay berates death continually, now with anger and defiance, now with simple pain, but it was not until she was faced with the shame of the Sacco and Vanzetti case that she was stirred to comment on another kind of iniquity; nor are her poems on justice denied in Massachusetts among her best work. The simplicity of her language parallels Housman's liking for plain Saxon monosyllables, although she is more "poetic" in her frequent mention of such figures as shepherds, clowns, and scullions, and in her quaint expletives, as she is also more anti-poetic in her easy references to such matters as brooms and barrels, breakfast and taxes. Metrically, her performance is more interesting than his, because she has experimented with a greater variety of forms, although she achieves her best results with the more familiar schemes.

In one of his several tirades against the virginal, untemptable stupidity of the public, Pound says of certain of his songs:

I was twenty years behind the times
so you found an audience ready.

Miss Millay's poetry, like Housman's, like the delicate lyrics
of Sara Teasdale, has found favor with a wide public because
it is, after all, behind the times. She uses a traditional technique to express traditional themes, while her clear-eyed irony
and the individual character of her verse, partly a matter of
musical phrasing, partly of vocabulary, give it a freshness
which surprises without alarming. One has but to contrast her
performance with that of such contemporaries as Pound, Eliot,
Edith Sitwell, Hart Crane, to make no mention of younger and
equally audacious poets, to appreciate how old-fashioned is her
method of attack, and how far she is from the pressure of contemporary thought. Her modernity lies in her willingness to
let the commonplaces of daily living and dying intrude upon
her verse, and in her acknowledgment that the relation between the sexes is not what it was painted by the poets of romantic love. But even these aspects of her work are not essentially of our own time. Her commonplaces are not those of the
worker or the thinker caught in the wheels of our mechanical
civilization, but those of a rural housewife, an artist in an attic,
or an exile from some village on the east coast. If her attitude
toward sex differs from that of Tennyson and Arnold, even
from that of Keats or of Shelley, it can readily be paralleled
in the verse of the Cavalier poets. Some of her happiest lyrics
are those in which she uses such models as Suckling's

> Out upon it, I have loved
> Three whole days together!
> And am like to love three more,
> If it prove fair weather...

or Marvell's

> Had we but world enough, and time,
> This coyness, Lady, were no crime,

or prettily parodies Crashaw's *Wishes to his Supposed Mistress.*
Even her later and more sober love poems and the sonnet se-

98

quence entitled, after Donne, *Fatal Interview*, do not probe the emotions with the peculiar sensitiveness of her contemporaries, but might rather be set alongside sonnets written before they were born: George Meredith's *Modern Love*. The thwartings, the conflicts, which harrow D. H. Lawrence, T. S. Eliot, Conrad Aiken, Robinson Jeffers, and which they expose, with varying success but unrelenting candor, are not fully admitted in her verse, or are confessed in a manner so archaic that it robs them of half their sharpness. It is in the gay rebellious lyrics of her youth that she strikes a more modern note. But the challenge which she flung a stodgy generation rings somewhat falsely on ears which have heard the cries wrung by a tyranny she has scarcely questioned. One returns to Miss Millay's poems less because they give the quality of contemporary experience than because they utter so piercingly the perennial cry against death of the lover of the sensual world.

One equally haunted by the fact of death, but given rather to ironic reflection than to lyric protest, was the long-lived Victorian, Thomas Hardy. Hardy's performance is of special interest because, while he began writing in the mid-nineteenth century, the thick volume of verse which he launched some fifteen years ago won him more laurels from his juniors than had been accorded him by his contemporaries. The Georgians are less akin to him than to Housman, but he may be considered here since he, too, was concerned with the rural scene and the old agricultural order, and if he looked persistently at the grimmer aspects of life, he presented what he saw in a traditional manner. A writer as uneven as he was prolific, he published a quantity of inferior verse. When he dealt with what he liked to call life's little ironies and satires of circumstance, he was apt to overweight the irony and stress the satire in a way that cheapened the poem. Drama became melodrama, and sentiment, sentimentality. Technically he was capable of gross errors, dancing metres which have a lilt inappropriate to the theme; obtrusive feminine endings; rhymes which chime too noticeably, and verbal idiosyncrasies which rival Browning's, introduced solely for the rhyme's sake. Possibly his worst fault is a prevalent tone of melancholy and negation suggesting rather a lack of vitality than the stoicism upon which he prided himself.

In one of his last and feeblest lyrics, written at the age of eighty-six and entitled, *He Never Expected Much,* he confesses that the world had not promised him more than "Just neutral-tinted haps and such," and that, for his part, not having failed to take this warning, he

> hence could stem such strain and ache
> As each year might assign.

It is this sense of a neutral-tinted experience, relying for its color on vicarious drama, often purely imaginary, and accepted with so much composure of spirit, it is this want of intensity, that spoils so much of his performance. Browning, whose life was easier than Hardy's, and the major part of whose poetry was the dramatization of others' experiences, had an energy which quickened and sharpened whatever he had to say. The difference was not as between the optimist and the pessimist, between a man who believed in the goodness of God and the immortality of the soul and a man who asked bitterly why the "purblind doomsters" had not strewn blisses instead of pains about his path. It was between a man exuberantly alive and aware of the world and a man sadly or sardonically enduring the long neutral-tinted years.

If this were all that could be said of Hardy's poetry, it would have small meaning for us, but it has several virtues of an order that are prized by poets of a later day. For one thing, he stubbornly refused to look away from the facts as he saw them. Tennyson, puzzled and saddened by the findings of the scientists, tried to reconcile what they told him with faith in some far-off divine event. Matthew Arnold, no less troubled by the attack upon received belief, could scarcely bite back his cries of pain. Hardy had the courage to face the music with

100

an occasional grimace, but without a whimper. His attitude—expressed in one of the three *In Tenebris* poems written some forty years ago—was that "if way to the Better there be, it exacts a full look at the Worst." He agreed with Arnold that poetry meant "the application of ideas to life" (it is perhaps significant that Hardy omitted the adjective "powerful" in quoting the phrase), and it was his conviction that only by exploring reality could one find the road to what he called "evolutionary meliorism." He was not quite as clear-eyed as he thought himself to be. His very anxiety to look full at the worst seems to betray a secret sense of disillusion. Later poets have been able to accept the teachings of Darwin and Huxley without such gritting of the teeth. Nor did Hardy's readiness to face the indifference of Nature imply a radical concern for the plight of man on earth. In 1913 he wrote a poem called *His Country* to which he appended a marginal note describing the poet as unable to discover the boundary of his native land, or the end of his duties to his fellows, or "who are his enemies." Yet he seems to have thought differently when the Boer War was in progress. Even in 1915 he was able to see war as an "artificial rage" and to acknowledge that a blind lust for empire is one of its strongest roots. Yet the World War was only a month old when he composed a soldier-song with the refrain, not ironically intended, "Victory crowns the just," and in March, 1917, he sent forth *A Call to National Service* as simple-minded in its patriotism if not as plain-spoken in its expression as one of Kipling's ringing tributes to the imperialist ideal. Yet if he did not always explore reality to its blackest depths, his willingness to do so constitutes one of his great claims to recognition. Believing that "delight is a delicate growth, cramped by crookedness, custom, and fear," he sought to expose those hampering weeds. Few poets have examined at once so gently and so thoroughly that delicate growth, for which delight may be another name, the relation between man and woman. It is not only in his occasional queer rhymes that Hardy recalls Browning and anticipates his juniors—it is also in his sense of drama and in his understanding of the more tenuous aspects of human interchange.

He was a modern, too, in his feeling for language, preferring it to be forthright and plain, even though his locutions might be strained for the sake of metre or rhyme. Such lyrics as *Drummer Hodge* and *In Time of the Breaking of the Nations,* recall Housman in the simplicity of the diction as well as in the metre and the tone. With his liking for homely words, Hardy antedated the imagists in their care for exactness by using the local idiom wherever it seemed suitable. As early as 1898 he prefaced his Wessex poems with the remark that he had used the old legitimate local words which had no English equivalent wherever they seemed the most natural or perhaps the only expression of a thought. And so one finds such words as "totties" for "feet," "bivering" for "chattering teeth," and "caddle" for "quandry," all in one poem, while words like "wight" for "fellow," and "hap" for "chance" recur frequently. The same gift for using the right colloquialism appears in D. H. Lawrence's dialect poems, as also the feeling for the dramatic interest of everyday life. Lawrence did not keep to this mode of writing, but the little that he did with it was finely felt, and he enriched whatever he learned from the elder poet by his own vitality.

Hardy was perhaps overfond of writing to melody, with the result that his verse is hampered by obtrusive anapaests and dactyls, but his many failures must not cloud the remembrance of those lyrics in which the tune of the notes and of the words run happily together. One instance is the *Lines Written to a Movement in Mozart's E Flat Symphony,* a poem which recalls, if it cannot quite match, Hopkins's felicitous use of alliteration and onomatopoeia. Such a charming trifle as *The Dark-Eyed Gentleman* gives the very tang and savor of balladry, and *An Ancient to Ancients,* with its recurrent formal word of address, "Gentlemen," coming in the same place in each stanza but spoken in varying tones, has a singing quality which does not impugn the thought.

102

BEARERS OF TRADITION

Hardy's earliest poem is dated 1865, his latest: 1927, and in the sixty years and more which lay between the two dates the temper and the manner of his work changed remarkably little. In this respect, as in some others, he suggests another ironist and traditionalist, his junior in years but his contemporary in feeling, the late Edwin Arlington Robinson. With the exception of that unwieldy panoramic chronicle, *The Dynasts*, Hardy attempted no poem as sustained as Robinson produced in his many novels in verse. Yet Robinson's elaborate fictions are but a more roundabout way of presenting the frustrate puzzled characters encountered in his first book, significantly entitled, *The Children of the Night*, and of reiterating the melancholy wisdom which is there set down. In his later work he did not explore more complex personalities than Cliff Klingenhagen, smiling over his wormwood while his friend drank the wine he offered, or Richard Corey, the glittering gentleman who found nothing better to do than put a bullet through his head. The poet merely allowed such characters further words and more gestures. Nor did his philosophy alter from that expressed in his earnest sonnets to Crabbe, to Zola, to Verlaine, in his prosy "octaves," and in the French forms consecrate to light verse—triolet, villanelle, ballade—into which he poured the solemn reflections and bleak moods of the early years.

Robinson saw enough of starved, diseased, misshapen lives to need a dose of stoic bitters every so often, yet he was more of a platonist than Hardy, and his verse keeps recurring to some vague, ultimate, sovereign solace which he called "the Light." Acknowledging in his early *Credo* his inability to find his way when there is not a star "In all the shrouded heavens anywhere," he yet maintained an intimation of "the coming glory of the Light," and he affirmed a like belief, however labyrinthine his argument, in the long title-poem of the volume called *The Man Against The Sky*, published nearly twenty years later. In some dim fashion he appeared to repeat it at the conclusion of his second Arthurian narrative poem, *Lancelot*, and throughout his work one finds him, the night

103

which frightened Arnold on Dover Beach still around him, the light which Browning struggled to show his fellows, still before. His poems may almost be read as a series of fugues and sonatas on the themes of Dover Beach and Self-Dependence.

It was not merely in his attitude toward a world

> . . . where bugs and emperors
> Go singularly back to the same dust,

nor the violence he felt

> Laid on his humor and intelligence
> When infant Science makes a pleasant face
> And waves again that hollow toy, the Race,

it was not alone his insistence on the necessity for facing grim reality, nor the trust he put in the brave mind and the compassionate heart which aligned Robinson with the poets of the latter half of the nineteenth century. It was the meditative character of so much of his writing—even in his narrative poems on romantic themes his protagonists are more apt to reflect at length upon their feelings for one another than to show their naked emotions at play. The tenuity of the situations in which his characters are frequently placed, the velleities which mark their behavior, deny the stern realism of which he had so much say. The body of his work leaves the impression of a poet who was intellectually sincere, but the greater part of whose life was so remote from the crude experience of most men that he was compelled to deal in romantic fictions and to set himself abstract psychological problems.

The effect is partly a matter of style. His diction is extraordinarily full of polysyllabic abstractions, his metaphors wanting in concrete detail, being largely a matter of lights and shadows, music, discords, and silences, and his involved locutions reminiscent, in their hesitancies and qualifications, of Henry James. Indeed, like James's, his characters, be they Guinevere and Lancelot or twentieth-century Americans, have a habit of talking almost in the same fashion as their author.

The brooding sense of frustration, the barren spiritual victories, apparent equally in his long narratives and his briefer lyrics, are tokens of the New England temper which the novelist, too, was so often compelled to record. Robinson sometimes depicted that locality with a cruel brush, but his work betrays a strong undercurrent of affection for its peculiar genius. As against his derogatory sonnet on New England, where passion is "a soilure of the wits," Joy "shivers in the corner," and

> ... Conscience always has the rocking-chair,
> Cheerful as when she tortured into fits
> The first cat that was ever killed by Care,

one may set his constant preoccupation with shivering joys and cheerful consciences. And though, if not always explicitly, in one poem after another he pitted Dionysius against Demos, what he appears actually to have desired was to retrieve for our bewildered period the New England idealism of a simpler age.

Tristram, which was easily twenty years behind the times, was Robinson's most popular poem. Some of his happiest achievements are to be found in a much earlier book: *The Man Against The Sky*. The title poem is a lengthy meditation on man's fate, shot with a sharper irony than Hardy's, if shadowed by a kind of solemnity which addresses the mind without speaking to the emotions. But the faults which mar his more ambitious productions are scarcely evident in this collection as a whole. The scenes are plainly present to the senses, the persons who figure in them are tenderly and acutely drawn. The broken millionaire, Bewick Finzer, with his cracked voice, his withered neck, his indigent cleanliness, his desperate brilliance, who returns,

> Familiar as an old mistake
> And futile as regret,

is a memorable portrait; so too is *The Poor Relation*, a truly

105

Jamesian creation; *The Man Flammonde*, and half a dozen others, not least the Shakespeare drawn for a fellow townsman who is being entertained in London by Ben Jonson. Here are many lyrics showing the incisive irony, the compassionate intelligence, which characterize the poet at his best.

For a picture as authentic as those presented here one must go back to the early piece, *Isaac and Archibald*, or to the later and more famous, *Mr. Flood's Party*. In the first poem one is made to see two old men, from the viewpoint of a little boy who walked with them to and from one another's farms, went down cellar with them to fetch cider, and sat with them in the orchard while they played seven-up and made sly innuendoes on the subject of old age. The other poem is a half humorous, wholly tender sketch of a solitary drinker of Tilbury Town, "convivially returning with himself" from his lookout on the hill to his jug, and when his modest orgy is over, more than ever alone. It is significant that Robinson was most effective when he was dealing with his remembrance of things past, the places and people who touched his imagination in childhood and in his early youth, or with figures whom history had somewhat actualized for him yet left at a distance, such as Shakespeare, Rembrandt, or Napoleon. When he went too far back, as in his Arthurian poems, or tried to grapple with immediate problems, as in his blank verse novels of modern life, he became vague, verbose, and romantic in the worst sense.

Like Housman's and Hardy's, his poetry dwells upon man's plight in a world where death is the sole certainty and change the one enduring fact. If it is, on the whole, more cheerful than theirs, it is nonetheless candid about such matters as the cruelty of poverty, the frequency of failure, and the needless pain inflicted by friends as well as foes. Not even the poems debating the question of prohibition and other doubtful blessings of democracy, however, prove it to be more alive than the verse of the Georgians to the conflicts which beset this generation. Indeed, he seems most remote from the present when he has to do with men and women who are our contemporaries and compatriots. Their drama is always of that entirely private kind which holds its interest irrespective of the particular settings and movements of history. It is the drama of character, and its theme more often than not is the paradox that apparent success may be actual failure, while the absence of tangible achievement can yet leave a man in possession of something that is no less gold for being "not negotiable."

The impressions of a child bred in a New England village overlooked by a deserted manor house pervade a large part of his work. The Puritan consciousness, the Puritan conscience, are offered repeated, if somewhat involved and obscure, testimonials. Robinson wrote like the Concord transcendentalist chastened by observing the material decay and the spiritual sickness of his native place, but clinging all the more firmly to the values it nurtured. He lived too far away from the world to be the realist he praised in his sonnet on Zola, yet he persistently reiterated the necessity for looking truth in the face. And for all his personal asceticism he retained the tolerance which dictated his youthful verses on Verlaine, a tolerance based on faith in the ultimate virtue of beauty. Perhaps to keep his faith, he often had need to retreat from melancholy contemplation of the present into the less troubling quarrels of the past. Technically his work is of interest only insofar as it shows how individual phrasing is an index to style where a man is using the accepted forms of an older day. His preference for blank verse and his avoidance of run-on lines enhance the old-fashioned effect of his verse. It is honest, serious work, and represents, in the old phrase, the application of ideas to life. Where it fails, as the bearers of tradition not seldom fail, it is where the ideas have reference to a picture of the world which was more actual to our grandfathers than it can be to us, or where the life has elements not sufficiently real to the poet who would deal with them.

CHAPTER V

HEIRS OF THE SYMBOLISTS

Et, dès lors, je me suits baigné dans le poème
De la mer infusé d'astres et latescent,
Dévorant les azurs verts où, flottaison blême
Et ravie, un noyé pensif parfois descend, . . .

J'ai vus des archipels sidéraux, et des îles
Dont les cieux délirants sont ouverts au vogueur:
Est-ce en ces nuits sans fond que tu dors et t'exiles,
Million d'oiseaux d'or, ô future Vigueur?

Rimbaud.

THE POET who writes:

No rose that in a garden ever grew,
In Homer's, or in Omar's, or in mine,

but must incarnadine the air of later summers for other lovers,
leaves the reader more aware of literature than of love. The
one who charms us with the melody:

Very old are the woods;
And the buds that break
Out of the brier's boughs,
When March winds wake,
So old with their beauty are—
Oh, no man knows
Through what wild centuries
Roves back the rose,

recalls not only the garlands woven by the Cavalier poets, by Spenser and Ronsard, the flower which graced the Wars of the Roses, the luxurious odors and the memories of Venus which made fragrant Graeco-Latin verse and came to sweeten the bowers of Ausonius in the fourth century of our era, but by the very vagueness of his reference reminds us of

> The flour sprong in heye Bedlem,
> That is bothe bryht and schen:
> The rose is Mary hevene qwyn,

and with it the breath and bloom of yet more ancient gardens. The poet who identifies the "Red Rose, proud Rose, sad Rose" of all his days with Shelley's image of intellectual beauty intertwines past and present yet more subtly, while the later lyricist who sings

> in the nickel-in-the-slot piano jogged
> "Stamboul Nights"—weaving somebody's nickel—sang—

> *O Stamboul Rose—dreams weave the rose!*

crowds the past upon the present with startling violence, making the coarse actuality throb with the rarest beauty that the imagination of man has created.

It is of the nature of this kind of poetry that the poet should suggest rather than state, that he should prefer a musical vagueness to definiteness of shape, and that he should evoke at once the movements of the mind and the awareness of a reality beyond the world of sense. When Poe wrote that the music of poetry should be suggestive and indefinite, by its very vagueness producing a spiritual effect, he was laying the foundations of symbolist theory. For him, and for the French school that one associates with his ideas, the image had to be indefinite or there had to be a succession of vague images, because only thus could one obtain the elusive shades, the finer vibrations, which would stir in the reader the feeling of the writer. The indecisiveness of these metaphors, melting into one another

109

like wavering bands of smoke, or transformed into something else at the instant of being perceived, like sculptures of cloud, would give the fluent quality, the multiple effects of sensation which prose is so clumsy at conveying. And by approaching more nearly the art toward which Pater declared all the others move, the poem would open the gates upon the spiritual universe which lies, for the mystic, behind the veil of appearances. Pater was one of the tutelary geniuses of symbolism in English verse, but the main impulse came from Stéphane Mallarmé, to whom, in the last years of the last century, young poets from across the channel made their pilgrimages. Faint belated traces of his influence may be discovered today in the surréalistes' surrender to fantasy, in their unappeasable inquisition of the psyche, and, more clearly, in the untranslatable subtleties of Paul Valéry.

Mallarmé's devotion to his art, his mastery of verbal magic, his care for the esoteric nuance, were partly responsible for the manner of the early lyrics of William Butler Yeats. Their tentative, suggestive, musical quality easily allows him to be called, as he has called himself, a symbolist poet. Although the verse of his later years exhibits elements of a different order, he has never ceased to employ images which have profound as well as apparent meanings. However he may have changed his approach and trimmed his style, his poetry has but altered its shape to suit the growth of the soul that animates it: it is symbolical still.

It is not without significance that the first line in his *Collected Poems* should be:

Words alone are certain good.

The fascination of the word, with its magical associations, an ear sensitive to verbal melody, and a strong religious instinct, combined to make Yeats attentive to symbolist doctrine. He has told us in his autobiography how, deprived by his father of a faith in which to rest, he made for himself a religion of his own, a kind of church of poetic tradition, legends of super-

110

human men and women, hungers and hatreds unforgettably expressed, handed down from one generation to another, by artists and philosophers. He wanted to give shape and vitality to those heroically imagined figures whose personalities had grown, he felt, out of man's deepest instinct—Platonic patterns of human excellence. And he thought to do this with a vocabulary so sensuous and musical that it would be the natural heritage of Irish poets to come.

There is no question but that he summoned up before his race an image of greatness, but it is doubtful whether he or any man could perfect a vocabulary to be transmitted to later generations of poets. Every writer must make his own style, as every man makes his own memories. Yeats came to realize this, and has written more than one lyric upbraiding those beggarly followers who aped what they could not create.

> I made my song a coat
> Covered with embroideries
> Out of old mythologies
> From heel to throat;
> But the fools caught it,
> Wore it in the world's eyes
> As though they'd wrought it.
> Song, let them take it,
> For there's more enterprise
> In walking naked.

His early work, however, drew as heavily upon Irish myth and folk-tale as upon the verse and the theory of the French symbolists. It is peopled with supernatural figures out of Celtic legend and with images of fantastic creatures, like the boar without bristles signifying winter and death, and the hound with one red ear who pursues the deer with no horns, signifying sexual desire. His verse took flame from the intellectual fire of Shelley's *Prometheus Unbound*, but Yeats was too wise to lapse, as Shelley sometimes did, into flat allegory. His study of the symbolical books of Blake and of the philosophy of the Hindu mystics came to nourish in other ways his faith in the

111

miracle-working image, the living, invigorating symbol which the poet takes from his people and from the genius of his native place.

When he became involved in Ireland's political struggle he abandoned the color and elaboration of his early lyrics for a looser, unrhetorical rhythm and a more direct, natural phraseology. But if he gave up the richness of his first manner, he continued to find in Irish mythology, in the dream of a free Ireland, united culturally as well as economically, in the imagery suggested by his native landscape, no less than in dream and vision, a stintless source for his art.

His youthful adventures in spiritualism had paved the way for an involved theory concerning the cycle of existence, the recurrence of certain phases of life, certain types of personality, the conflict between the incarnate self and the soul striving to realize an image of that self's antithesis. Many of his later poems express a philosophy which developed out of the doctrine of the Oriental sages, colored by curious personal experiences connected with Yeats's discovery that his wife had the powers of a medium. The symbols here differ from those of the early lyrics: the sun and the changing moon, the hawk's blind logic and the butterfly that is the soul, the gyre and the tower, replace the rose and the waves and the druid imagery. These are difficult poems for one unprepared to accept Yeats's archaic system, with its Zodiacal signs and its Byzantine remoteness. But they are instinct with a vitality which saves them from dry abstraction, and they are rich with a wisdom found nowhere else, unless it be in Blake's *Marriage of Heaven and Hell*. The thoughts which fill them are the thoughts of Blake:

Energy is Eternal Delight.
The road of excess leads to the palace of wisdom.
Improvement makes strait roads; but the crooked roads
    without Improvement are roads of Genius.
One Law for the Lion & the Ox is Oppression.

An exalting of the imagination, a hatred of the "levelling, rancorous, rational sort of mind" that never looked out of the eye of drunkard or saint, an inexhaustible energy of body and fantasy, these turn all his strangeness into fiery beauty, into heartbreaking nobility.

A dreamer and a visionary, he has confessed that he does not always understand his own imaginings, nor always interpret them in the same way. If the poet is puzzled about the meaning of his poem, it is not surprising that his reader should be so, and when, like Yeats, he trafficks in medieval magic and Indian philosophy, it is natural that the modern mind should be bewildered and repelled. He is too ready to give emotional credence to ideas which his reason rejects. But he has the capacity with which he credits Donne for being as metaphysical as he pleases because he can be as physical as he pleases. No poet of our time has such sensual vigor, a vigor which brings both pathos and a certain healthy coarseness into some of the work of his old age. This physical exuberance ("Exuberance is Beauty," said Blake), irradiating even his more abstruse poems, redeems them from unreality and abstractness. Plagued by the infirmities which the strongest man must bear at seventy years, ravaged by the fierce winters of Ireland's discontent, he maintains his integrity. He has found a lively symbol in the person of Jonathan Swift, whom he regards as his prototype. The stern pride and savage indignation of this eighteenth-century Irishman seem to link him to the poet who so delights in tradition, ceremony, and discipline. It dare not be forgotten that Yeats's obedience to the ascetic demands of the mind must take its turn with obedience to the demands of an active patriotism and of his own passionate nature. Hostile to reason, though marked by a nimble wit and an acute intelligence, Yeats's genius cannot interpret this age to itself. But the very body of myth and symbol which has stood like a cloud between him and his more tough-minded contemporaries has lifted his poetry to a height to which, burdened by brute fact and confused by the disorders of the moment, they could not climb.

A later generation, going to France for lessons in technique, paid its respects to the symbolists in a more naïve fashion. More than one of the writers who allied themselves with the imagists—Pound, in a few isolated lyrics, and more obviously, Amy Lowell and John Gould Fletcher, emulated the discursive music, the elaborate ornament, of Mallarmé's successors. Miss Lowell was so vigorous a publicist, so confused a thinker, and so imitative a writer, that in the course of her battle for imagism she succeeded in gaining a public for something very different: those lengthy, brassy-sounding, brightly decorated poems of hers which followed, at a distance, the work of Henri de Régnier, Francis Jammes, or, more particularly, Paul Fort. The fact that she based her experiments in polyphonic prose not upon the rhythms of verse but upon those of oratorical prose, is an additional testimony to her divergence from imagist principles, and, indeed, from any principles worth holding, for oratory implies an insincerity which is the destroying worm of poetry. Her more gifted confrère, John Gould Fletcher, although at one time calling himself an imagist, has written poems characterized by a diffuseness, a vagueness, and a care for orchestration, which alike link him to the French poets whom he admires. He has paralleled their performance rather than advanced upon it, but his most successful pieces are distinguished by an unusual richness of color and a sonorous music. Such lines as

Lacquered mandarin moments, palanquins swaying and
    balancing
Among the vermilion pavilions, against the jade balus-
    trades,

stick in the memory, and his symphonic paintings of clouds rolling through a wide midsummer sky, of an old house cobwebbed with melancholy recollections, of clipper ships straining in the wind, are more than competent.

One would be hard put to it to discover a poet of importance writing during the War years who was untouched by French influences. But since even those who devoted themselves to similar experiments differed as widely as Mallarmé from Laforgue, and since the Anglo-Americans chose a variety of men on whom to model themselves, the formula for symbolist poetry in English is reduced to something as subtle and ambiguous as a symbolist poem. A good many words have been spent in trying to prove that Pound derives from this group and its descendants, and indeed it is possible to find in his *Return* the weighted rhythms of de Régnier, in his *Alchemist* a hint of de Gourmont's *Litanies,* in several poems from *Lustra* the ironical accent of Laforgue, the wit of Corbière, the satirical savagery of Tailhade. But what Pound has in common with the symbolists is a passion for the solution of technical problems, a passion which set him to studying their predecessors: chiefly the Parnassian who so carefully pared and polished his enamels and cameos. *Hugh Selwyn Mauberley* is as obviously a tribute to Gautier as it is an attack upon those of Pound's contemporaries who had surrendered to what, with a flicker of the eyebrow at Miss Lowell, he has called "Amygism." Yet even in the *Mauberley* poems there is evidence that Pound draws upon elements which belong less to Gautier than to later comers. The familiar strophes are there, significantly distorted:

> The age demanded an image
> Of its accelerated grimace,
> Something for the modern stage,
> Not, at any rate, an Attic grace . . .

the introductory Ode for his sepulchre subtly recalls the Preface wherein Gautier nodded across the years to Goethe, and there are numerous explicit references to Gautier's verse and prose. The whole group of poems may be regarded as a sardonic commentary upon the unfading lines:

> Oui, l'œuvre sort plus belle
> D'une forme au travaile
> Rebelle,
> Vers, marbre, onyx, émail . . .

D'une main délicate
Poursuis dans un filon
     D'agate
Le profil d'Apollon ...

Tout passe.—L'art robuste
Seule a l'éternité.
Le buste
Survit à la cité ...

Sculpte, lime, cisèle,
Que ton rêve flottant
     Se scelle
Dans le bloc résistant!

And yet the very bitterness of Pound's irony:

The tea-rose tea-gown, etc.
Supplants the mousseline of Cos,
The pianola "replaces"
     Sappho's barbitos ...

the complexity of his references, his recurrent reminders of a civilization closer to that of the Third Republic than to that of the Second Empire, all combine to give *Mauberley* a symbolist cast. There are two poems in the group which are neither Gautier nor Corbière but Pound himself, and they are the best of the lot:

Died some, pro patria,
          non "dulce" non "et decor" ...
walked eye-deep in hell
believing in old men's lies, then unbelieving
came home, home to a lie,
home to many deceits,
home to old lies and new infamy;
usury age-old and age-thick
and liars in public places.

And:

There died, a myriad,
And of the best, among them,

116

For an old bitch gone in the teeth,
For a botched civilization,

Charm, smiling at the good mouth,
Quick eyes gone under earth's lid,

For two gross of broken statues,
For a few thousand battered books.

Here are Pound's fit words, Pound's personal cadences, here is Pound's lasting rage at the mob-minded money-lusting crew that holds the world in fee. These poems are not dictated by a desire to turn upon his followers, to adopt a new mode. They are the sublimed essence of the most violent of his *Cantos*.

The main part of *Mauberley* has its counterpart in Eliot's repeated attacks upon the *nouveau riche* who wears so awkwardly the appurtenances of a cultural tradition to which he was not born, in *Burbank With A Baedeker: Bleistein With A Cigar*, in the *Sweeney* poems and *The Hippopotamus*. But though Eliot, too, was for a while the votary of Gautier, he is not, except in a very limited sense, the classicist he sometimes claims to be. On the contrary, his nostalgia for the withered glories of the past (which are more strongly present to him than its ugliness), his terror of contemporary confusions and their issues, mark him plainly as a romantic. While insisting on the value of impersonality, and declaring that the poet may as readily make use of emotions which he has not experienced as of those with which he is familiar, Eliot at the same time confesses that "what every poet starts from is his own emotions." Even in creating a *dramatis persona*, he observes, the work "consists in the process of the transfusion of the personality, or, in a deeper sense, the life of the author into the character," and he says further that his personages, if they are to be alive, must dramatize, if in "no obvious form, an action or struggle for harmony in the soul of the poet." Although he has paid the tribute of imitation to the chiseled

117

precision of Gautier, his alliance with the symbolists is evident in those many poems of his which combine a sardonic naturalism with an extreme refinement of sensibility. No poet of this century writing in English has been so fully obedient to the maxims laid down by Poe, and by Coleridge before him, and exemplified by the French poets of the close of the nineteenth century, that poetry should rely upon music to produce effects which are at once vague and charged with suggestion.

Few poets in our time have exhibited such complete mastery of their instrument. Indeed, if Eliot has any claim to being called a classicist, it is because his technical excellence, like Pound's, derives in part from a close study of his predecessors, both French and English, in part from an ability to resume where they left off. Although at one time attacking the theory of free verse, declaring that "no *vers* is *libre* for the man who wants to do a good job," he has recently admitted that his own work may fairly be regarded as free verse. Its filiations are with Elizabethan blank verse and with the *vers libre* of Jules Laforgue. In both instances, as he has himself pointed out, you have the stretching, contracting and distorting of a traditional measure. It is this mingling of sixteenth-century English and late nineteenth-century French influences which allows his verse the dramatic vigor of the one and the supple ironic grace of the other.

What makes for the peculiarity of his style is his habit of borrowing, not merely technical devices, nor even musical phrases and felicitous images, but entire passages from those poets whom he admires. *The Waste Land* is a famous museum of such spoils. There is Elizabethan blank verse and Shakespearean song. There is the rhythm of the Old Testament, the echo of the Psalms:

By the waters of Leman I sat down and wept . . .

immediately succeeded by that of Spenser's *Prothalamion:*

Sweet Thames, run softly till I end my song,

and this again followed by Marvell's:

> But at my back I always hear
> Time's winged chariot hurrying near;

altered to:

> But at my back in a cold blast I hear
> The rattle of the bones, and chuckle spread from ear to ear.

The reader is startled by the novel context set to the familiar tune, no less than by the sudden shifts from a sixteenth-century air to the cadences of common speech and thence to a bit of jazz:

> Those are pearls that were in his eyes.
> "Are you alive or not? Is there nothing
>   in your head?"
>   But
> O O O O that Shakespeherian Rag——

Occasionally a knowledge of Eliot's sources may impair rather than contribute to one's pleasure in his accomplishment. Thus, familiarity with Gautier's poem beginning

> Carmen est maigre,—un trait de bistre
> Cerne son œil de gitana...

is not unapt to distract one by reflections on literary cross-pollination from the neatness of Eliot's

> Grishkin is nice: her Russian eye
> Is underlined for emphasis.

On the other hand, the recollection of Gautier's poem on the hippopotamus can only add to one's enjoyment of Eliot's satirical paraphrase. Appreciatively he quotes Ben Jonson's dictum that it is the requisite of a poet "to be able to convert the substances, or riches of another poet, to his own use," and his work is a store-house of old treasure looted indifferently

119

from the Elizabethans, the metaphysicals, the symbolists, and some less likely sources. His mentality is naturally less close to that of a Shakespeare or a Webster than to that of a Laforgue, dying, acutely conscious of his own physical malady and not unaware of the spiritual malaise of his time, in the industrialized Paris of the seventies. And so one finds Eliot's verse expressive of the indecisions, the visions and revisions, all the tentative, hesitant movements of a mind troubled by the complexities and contrasts of a civilization which is the uncomfortable heir of all the ages. Like Laforgue, he mixes the argot of the street with the question phrased only to himself by a half-lunatic Hamlet, moves easily between the monuments of the past and the tenements of the present, transposes a sentimental velleity into a witty conversational key, and sharpens the impression of the noble and the grotesque by placing them in close juxtaposition.

In his early work one found chiefly the lineaments of Webster, Laforgue, and Gautier: the grimace of a man who saw the skull beneath the skin; the irony of a man who attributed to the moon, as to the telegraph wires, the humiliations lying in wait for the feeble human organism; the imagery of a man who recorded his observations with the sensitiveness and accuracy of a fluoroscope. He was preëminently the poet of the city, not because its tall buildings, its restless surge, its "million people, surly with traffic" moved him by their greatness or their pathos, but because the crowd, the stench of commerce, the meanness to which life is reduced in the experience of the least common human denominator, exacerbated his nerves. Certain commentators on Eliot's work repeatedly express a fear of offending him by a too "vulgar" understanding of his intention. In this excessive timidity they pay a tribute to the effectiveness of his performance, for his first poems, whether, as in *The Love-Song Of J. Alfred Prufrock,* they record the impotence of a prudent man in a frock-coat fallen among the potential thieves of his virtue, or, as in other pieces, they deal with the misdirected efforts of a middle-aged lady to secure

120

an ambiguous affection, the death of a maiden aunt, a romantic interlude in a garden, or moments of cruelly intense awareness on sordid back-streets, all testify to Eliot's shrinking from and hatred of vulgarity. In this, too, he is allied to the symbolists, who, where they essayed naturalism, did so in order to expose the ugliness of that tawdry life from which they were in flight.

He has not admitted, as they did, a concern with his own sensations and emotions, but the obscurities of his work are nearly always due to the methods and purposes of symbolism. A phrase from some poet or philosopher he has studied, a reference to some figure in history or fiction comprehends, for him, a certain definite, if admittedly transient and elusive state of mind. He introduces the phrase or the allusion into his poem, sometimes merely the melody of the phrase transposed into his own words; he compresses, he selects, he intimates, and thus he creates an atmosphere, records a mood, in verse so charged with elliptical associations as to be a kind of musical shorthand. His *Rhapsody On A Windy Night* is a perfect example of this:

> Twelve o'clock.
> Along the reaches of the street
> Held in a lunar synthesis,
> Whispering lunar incantations
> Dissolve the floors of memory
> And all its clear relations,
> Its divisions and precisions,
> Every street lamp that I pass
> Beats like a fatalistic drum,
> And through the spaces of the dark
> Midnight shakes the memory
> As a madman shakes a dead geranium.
>
> Half-past one,
> The street-lamp sputtered,
> The street-lamp muttered,
> The street-lamp said, 'Regard that woman
> Who hesitates toward you in the light of the door

Which opens on her like a grin.
You see the border of her dress
Is torn and stained with sand,
And you see the corner of her eye
Twists like a crooked pin.'

The memory throws up high and dry
A crowd of twisted things;
A twisted branch upon the beach
Eaten smooth, and polished
As if the world gave up
The secret of its skeleton,
Stiff and white.
A broken spring in a factory yard,
Rust that clings to the form that the strength has left
Hard and curled and ready to snap.

Half-past two,
The street-lamp said,
'Remark the cat which flattens itself in the gutter,
Slips out its tongue
And devours a morsel of rancid butter.'
So the hand of the child, automatic,
Slipped out and pocketed a toy that was running along
    the quay.
I could see nothing behind that child's eye.
I have seen eyes in the street
Trying to peer through lighted shutters,
And a crab one afternoon in a pool,
An old crab with barnacles on his back,
Gripped the end of a stick which I held him.

Half-past three,
The lamp sputtered,
The lamp muttered in the dark.
The lamp hummed:
'Regard the moon,
La lune ne garde aucune rancune,
She winks a feeble eye,
She smiles into corners.
She smooths the hair of the grass.
The moon has lost her memory.
A washed-out smallpox cracks her face,

Her hand twists a paper rose,
That smells of dust and eau de Cologne,
She is alone
With all the old nocturnal smells
That cross and cross across her brain.'
The reminiscence comes
Of sunless dry geraniums
And dust in crevices,
Smells of chestnuts in the streets,
And female smells in shuttered rooms,
And cigarettes in corridors
And cocktail smells in bars.

The lamp said,
'Four o'clock,
Here is the number on the door.
Memory!
You have the key,
The little lamp spreads a ring on the stair,
Mount.
The bed is open; the tooth-brush hangs on the wall,
Put your shoes at the door, sleep, prepare for life.'

The last twist of the knife.

This poem is one of the bridges between Eliot's *Preludes*, with their evocations of drab streets and sordid rooms, and his symphony of modern disorder and desperation: *The Waste Land*. The voice here may be the voice of Laforgue, but the hands which arranged these images with such terrible suggestiveness are the hands of Eliot. They are images which repeat themselves in his work and so take on the character of symbols. There is the woman whose eye twists like a crooked pin, recalling Prufrock, fixed by a formulated phrase, himself "formulated, sprawling on a pin." There is the helpless stubborn crab which reminds one again of Prufrock and his unhappy notion that he should have been

a pair of ragged claws
Scuttling across the floor of silent seas.

There is the moon conceived as twisting a paper rose, as the
Lady in the *Portrait* slowly, nervously twists the lilac-stalks.
There is the lamp whose ineffectual light shines on so many
dismal streets. There is the child with nothing behind his eye—
the natural offspring of Apeneck Sweeney, or perhaps young
George himself, the unwanted youngest son of Lil and Albert
in *A Game of Chess*. Not least significant are the lines:

> Memory throws up high and dry
> A crowd of twisted things.

The dryness of barren shore which will take on monstrous
proportions in *The Waste Land:* "Rock and no water and the
sandy road" becoming the symbol of infertility and spiritual
famine, is thus one of Eliot's earliest images. The crowd of
twisted things anticipates the distortions which, in the larger
poem, cry out that the times are out of joint.

In one of his several apologies *pro domo sua,* Eliot observes
that it is possible to respond to a poem without wholly understanding it. This is true of his own work because it carries,
even for the uninstructed, certain associational values, and
never fails of technical beauties. Yet his reliance upon allusion
is so great, and the learning which produces his references
frequently so esoteric, that even the sympathetic reader is often
held off by these bars to comprehension. The reception accorded
The Waste Land upon its appearance, and the confusion among
its interpreters, may be accounted for partly by the privacy
of many of its references, if partly, too, by its quality of dream-
life. In this poem, as in dreams, objects seem to grow out of
emotion, instead of emotion, as in waking life, centering itself
upon the object. The enormous influence which *The Waste
Land* has had upon later poets would seem to bear out Eliot's
contention as to the possibility of enjoying a work before one
understands it.

The theme of the poem is a variation upon the theme of so
much of Eliot's poetry: the relation between sexual incompe-
tence or inability to love and spiritual defeat. Here the idea

124

that the abuse of love has meant the denial of life is treated as a musician might handle it, although perhaps never as directly. It is implied rather than stated, but the suggested idea is introduced, counterpointed, repeated, complicated, transposed and developed with musicianly skill and symphonic effect.

The romantic legend on which the poem is based derives from the fertility myths of Tammuz, Osiris, and Adonis, translated into Christian symbolism. The tale relates how potency is magically restored to the sick Fisher King, and fertility brought back to the land over which he reigns, a land laid waste by a drought sympathetically connected with his malady. The cure is effected by the Pure Knight, who fares forth to the Chapel Perilous to find the Lance and the Grail, obvious phallic symbols, representing the instruments of life. The poem is further complicated by the fact that it offers the material implicit in the legend as present to the consciousness of Tiresias, the seer who has been both man and woman, and who has foreknown and foresuffered all. This Tiresias is aware, moreover, not only of the dooms that Homer sang, but of the history of the ensuing three thousand years, and of all that went before, as grasped by a contemporary who looks at the war-stricken world, remembering the work of Freud and Frazer, along with the vision of Dante and the wisdom of the Rig-Veda.

None of the symbolism in the poem is fortuitous, though much of it is obscure. Thus the Tarot pack, which superficially appears to have no relation to ancient myth or modern skepticism and despair, is a pack of cards, still used by gypsies for telling fortunes, which may be traced back to an ancient Egyptian calendar recording the rise and fall of the Nile, and to a Chinese monument commemorating the recession of the waters of the Flood. Thus "Madame Sosostris, famous clairvoyante," with her "wicked pack of cards," one of which is the Hanged Man, whom the poet associates with the Hanged God, sacrificed for the sake of life more abundant, darkly emphasizes the suggestion of the freeing of the waters which will renew fertility. The four suits in the Tarot pack: Cup, Lance, Sword and Dish, have a mystic significance obviously related to fertility symbols.

The poem weaves back and forth between the Elizabethan court and post-War London, with brief sharp glimpses of royalty floating with the beloved on the Thames, slum-dwellers in a public-house rehearsing the sordid realities of marriage as they know it, a typist conducting a meaningless affair in her hall-bedroom, a lady hysterical with loneliness in her richly furnished mansion. Reminiscences of Phœnicia and Smyrna, of ancient and modern trade, of Dante's hell and no-man's land, serve to heighten the contrasts and to intensify the sense of futility and waste. And all these fragmentary scenes, enacted—as the walls of Troy were built, and the Long Walls of Athens destroyed—to music, point to the incoherence, the shabbiness, the emptiness, of a loveless infertile world. The poem ends, unintelligibly for most of us until we have pondered the notes appended to it, with a line from the Buddhist fire-sermon, the fire being the three-fold fever of greed, hate, and infatuation, which must be extinguished before the soul can enter upon its real life.

The method of the symbolists is not least evident in that passage from The Fire Sermon which deals in unmistakably plain terms with the mechanical intercourse of the typist and the carbuncular young clerk with the bold stare:

> One of the low on whom assurance sits
> As a silk hat on a Bradford millionaire.

There is a vague allusion to Sappho's familiar lyric on the evening which brings all things home, bringing the typist home at tea-time, to clear away her breakfast, light her stove, lay out tinned food, beside the window where are spread

> Her drying combinations touched by the sun's last rays.

The allusion suggests sharply the contrast between the loves of the dead Greek poet and the facile physical surrender of the

126

stenographer. The scene is briefly presented: the vanity of the clerk, the boredom and indifference of the typist, the quick termination of a meaningless episode; and a line of Goldsmith's again points the disparity between the conventions of the eighteenth century and those of our own, between the sensibilities of a girl who has indulged in a rash gesture of tenderness and those of one who has vainly tried to alleviate an unappeasable tedium:

> When lovely woman stoops to folly and
> Paces about her room again, alone,
> She smoothes her hair with automatic hand,
> And puts a record on the gramophone.

The effect of these lines is heightened by a quotation from *The Tempest* which follows directly upon them:

> 'This music crept by me upon the waters.'

The symbolical character of the poem is not merely due to the fact that it is all compact of allusions, and moves between dream and nightmare, nor even because its exquisite cadences, its mixture of archaisms and modern slang, scholarly cant and conversational ellipses, show the technical influence of the French. It is also bound up with the poet's submission, more evident in his later work, to a religious view of life.

The skepticism which seasoned his early lyrics with desperate irony is more and more suppressed, so that in *Ash Wednesday*, with its ritual supplication, and in his more recent poems, one finds Eliot striving toward an attitude to which his pyrrhonic contemporaries cannot subscribe. Eliot is not a mystic. He seems unable to follow Yeats, from whom *Ash Wednesday* has borrowed a few archaic ornaments, in believing with his emotions what he does not believe with his mind. He lacks the power of Hart Crane, tutored by Rimbaud, Whitman, and Emily Dickinson, to communicate the conviction of a spiritual universe. There is a relative thinness about the poems subsequent to *The Waste Land,* although his mastery

of music remains unquestioned, and the allusions with which
he troubles his lines make widening circles on the yielding
surface of his verse. He has spoken more convincingly of
confusion and doubt than of a difficult serenity. The picture of
desiccation in *Gerontion,* the precursor of *The Waste Land:*

> Here I am, an old man in a dry month
> Being read to by a boy, waiting for rain,

is repeated in varying tones in later poems. *The Journey of the
Magi,* which is as close to Pound's technique as Eliot has ever
come, has more to say of death than of birth:

> ... There were times we regretted
> The summer palaces on slopes, the terraces,
> And the silken girls bringing sherbet.
> Then the camel men cursing and grumbling
> And running away, and wanting their liquor and women,
> And the night-fires going out, and the lack of shelters,
> And the cities hostile and the towns unfriendly
> And the villages dirty and charging high prices:
> A hard time we had of it...
>
> All this was a long time ago, I remember,
> And I would do it again, but set down
> This set down
> This: were we led all that way for
> Birth or Death? There was a Birth, certainly,
> We had evidence and no doubt. I had seen birth and death,
> But had thought they were different; this Birth was
> Hard and bitter agony for us, like Death, our death.

A Song for Simeon is *Gerontion* transposed into a religious
key:

> My life is light, waiting for the death wind,
> Like a feather on the back of my hand.
> Dust in sunlight and memory in corners
> Wait for the wind that chills towards the dead land...
>
> Before the time of cords and scourges and lamentation
> Grant us thy peace.
> Before the stations of the mountain of desolation,
> Before the certain hour of maternal sorrow,

Now at this birth season of decease,
Let the Infant, the still unspeaking and unspoken Word,
Grant Israel's consolation
To one who has eighty years and no to-morrow...
I am tired with my own life and the lives of those after me,
I am dying in my own death and the deaths of those after me.
Let thy servant depart,
Having seen thy salvation.

The promise expressed in the more recent *Marina* poem is as tenuous as it is tender. There is more conviction in *The Hollow Men*, with its satirical parody of the old nursery rhyme:

> *Here we go round the prickly pear*
> *At five o'clock in the morning,*

its aching, halting cadences, its ghastly finale:

> Between the idea
> And the reality
> Between the motion
> And the act
> Falls the Shadow
>
> > *For Thine is the Kingdom*
>
> Between the conception
> And the creation
> Between the emotion
> And the response
> Falls the Shadow
>
> > *Life is very long*
>
> Between the desire
> And the spasm
> Between the potency
> And the existence
> Between the essence
> And the descent
> Falls the Shadow
>
> > *For Thine is the Kingdom*
>
> For Thine is
> Life is
> For Thine is the

129

This is the way the world ends
This is the way the world ends
This is the way the world ends
Not with a bang but a whimper.

One feels that the poet has only partially escaped the repressions and frustrations which he mocked so bitterly in the lyrics of his young manhood. The spirit of renunciation implicit in his later work, albeit renunciation for life's sake, may possibly have some subterranean link with the inhibitions of the child perplexed and offended by "The heavy burden of the growing soul," the simple soul

                    taking pleasure
In the fragrant brilliance of the Christmas tree,
Pleasure in the wind, the sunlight and the sea...

Content with playing-cards and kings and queens,
What the fairies do and what the servants say;

the small soul curled up in the window seat "Behind the Encyclopedia Brittanica," the soul

Unable to fare forward or retreat,
Fearing the warm reality, the offered good,
Denying the importunity of the blood,
Shadow of its own shadows, spectre in its own gloom,
Leaving disordered papers in a dusty room;
Living first in the silence after the viaticum.

It is not for the warm reality, the offered good, that one returns to Eliot, nor yet for the empty evocations of emptiness with which his *Agon* is occupied. It is for his richly allusive, ironical records of a grotesquely disordered civilization. It is for that perfection of form which is the bodiment of a poet's integrity, for the miraculously close approach of his verse to the art of music. Above all, it is for his gift of conveying, in however veiled and private a fashion, the insights of a cultivated intelligence, the tentative and complex movements of a heavily burdened soul.

130

Eliot is the most influential of those who have made symbolist technique an active principle of English verse, and one has only to examine the lyrical output of the decade between 1917 and 1927 to see how deeply, if belatedly, this influence penetrated Anglo-American work. It is responsible for the emphasis upon musical nuances; the interest in a subtler and more involved consciousness; the use of a more flexible, more various vocabulary, juxtaposing the lyrical and the anti-poetic, to convey these shades; the ready resort to synesthesia: expression of an experience in terms of a sense other than that which first apprehends it, as the blind man explained scarlet to himself by the clangor of a trumpet.

Thus one finds in the carefully modulated music, the light irony, the faintly exotic elegance of Wallace Stevens a characteristically Gallic note. Some of his choicest lyrics are pure imagism: *Peter Parasol, The Load of Sugar Cane, Bowl:*

> For what emperor
> Was this bowl of earth designed?
> Here are more things
> Than on any bowl of the Sungs,
> Even the rarest:
> Vines that take
> The various obscurities of the moon,
> Approaching rain,
> And leaves that would be loose upon the wind;
> Pears on pointed trees,
> The dresses of women,
> Oxen...
> I never tire
> To think of this.

But such work as his own favorite, because it contains "something of the essential gaudiness of poetry": *The Emperor of Ice-Cream,* or *Peter Quince at the Clavier,* or *The Weeping Burgher:*

> Ah! that ill humors
> Should mask as white girls.

131

And ah! that Scaramouche
Should have a black barouche...

read like translations from the French.

Again, when cleared of its melodramatic entanglements, the later work of Conrad Aiken, especially his touching, if somewhat repetitious *Preludes* (leading, one wonders, to what overwhelming question), represents an exploration of the psyche which owes as much to Eliot and Laforgue as to the Viennese doctors. Aiken once wrote in a private letter to the author that his long poem, *The House of Dust*, is "a complex, of which mortality is one motif, crowd-awareness another, the inter-relation of the crowd and the individual a third," and a fourth the expression of the poet's identity "in terms of a huge panorama of scenes, actions and opinions," adding: "... in the latter regard it resembles *The Waste Land.*" One must substitute feelings and apprehensions for opinions, which do not enter into Eliot's poem as such; but the prevalence of what one might call the psychological panorama in modern verse is definitely due to Eliot, and is an offshoot of the interest that the contemporary poet shares with the early symbolists in the more obscure movements of the mind.

The richly evocative pastorals and savage satires of Edith Sitwell depend for their effect upon a train of associations, often of so private a nature as to seem bizarre at first reading, and marked by an extreme sensitiveness to synaesthetic modes of awareness. Miss Sitwell delights to praise the English poets of the Augustan age, but her own work has neither the objectivity, the lucidity, nor the neatness of neo-classical verse. On the contrary, it is personal, involute, trailing clouds of story, and of allusion all compact. It is also highly civilized: only one familiar with the history of costume as well as with less recondite matters can fully enjoy her *Elegy on Dead Fashion.*

Her greatest gift is her understanding of verbal texture. One must go back to the poet who discovered how to build palaces to music, to find an enchantment to which hers is akin. Nurtured upon an aristocratic tradition which she is left, in maturity, to lament, she is always seeking the key to a fabulous past. And when she finds it, the gardens unlocked by her verse seem the haunt of one who on honey-dew has fed and drunk the milk of Paradise.

> Where reynard-haired Malinn
> Walks by rock and cave,
> The Sun, a Chinese mandarin,
> Came dripping from the wave...
>
> The flowers that bud like rain and dream
> On thin boughs water-clear,
> Fade away like a lovely music
> Nobody will hear,
>
> And Eolus and Boreas
> Brood among those boughs
> Like hermits haunting the dark caves
> None but the wise man knows.
>
> But Malinn's reynard-coloured hair
> Amid the world grown sere
> Still seemed the Javanese sunrise
> Whose wandering music will surprise
> Into cold bird-chattering cries
> The Emperor of China
> Lying on his bier.

One must yield wholly to the spell of skillfully managed vocables and fluid images tinctured with rich associations, to relish this poetry. But submission means the freedom of a country as fair as it is fantastic.

The obscurity of modern verse is almost equally due to the intellection which goes into its making and to the extreme distrust of reason which has been fostered by those scientists and philosophers whose study is the mind of man. Under this influence the writer may discard logic altogether, and offer a poem as unreasonable as a dream. But in doing this he is aware that the more fantastic the dream, the deeper its significance may be. He is not seeking to evade reality. He is using new means of coming to closer grips with it. His audience, accustomed to the logical procedures of the older poets, reads it as prose, and naturally makes nothing of it. Only by a complete surrender to the flux of images and to the multiple phonetic meanings, only by the willing suspension of disbelief which Coleridge demanded, combined with an alert appreciation of imaginative sleight-of-hand, can one enjoy it.

The Ultima Thule of symbolism is achieved by James Joyce in his *Work in Progress*. This prose poem appears to be a more elaborate, more profound, and immeasurably more difficult counterpart of *Ulysses:* a legend not Homeric but pan-human, centering around Dublin, and involving the self-portrait of a mind during a single night, when, consciousness having abdicated, the subconscious plays with history and pre-history in the dimension of dreams. The scene is ostensibly a tavern in Phoenix Park, Dublin, but it is equally any place to which the playful imagination turns. The hero, Humphrey Chimpden Earwicker, is also the bearer of the good Irish name, Sir Perse O'Reilly, since earwicker means pierce-ear, in French: *perce-oreille*; but he is furthermore Adam and Napoleon and Dean Swift; his initials H.C.E. representing the words, Here Comes Everybody. He is, in fine, the man of all time, as his wife, Anna Livia Plurabelle, is the woman of all time, and their children, Shem and Shaun, are all children, and their dreams the myths of the race. Fully to appreciate it one must be able to follow the secret passages of Joyce's labyrinthine and extravagantly furnished mind in all their windings and dippings. This is the more difficult inasmuch as he uses every resource not only of the English tongue, but of a dozen other languages, and does not hesitate to create new words, for the sake of the significance of the sound or the value of telescoped meanings. Anna Livia Plurabelle is at once womankind and the river Liffey (*amnis Livia* in Latin) and the beauty made of many beauties, as the river is the confluence of many streams. As the two washerwomen—themselves semi-mythological figures—

134

recount her story to their paddling of the dirty clothes on the stones, they bring the names of hundreds of rivers into their talk. One of them cannot hear well, for the cotton in her ears: "It's that irrawaddy I've stoke in my aars. It all but husheth the lethest sound," she says. This is not mere rendering into a lisping brogue of the words: "It's this here wadding I've stuck in my ears. It all but hushes the least sound": it is the evocation of Lethe, the stream that flows through Hades, of the Aar river in Switzerland, of the Stoke, in England, and of an Indo-Chinese river, the Irrawaddy. Some of Joyce's neologisms need no elucidation. A word like "bluddlefilth" concentrates the idea of blood, bludgeon, filth, and battlefield with admirable economy and force. A word like "thonthorstrok" carries more literary suggestions, combining as it does the idea of thunder-bolt, stroke of lightning, and Thor, the Hammerer, the Norse god of thunder. It is an acute ear that is able to catch the finer vibrations of Joyce's symbolical thonthorstroks, but that is perhaps the least of the difficulties which the text presents.

The reader has no time to orient himself before he is snatched from the scene, since time, too, is telescoped: the past impinges upon the present, the movement is as readily backward as forward, and the sense of dream-life is enhanced by the palimpsest character of the objects presented, which merge into one another and emerge from one another with the illogical rapidity of associated images. These objects have the imma-terial quality of things in dreams. One hears them more readily than one sees them, for Joyce's ear is as sensitive as his mind is quick. In his handful of short lyrics the melodies are so clear and simple that one seems to catch the accompaniment of struck ivories or plucked strings, as in "Rain on Rahoon is softly, softly falling," or the more Joycean *On The Beach At Fontana:*

> Wind whines and whines the shingle,
> The crazy pierstakes groan;
> A senile sea numbers each single
> Slimesilvered stone.

In *Work In Progress* the music is more suggestive, as in the famous closing part of *Anna Livia Plurabelle*, where the gossip of the washerwomen in the falling dusk eventually flows into the voice of the river muttering to itself over the stones under the elmtree:

Can't hear with the waters of. The chittering waters of. Flittering bats, fieldmice balk talk. Ho! Are you not gone ahome? What Tom Malone? Can't hear with bawk of bats, all the liffeying waters of. Ho, talk save us! My foes won't moos. I feel as old as yonder elm. A tale told of Shaun or Shem? All Livia's daughtersons. Dark hawks hear us. Night! Night! My ho head halls. I feel as heavy as yonder stone. Tell me of John or Shaun? Who were Shem and Shaun the living sons and daughters of? Night now! Tell me, tell me, tell me, elm! Night night! Telmetale of stem or stone. Beside the rivering waters of, hitherand thithering waters of. Night!

Joyce is most intelligible where he is most lyrical. And it is of some interest that the few pages which have been rendered into Basic English: the 850 simple words essential to communication, retain the fine rhythms of the original. It is such passages as the one quoted above that remind us of the fascination that Vico's philosophy holds for him, and which is said to inform his strange and impressive work.

Gianbattista Vico was an Italian jurist of the seventeenth century who anticipated several contemporary thinkers, including Spengler. He held that the business of the philosopher was to discover the laws of God by studying the mind of man and the development of history. God, according to Vico, gave man a sense of justice, what he called "poetical wisdom," and this irrational conscience, of divine origin, gradually developed into civil law. This development was history. But history, for Vico, did not mean progress, though the idea of progress was not wholly incompatible with his law of cycles. Nations passed, in his view, through three stages: the divine, the heroic, and the human. In the first, primitive period the government is a tyranny, maintaining itself by control of language and literature. In the second—a revolt against the first—the government is democratic, and authority a matter of jurisprudence. This in turn leads to the rise of imperial power, the civilized rule of the few over the many; but it, too, becomes corrupt and falls again into barbarism, and the cycle repeats itself. It is possible —though extremely doubtful—that a thorough study of *Work In Progress* would reveal it as an elaborate symbology of Vico's theories. There is no doubt, however, that certain strains in Vico's thought have profoundly colored this dream epic. The idea of seeking the laws of history in the nature of the human mind; the conception of time as an absolute; the effort to understand humanity by recovering the mythopoeic faculty which distinguished the childhood of the race and is still the property of the unspoiled child; the strong feeling for language as an instrument of power, verging upon magic—all these are evident in Joyce's creation, not less because it is the creation of a highly sophisticated, widely ranging modern mind.

The sophistication makes for a quality not often associated with poetry, though fairly frequent in contemporary work: an aggressively lively humor. It ranges from the witty transposition of familiar quotations, as in "where the bus stops there shop I, here which ye see yea reste," to the rich bawdiness of this passage from *Haveth Childers Everywhere:*

Mr. Answers: Bringem young, bringem young, bringem young!: in my bethel of Solyman's I accouched their rotundaties and I turnkeyed most insultantly over raped lutetias in the lock: I gave a bax of biscums to the jacobeaters and pottage bakes to the esausted; I dehlivered them with freakandesias by the constant droppings from my smalls instalmonths while I titfortotalled up their farinadays for them on my slataper's slate with my chandner's chauk: I juanted on my jingelbrett rapt in neckloth and sashes, and I beggered about the amnibushes like belly in a bowle.

Here Brigham Young and Jacob and Esau, the turn-key strutting like a turkey and the satisfied sultan, the speakeasy and Lutetia: "the mudtown of the Parisii," dissolve into one another in a giddy licentious fantasia. Indeed, Joyce's performance might be described as a monstrous, quasi-mythological,

Rabelaisian Jabberwocky, in which almost every word has several meanings, partly revealed, partly overlaid by frequent puns, the whole intricate symbolism and the sonorous lilting rhythms, occasionally punctuated by rhyme or turned into emphatic metre, all working together to reach downward to memories and anticipations astir like sub-sea life in the waters of sleep. It is an heroic if very possibly vain attempt to master material which has never before been handled so intimately in literature. And like *Ulysses*, it may also be taken as a terrible commentary on the workings of the average sensual mind as perceived by a man of genius.

Among the paraphrases of nursery rhyme in which it abounds there is one which seems to offer a metaphorical description of Joyce's method:

Hadn't he seven dams to wive him? And every dam had her seven crutches. And every crutch had its seven hues. And every hue had a differing cry.

One may think of the soul as a lame beggar—Yeats represents it so in one of his plays—and without making too strict an allegorical interpretation, conceive of it as companioned by the body, which goes on crutches, too, but those crutches: sensations, emotions, ideas, stump along in Joyce's dream in multiple colors, and with multiple cries. By the very multiplicity of its meanings, the work tends to make meaning meaningless, and so discourage all but the most passionate Joyceans. The reader is apt to cry out in a Joycean phrase: "My sights are swimming thicker on me by the shadows to this place." But this sentence, like its fellows, may be read in more ways than one: it says that the tunnel of the subconscious is so dark as to make a man feel blind; but it also says that if one goes deep enough, one becomes accustomed to the dark and sees things which are not to be beheld in the light of common day.

At the opposite pole from Joyce stands Gertrude Stein, who has made a stupendous exhibition—which has taken in a number of otherwise discerning folk—of tenderly unbuttoning herself, but whose fingers are cramped by early addiction to the ouija-board. Her strong sense of rhythm is abrogated by her lack of feeling for verbal texture. Music bores her. She has an interest in the metaphysics of language which leads her to emphasize words like "as," "and," "or," representing abstract relations, and to prefer participles, with their suggestion of continuity. This unique type of symbolism, combined with her dread of using words for their connotative values, and her belief that repetition is clarifying, results in what Wyndham Lewis has called "a sort of gargantuan mental stutter." Her occasional flashes of irony would make her work amusing if it were not so tedious. It is significant that she has had so strong an influence on writers like Hemingway and Sherwood Anderson, and no influence on poets. The few who enjoy her, like Edith Sitwell and the Scots poet, C. W. Grieve, who goes by the name of Hugh MacDiarmid, never imitate her, and seem to admire her for what she is *not* doing: Miss Sitwell for her ability to make words do what they have never done before, MacDiarmid for showing the futility of average cerebration. On the contrary, Miss Stein approaches words with the excitement of a child to whom grammar is a discovery, and the futility of much of her work is the result of her own intellectual poverty. She has some nice insights, as when she observes, "In the midst of our happiness we were very pleased," but the proper response to her performance may be found in Scene VIII from her own mocking and relatively lucid production: *I Like It To Be A Play:*

> You were astonished by me.
> All of us complain.
> You were astonished by me.
> Don't you interested trying.
> Don't you interested trying to stammer.
> No indeed I do not.

She can regard herself humorously, but she is incapable of sensitiveness to anything outside herself. When, in her autobiography, she describes her friend Elmer making Captain Peter "admit that it was a nice war," it is plain that she feels this to be "a great triumph." In the face of this egocentric callousness, astonishment and complaint are equally irrelevant.

Poets writing in English, with the possible exception of Thomas McGreevy, have not gone to the lengths of the French in exploring the realm of dreams. Even Joyce, in his effort to conquer a portion of that wild territory, has been alert to curb and rudder by the exercise of the intellect what Coleridge called "the streamy nature of association." Those who would deny the need for such curbing and ruddering belong, like the surréaliste extremists, with their interest in pure psychic automatism, in the company of psychical research students. Yet if the poet abandons control of the imaginative process at the risk of his art, it has become a truism that all poetry, even the most serious, even the wittiest, has its sources in the darker places of the mind. For some it is an escape from the harsh actual world into the land of Nod. For others it is an intensification of experience, whether a love colored by delight, or the cruel pains which beset the flesh and spirit of man on his brief journey between two oblivions. In either case, the process involves a withdrawal into that privacy where the psyche is alone with its memories and desires.

This region below the threshold of consciousness is stored with all that the poet has ever heard and seen, all he has touched and smelled and tasted, all he has ever felt, and read, and been told. It is like a cavern of old ocean where things suffer a sea-change into something rich and strange. The more aware, the more intense, his conscious life is, the more things will have fallen away to lie waiting in the cavern, the richer and stranger will be the treasure thrown up by the tide. Yet he does not therefore forego the conscious shaping and polishing of those fragments. In the game that the poet is committed to play, reason and fantasy, sense and spirit perpetually act upon one another, producing in the end something which seems as natural and inevitable as a flower or a rock. The genius is one whose subconscious mind gives him the richest materials to work with, whose conscious mind is in the most complete control of those materials.

An American who closely approximates this definition, one who plunged adventurously into life and desperately to his early death, was the author of that superb symbolist poem of our own time and place: *The Bridge*. A mystic, like Yeats, deprived, like him, of a religious tradition in which he could be at ease, longing, like him, for a sacred myth acceptable to his compatriots and contemporaries, but far more keenly alive to the disruptive elements of our urban, industrial civilization, Hart Crane found in the Brooklyn Bridge a symbol adequate to his purpose. The bridge became for him the key, not alone to the spanning of a continent, but to the ultimate union of mankind. It was the outward and visible sign of man's dynamic nature, the mechanical extension of his being which pointed to vaster ideal horizons. Where Crane telescopes sensations and emotions, or with a cinematographic touch allows the close-up of a remembered moment to open into scenes rapidly shifting time and place, he presses upon the nerve of modern sensibility. Where the light of intellectual beauty sheds its radiance on the given experience, the poet transcends all his contemporaries.

The poem proper begins with the vision of Columbus, a navigator having the stature of a mythical hero, and moves on across moving landscape and seascape, to a passage toward the close which apostrophizes once more the vision with which it opened:

> ... still one shore beyond desire!
> The sea's green crying towers a-sway, Beyond
>
> And kingdoms
>   naked in the
>   trembling heart—
>   Te Deum laudamus
>   O Thou Hand of Fire

Crane could more easily soar than saunter. Of the eight parts which compose the whole, the least successful are the *Three Songs* and the short canto, *Quaker Hill*, which center, like the lyrics, upon a personal reminiscence. *Powhatan's Daughter* identifies the Indian princess with the American earth, traversing its history since the white men took possession of it. *Cutty Sark* is the résumé of a shore leave which tenders exciting, half pathetic, half romantic intimations of journeys through the seven seas and fairer adventures of the mind. *Cape Hatteras* recalls the slow growth of the continent, lifting its peaks out of the ancient waters; the rapid rise of commerce and industry, changing the aspect of empire; the conquest of the air-ways, enormous with promise, but sowing death; the hope Walt Whitman cherished: the dream of a bridge across the gulfs of man's consciousness,—

Years of the modern! Propulsions toward what capes?

The Tunnel, one of the major parts of the poem, sees the poet descend into the subway, with its cumulation of sordid horrors, its evocation of Poe's mechanic infernos, but as he makes his exodus to the harbor, his dream revives, crossed with the pain of all he has suffered. The final section, *Atlantis*, completes the transfiguration of the bridge into a symbol of ineffable beauty and dynamic thrust—

> Migrations that must need void memory,
> Inventions that cobblestone the heart,—
> Unspeakable Thou Bridge to Thee, O Love.
> Thy pardon for this history, whitest Flower,
> O Answerer of all,— Anemone,—
> Now while thy petals spend the suns about us, hold—
> (O Thou whose radiance doth inherit me)
> Atlantis,—hold thy floating singer late!

The epigraphs from Blake and Plato help to elucidate the mystic strain which marks the whole poem, and particularly the line from the *Symposium* which Crane renders: "Music,

142

then, is that which relates to love in harmony and system."
This suggests Rimbaud's prophecy: "Always full of *Number*
and *Harmony*, poems will be made last. At bottom this should
have in it again something of Greek poetry." One is reminded,
too, of the prayer of the Pythagoreans which began: "Bless
us, divine number, thou who generatest gods and men!" and
of Nicomachus' words: "All things that have been arranged by
nature according to a workmanlike plan appear, both individu-
ally and as a whole, as singled out and set in order by Fore-
knowledge and Reason, which created all according to Number, conceivable to mind only and therefore wholly immaterial;
yet real, indeed, the really real, the eternal." Neither Crane nor
Rimbaud relied much on reason, but both were in search of
reality, and both revered the immaterial beauty of ideal
patterns.

There are several passages in *The Bridge* which read like a
fulfillment of the extravagant prophecies of Rimbaud, whom
Crane professed himself unable to read in the original (a piece
of mockery which one is at liberty to doubt). The poem is an
apotheosis of the stormy voyages and far explorations, the
energy, the agony, the exaltation evoked by the author of *The
Drunken Boat* and *A Season In Hell*.

This precocious French provincial at nineteen had exhausted
all that complete surrender to sensation, all that the intense
life of the imagination, feeding richly and rapidly on history
and science, could yield. Ironically enough, Rimbaud received
posthumous honors in his home town as a pioneer whose
industry had opened up markets for the manufacturers of the
Republic—a bronze bust of him set up during the ceremonies
was melted down during the German occupation. A sheaf of
poems, a couple of letters, the superb delirium of his testament: *Un Saison En Enfer*, his reports to the Geographical
Society, and the legend of a career which carried him from
Parisian bohemia through military adventures into the practical tasks of an African trader—these compose his legacy. But
the force of the boy who cried that the poet must be a vision-

143

ary, must make himself a visionary, that he is "truly Thief of fire," is felt in a work composed nearly sixty years after he stopped writing. Rimbaud regarded the poet as an explorer of unknown fields of consciousness, a seer, a maker, an inventor, an "alchemist of the word." He was no thin-blooded dreamer. He would have mounted the barricades with the Communards. He was acutely sensible of the gifts of science: but they were insufficient. He expected a future that would be materialistic. But above all he was a visionary. His poetry anticipated the kaleidoscopic changes and dislocations of the cinema, the cross-currents of the radio. Sensations and ideas swarmed upon him with a rapidity which made his utterance seem the dreams of a man inflamed by some powerful drug. In its ecstatic rhythms, its swift, kindling images, its semi-colloquial, elliptical notations of the actual scene as it crowds upon a shelterless sensibility, Crane's work testifies to the kinship between two men separated by the barriers of race, country, time, and circumstance.

In spite of the debt to Rimbaud, the poem has a native indigenous character which separates it from work centered, as so much contemporary poetry has been, more upon literary than upon personal experiences. The American element in Crane's performance is emphasized alike by the allusions to Herman Melville and Isadora Duncan, and by the references to Times Square and Hollywood, to Rip Van Winkle and to the hobo-trekkers behind his father's cannery works:

> John, Jake or Charley, hopping the slow freight
> —Memphis to Tallahassee—riding the rods,
> Blind fists of nothing, humpty-dumpty clods.

The scene is America: the Atlantic coast, the harbor of the empire city, with its "gaunt sky-barracks," its subway, its elevated, its "thousand theatres, mysterious kitchens," the country through which the Twentieth Century whizzes over the rails, and the Mississippi mightily moves. The spirit is American: the spirit of Walt summoning his comrades to more generous loves, of Emily Dickinson reding the riddle of identity.

One of the reasons why *The Bridge* is so full of interest is that the poem draws together three significant elements in American poetry: it opens upon the democratic vistas of Whitman; it employs the symbolist method of Poe to record his nervous terror; it celebrates the inviolable self to which Emily Dickinson clung. The *Cape Hatteras* section opens with an epigraph from Whitman:

> The seas all crossed,
> weathered the capes, the voyage done...

and moves on to apostrophize him as an elder brother:

> "—Recorders ages hence"—ah, syllables of faith!
> Walt, tell me, Walt Whitman, if infinity
> Be still the same as when you walked the beach
> Near Paumanok—your lone patrol—and heard the wraith
> Through surf, its bird note there a long time falling...
> For you, the panoramas and this breed of towers,
> Of you—the theme that's statured in the cliff.
> O Saunterer on free ways still ahead!

In the *Quaker Hill* section, which takes one of its epigraphs from Emily Dickinson, the poet surveys the Promised Land of the Fathers turned into tracts glorified by the suburban land agent in bootleg roadhouses, and having asked (knowing too well the answer):

> Where are my kinsmen and the patriarch race?

cries:

> ...yes, take this sheaf of dust upon your tongue!
> In one last angelus lift throbbing throat—
> Listen, transmuting silence with that stilly note
>
> Of pain that Emily, that Isadora knew!

This passage is immediately followed by *The Tunnel:* the journey in the subway, through the subterranean darkness, symbol

of the hell of urban America, where the poet encounters another traverser of that lightless corridor:

> Whose head is swinging from the swollen strap . . . ,

> And why do I often meet your visage here,
> Your eyes like agate lanterns—on and on
> Below the toothpaste and the dandruff ads?
> —And did their riding eyes right through your side,
> And did their eyes like unwashed platters ride?
> And Death, aloft,—gigantically down
> Probing through you—toward me, O evermore!
> And when they dragged your retching flesh,
> Your trembling hands that night through Baltimore—
> That last night on the ballot rounds, did you
> Shaking, did you deny the ticket, Poe?

These references are plain for him who runs to read. But it
is the poem as a whole which conveys at once Poe's horror of
the soulless machine, Emily's delight in the American landscape, her piercing intensity, Walt's vision of the rapid development of these States, and the revolutionary ideal upon which
they were founded. Such lines as

> —And did their riding eyes right through your side,
> And did their eyes like unwashed platters ride?

where the motion of the train, the pressure of the mob, the
suggestion of the kitchens and cafeterias where they snatch
the food which sustains them between dull job and duller
play, blend in one image of meaningless haste and needless
squalor, offer a piece of symbolism showing both Crane's
technical debt to Rimbaud and his pain at the distortion of
Whitman's America.

The poem is not without flaws. It is unnecessarily obscure,
sometimes because of the too private nature of the references,
sometimes because of too great compression of meaning,
aggravated by the use of a technical nautical terminology. The
exalted character of the writing is not always sustained at the

right level, but occasionally produces a strained, rhetorical effect. Yet, like the best symbolist poetry, it yields richer meaning with each re-reading. Such a sleight as the transformation of "dreams weave the rose" to "drums wreathe the rose" is more than a technical trick: in its context the twist of the phrase suggests the whole complex of sensations, ideas, and emotions which agitate a modern Platonist drinking with a sea-worn sailor in a South Street café to the sound of a mechanical piano grinding out *Stamboul Nights*. A simpler passage carries a like suggestiveness:

> Be minimum, then, to swim the hiving swarms
> Out of the Square, the Circle burning bright—
> Avoid the glass doors gyring at your right,
> Where boxed alone a second, eyes take fright
> —Quite unprepared rush naked back to light:
> And down beside the turnstile press the coin
> Into the slot.

Here one is conscious of the pressure of the crowd at Times Square, the brilliance of Broadway, and the lights and noises at Columbus Circle, the agony of keeping a hold on one's identity in the city mob, the terror that lurks in mirrors; and one is again reminded of the Pythagorean mystics, of the vain efforts to square the circle, so that the physical stress becomes fused with the psychological strain and this with the intellectual effort, until the whole man is involved. Throughout, the fluent prismatic colors of the imagery, the resonance of the syllables, mingle to suggest a vision which neither the definite art of painting nor the logical art of prose nor the abstract art of music can summon up. At the same time the poem is to such a degree grounded in common factual experience, so quick with conversational idiom, as to keep a lien upon reality.

Crane, in his impatience to meet death, forwent the fruits of maturity. He did not achieve the ripeness which belongs to Yeats, the technical felicity of Eliot (it is worth remarking that a posthumously published poem, *The Hurricane*, bears the stamp of Gerard Manley Hopkins). But he escaped exhaustion and staleness, and his influence upon his contemporaries continues to be felt, as the work of Horace Gregory, Lola Ridge, Louis Grudin, Yvor Winters, variously attests. Before he was undone by the pressure of immediate evils he found the symbol which would survive him, to bear to later comers his intimations of a brave new world.

CHAPTER VI

FILIATIONS WITH THE METAPHYSICALS

For a Tear is an Intellectual Thing. . .

Blake.

POETRY, MORE obviously than the other forms of literature, is a hybrid. It is partly a kind of music—at its most primitive, a throbbing of tom-toms; at its most sensitive, an arrangement of vocables and phrases which is subtly moving. But since its substance is words, and words carry meaning, it is also a way of conveying, with a clarity impossible to its sister art, a statement of fact or an idea. The practitioners of "pure poetry" have approached, but never attained to the abstract passion of music. The most thoughtful, the most logical of poet-philosophers could not be satisfied with the dispassionate abstraction of practical prose. The heirs of the symbolists, not more concerned with technical problems than with the task of setting down elusive and involved states of consciousness, turned naturally to those English poets of an elder day whose interests and perplexities were remarkably akin to their own: the metaphysicals.

Alert intelligences in the seventeenth century confronted a world which, in its disruptions and its promises, somewhat resembled the world of the twentieth-century poet. The political and religious confusion of the period is indicated in a passage from a devotional work by Henry Vaughan: "We could not have lived in an age of more instruction," he wrote, "had we been left to our own choice. We have seen such vicissitudes and examples of human frailty, as the former world (had they happened in those ages) would have deemed prodigies. We have seen Princes brought to their graves in a new way, and the highest orders of humane honors trampled upon by the lowest. We have seen Judgment beginning at God's Church and (what hath never before been heard of since it was redeemed and established by his blessed Son) we have seen his Ministers cast out of the Sanctuary, & barbarous persons without *light* or *perfection*, usurping holy offices. A day, an hour, a minute (saith *Causabone*) is sufficient to over-turn and extirpate the most settled Governments, which seemed to have been founded and rooted in Adamant."

The medieval synthesis had broken down. Science and technology were displacing magic and theology. If the eye, fixed more steadily upon the physical universe, saw the possibilities of subduing it, there was also a clearer insight into its intricacies and betrayals. Naturally, one can no more lump together indiscriminately the poets of this period than those of any other, yet a certain unanimity of apprehension and of method is observable in the work of those whom we designate the metaphysicals. Fascinated by the new learning, and unable to fit it into the framework of received opinion; adventuring among ideas as their forebears had adventured in foreign places, and likewise returning with a more elaborate picture of the earth and of man, the best minds could not produce verse that was "simple, sensuous and passionate." On the contrary, the outstanding work of the school is complex, intellectual and at times agonizedly skeptical.

The most representative of the group, and the most influential in our time, John Donne, was at Shakespeare's death a boy of fifteen, and when Milton was born, a man of thirty-five. If one sets him between these two poets, one gets a nice sense of the qualities which distinguish this preëminent metaphysical.

Where Shakespeare is so in love with English that almost every word is pregnant with metaphor, and Milton so conscious of his noble models that he is perpetually borrowing classical ornaments in which to dress his lines, Donne uses the plain fluent language of conversation:

> I am two fooles, I know,
> For loving, and for saying so
> In whining Poetry...

Shakespeare sings in the most honeyed of lyric strains, or else so loads and manipulates his blank verse to bear the weight of passionate meaning that only a miracle keeps it from breaking. Milton oftenest makes his verse march as though it had assumed the toga and the purple. Donne, always closer to the author of Hamlet than to the Puritan apologist for God, is more concerned to state his thought in all its intricacy than to give it a graceful or a rich vehicle, as in the *Hymne To God, My God, In My Sicknesse:*

> Whilst my Physitians by their love are growne
>   Cosmographers, and I their Mapp, who lie
> Flat on this bed, that by them may be showne
>   That this is my South-west discoverie
> *Per fretum febris*, by these streights to die,
>
> I joy, that in these straits, I see my West;
>   For, though theire currants yeeld returne to none,
> What shall my West hurt me? As West and East
>   In all flatt Maps (and I am one) are one,
> So death doth touch the Resurrection...

He is manifestly sensitive to verbal texture and capable of delightful melodies, but his lyrics surprise chiefly by an intellectual energy which troubles the smoothness of his numbers. It is this that sets his work apart both from the tragic wisdom of Shakespeare and the dignified splendor of Milton. Like a good talker, Donne mixes seriousness and wit, sense and sally, with a fiery element which makes his poetry the kindling thing it is.

His experience of life seems not to have been as various as Shakespeare's, nor his response to it generally as profound. Educated in the Catholic faith, but ultimately rejecting it to become one of the greatest of Anglican divines, he could neither build so integrated a structure as Dante's, nor rise, with the complacent ease of Milton, to the height of that serious soldier's great argument. For Shakespeare's delight in all sorts and conditions of men and women, Donne substituted a delight in the workings of his own mind. Milton's struggle was for liberty of conscience; that of Donne, with his more medieval sympathies, was for perfect faith. His energy was not the romantic ebullience of the early Elizabethans, nor did his thinking run in the comfortable channels of his eighteenth-century successors. He was an intellectual who examined his responses to love and to death almost as one engages in a game, which is akin to art alike in its discipline, its freedoms, and the different kinds of release it affords the participant and the spectator. His finest lyrics offer something of the pleasure that may be derived from watching chess procedure, and it is the same character which brings them so close to intelligent intercourse. But it must never be forgotten that if his poems exhibit a skillful player's cleverness, they show that he was possessed by the passionate player's intensity.

It has seemed worth while to dwell a little upon John Donne because the peculiarities of his time and his temperament have made his verse congenial to a number of contemporary poets. Their experiences could not, of course, parallel his. If his faith was shaken, it was not undone. If his career was broken, it was only apparently. If he had to adjust his conceptions of the universe to the discoveries of a Kepler and a Galileo, he was able to cling to some certainties unavailable to the twentieth-century mind. The doubts which assail men in our day were bred of events which outstrip mere personal misfortunes in magnitude and significance. But the spirit of inquiry lately abroad in the world has made us sympathetic with his tireless anatomizing. The War, in becoming a world industry, involved destruction and dislocations not confined to physical things, so that men could no longer maintain attitudes which had seemed satisfactory so short a time ago. The faith in "progress" which had been a balm to those injured by the implications of the struggle-for-existence theory was roughly ripped away. And the bitter, skeptical, ironical temper which men carried with them from the trenches, along with their lice, their wounds, and their nightmarish memories, was strengthened by new ideas of behavior which taught them to distrust their deepest instincts. The more recent findings of the psychiatrists and the anthropologists had much the disturbing effect that the teachings of the physicists had had in the seventeenth century, and the unease of the intellectuals was complicated by the beginnings, however vaguely sensed, of the breakdown of the accepted economic order.

Verlaine once said of Tennyson that when he should have been broken-hearted he had too many reminiscences. The poets of the post-War period were not falling into this trap. They looked back of Tennyson, with his melancholy tender-mindedness, back of Wordsworth, with his sublime confidence in a divine order, to men who, like themselves, knew "the ague of the skeleton," men for whom

> No contact of the flesh
> Allayed the fever of the bone.

So that T. S. Eliot, in his *Whispers of Immortality*, not even glancing at the glory and the dream whose friendly ghosts so haunted the sage of Grasmere, fixed his eye upon Webster and John Donne, concluding sardonically:

> But our lot crawls between dry ribs
> To keep its metaphysics warm.

These lines, with their startling marriage of the concrete image and the abstract idea, their colloquial use of "our lot," the

153

verb, which thrusts in one's path, as it were Yorick's skull, the worm of doubt, and with their confession of an agony which mocks itself, are a notable index to the kinship between poets three hundred years apart. One catches the note of Donne as well as of Laforgue in such a phrase as

> ... the evening is spread out against the sky
> Like a patient etherized upon a table.

The ability to turn to capital uses the intellectual currency of the day belonged as much to the English metaphysical as to the French symbolist, and Eliot has paid his devoirs to both.

Crossing the metaphysical element in his work with a stronger symbolist strain, Eliot never achieves as effective a logical pattern as Donne's elaborated conceits produce. He wants, moreover, the singular force of the elder poet. He offers

> What's not believed in, or if still believed,
> In memory only, reconsidered passion,

more often than the union of powerful feeling and lively imagery of:

> License my roving hands, and let them go
> Before, behind, between, above, below.
> O my America! my new-found-land,
> My kingdom, safeliest when with one man man'd,
> My Myne of precious stones, My Emperie,
> How blest am I in this discovering thee!

If he uses the language of ordinary speech it is not, as with Donne, in a moment of passion:

> For Godsake hold your tongue, and let me love,

but to express the tedium of the common hours:

> Oh, do not ask, "What is it?"
> Let us go and make our visit.

154

Filiations with Metaphysicals

There is a diffidence in the twentieth-century poet, infecting even his religious poems, which is not to be mistaken for the skepticism which links his early work so closely to the astringent analytical verse of this literary ancestor of his. It is not simply because they conform to the rules of his chosen form that Donne's *Holy Sonnets* have a vehemence and an integrity which sets them poles apart from such a piece of penitential music as *Ash Wednesday*. Where Donne turned his learning, which was great for his time, and his sensuality, which was great for any time, to the resolution in poetry of an emotional conflict, Eliot weaves literary references and melodious echoes into his discourse in a fashion which tends to render the emotion suspect. When he speaks of

> The Word without a word, the Word within
> The world and for the world;
> And the light shone in darkness and
> Against the Word the unstilled world still whirled
> About the centre of the silent Word,

neither acquaintance with the seventeenth-century theologian on whom he draws, nor delight in his verbalism and his music, can win as full a response from the reader as is given to those poems which Donne suffused with the fervor of his personal anguish. Yet if he lacks Donne's intensity, and is far less of a dialectitian, his contribution to modern poetry owes much to his sympathy with Donne's inquisitorial psychologizing and half-conversational, half-lyric style.

The contribution of Eliot, and, through Eliot, of Webster, Laforgue, and Donne, gave a particular cast to the poetry of the post-War period. Sometimes it is the desperate violence of the Elizabethans which is uppermost, sometimes the lyric irony, the swift contemporaneity of the Frenchman, sometimes the intellectual pattern, the self-searching candor of the metaphysical. Wit is impossible to Midas, who, though all he touches turns to gold, is condemned to wear ass's ears. The poets of the post-War generation were not always logical, but they were often witty. With satire, with irony, they revenged themselves on Midas *anno domini*. Thus even those who could not be described as metaphysical poets paid oblique tribute to the spirit of the prince of them all.

This tone is a distinguishing feature in the work of the self-styled Fugitives. These poets confessedly "never quite cared to define what they fled from," but were united in a distaste for "social optimism," and in a desire to cultivate their southern gardens. It is only of recent years that they have realized what they fled *to*, and in a symposium entitled: *I'll Take My Stand*, several of them: Donald Davidson, John Crowe Ransom, Allen Tate, and Robert Penn Warren, united with eight other writers, including John Gould Fletcher, to defend the agrarian economy, the traditional sanctities and amenities of their native place. It is singularly appropriate that Fletcher's essay bears an epigraph from Confucius. Their association, which began in 1921, culminated seven years later in the publication of an anthology of verse representing each man's choice from his own work. For all the differences among the eleven people included, the collection has unity, due to the markedly intellectual character of their poetry.

John Crowe Ransom may be singled out for consideration here, because his work is fairly characteristic of the group and obviously carries a metaphysical strain. It shows a lively wit toughened by physical vitality, and, what others eminent in the assemblage do not possess, a singularly nice ear. Ransom's verse has a kinetic energy which quickens his finest abstractions. His debt to John Donne is plain, not least in the fact that his poems should not be dismembered: it is only the lyric entire and intact which can convey the poet's meaning. Again, as with Donne, the thing presented is apt to be an idea transfigured by emotion, or an emotion intellectually apprehended. Thus in *The Equilibrists* the idea is stated in the couplet:

> Predicament indeed, which thus discovers
> Honor among thieves, Honor between lovers.

156

The emotion kindles and inflames the whole. The same union of thought and feeling is in the two sonnets: *Yea*, and *Nay*, and in *Winter Remembered*, with its echo of Villon in the final lines:

Two evils, monstrous either one apart,
Possessed me, and were long and loath at going:
A cry of Absence, Absence, in the heart,
And in the wood the furious winter blowing.

Think not, when fire was bright upon my bricks,
And past the tight boards hardly a wind could enter,
I glowed like them, the simple burning sticks,
Far from my cause, my proper heat and centre.

Better to walk forth in the murderous air
And wash my wound in the snows; that would be healing;
Because my heart would throb less painful there,
Being caked with cold, and past the smart of feeling.

And where I went, the hugest winter blast
Would have this body bowed, these eyeballs streaming,
And though I think this heart's blood froze not fast,
It ran too small to spare one drop for dreaming.

Dear love, these fingers that had known your touch,
And tied our separate forces first together,
Were ten poor idiot fingers not worth much,
Ten frozen parsnips hanging in the weather.

It is this mixture of wit and passion which gives so fresh a turn to his poetry, whether he engage in theological fencing, embroider with extravagant humor upon the bare fabric of a folk-tale, or paint a modern landscape with figures, young or old, that suddenly stretch out hands to squeeze the heart. There is Janet, who runs out into the morning to see how her brown hen is faring and who, finding it dead of a bee-sting, will "not be instructed in how deep" is the kingdom of death. There is the old man in war-paint and feathers dancing with his grandsons "around a back-yard fire of boxes," who to the

chiding of his son, their father, responds with a silence which
declares: "This life is not good but in danger and in joy,"
repents the "middling ways" of his own years of discretion, and
promises that he will "be more honorable in these days."
There are Jane Sneed and John Black, who are the typical
lovers of metaphysical poetry in being

> one part love
> And nine parts bitter thought...

as well as many another troubled pair and troubling solitary.
Ransom curbs his tendency to an orotund Latinity or a
cavalier elegance of style by resorting to a Saxon simplicity,
qualifies his acerb observation with a discriminating tenderness,
and objectifies his thought in homely images, as in his sonnet
sequence, *Two Gentlemen in Bonds*, the two gentlemen in question representing, if you please, body and mind, or being
simply the unfriendly brothers, Abbott and Paul. He delights
in juxtaposing things that seem worlds apart. In his handling
of the story of Judith of Bethulia every element contributes to
surprise: the rhythms, skillfully managed to induce a mount-
ing excitement, the subtle arrangement of masculine and feminine endings, the interplay of rhyme and assonance, the
mingling of the legendary and the contemporary:

> Beautiful as the flying legend of some leopard,
> She had not yet chosen her great captain or prince
> Depositary to her flesh, and our defense;
> And a wandering beauty is a blade out of its scabbard.
> You know how dangerous, gentlemen of threescore?
> May you know it yet ten more.

One becomes, as it were, half habituated to astonishment, and
thus prepared for the conclusion, which shows Judith, no less
than Holofernes, captive and stricken:

> The heathen are all perished. The victory was furnished,
> We smote them hiding in our vineyards, barns, annexes,

FILIATIONS WITH METAPHYSICALS

And now their white bones clutter the holes of foxes,
And the chieftain's head, with grinning sockets, and varnished—
Is it hung on the sky with a hideous epitaphy?
No, the woman keeps the trophy.

May God send unto the virtuous lady her prince.
It is stated that she went reluctant to that orgy,
Yet a madness fevers our young men, and not the clergy
Nor the elders have turned them unto modesty since.
Inflamed by the thought of her naked beauty with desire?
Yes, and chilled with fear and despair.

Perhaps because his background is not an urban one, the complexity of Ransom's verse is not as crowded as is that of much modern work. He is capable of using an ironic poetic shorthand, as witness his *Amphibious Crocodile*, which satirizes the would-be cosmopolitan provincial, *genus Americanus*, in a style deriving from Eliot's *Hippopotamus*, the *Sweeney* poems, and Pound's *Mauberley*. In a phrase here, a detail there, he recalls Eliot's earlier work, and in his ready rhymes and quickness of spirit shows a kinship with another admirer of Skelton: Robert Graves. But like his fellow Fugitives, his flight is from the confusions of our industrialized society into the comparative peace, the stable simplicities of his native region, though he turns a quizzical eye upon what he finds there. It is not for his wide scope but for his sharp wit, above all for his self-analytical passion and his mingling of the physical and the metaphysical, that he is remarkable. In the choice of much of his subject-matter and more of his imagery he is of his own place—the post-Reconstruction South, which yet refuses to admit the possibility of mechanization. In his ironical fancy, his juncture of ardor and intellectualism, he is of his own time, and therefore of the past that is kindred to it.

The intellectual bias of some contemporaries, one may instance Laura Riding and Allen Tate, has had a dangerously constricting effect upon their work. The hard angular character of the verse of the latter is due to the use of a vocabulary so abstract that it often arrests the feeling of which it should

159

be the very gesture. The detached statements of Marianne Moore exhibit a learning which is as amazing for its lack of emotional bias as for its encyclopedic range. She is apt to pleasure herself with dry notations of fact, as when, in contemplating a carrot, which she draws with thin sharp abstract lines, she concludes: "that which it is impossible to force, it is impossible to hinder." This piece is wittily entitled: *Radical*. Again, in admiring the tiger who pays no respect to his companions, she will obliquely remind the reader of Axel's admonition: "Live? Our servants will do that for us." She has an acute eye, a rich vocabulary, and an intelligence that allows her to use these tools in a delightful fashion. But her voracious mind sometimes makes her a mere cataloguer, and leads her to ornament her verse with quotations from such various sources as the *Literary Digest,* Dostoevsky, the Department of the Interior rules and regulations, the *Greek Anthology,* and the advertising section of *The New York Times.* She knows what poetry is. Not until the poets can present "imaginary gardens with real toads in them," she tells us, can we have it. Her own toads are all but real yet her gardens are not deeply imagined. Much of the time it is possible to accept her observations as straight prose, the prose of the eighteenth century, civilized, entertaining, and quite impersonal.

Appreciating the privacy of some of his references, the modern poet may seek a wider audience by confiding to his readers in a postscript, as Miss Moore has done, if not the premises upon which his work is based, at least the thought which has nourished it. T. S. Eliot set the precedent in his notes to *The Waste Land,* in which he stated that the poem owed much to Miss Weston's work, *From Ritual to Romance,* and to the Atthis, Adonis, Osiris sections of Frazer's *Golden Bough,* and mentioned the various poets and saints whose words are woven into his text. Pound has not been as explicit as Eliot, but it is common knowledge that for a full understanding of the *Cantos* one should be acquainted with the history of Provençe, with Andreas Divus's translation of Homer, with the subject-matter of Steffens's autobiography, and with the social credit theory of Major Douglas, among other things. A more recent comer, John Wheelwright, following Eliot, refers his readers to Baring-Gould's *Lost and Hostile Gospels*, the *Greek Anthology*, James's *Portrait Of A Lady*, a translation of a Nestorian novel on the Acts of Thomas, and quotes in a single poem the Hymnal, the Psalter, the Bhagavad Gita, Oliver Wendell Holmes, Stonewall Jackson, and an anonymous ejaculation made during the flood at Jamestown. Wheelwright is at once more abstruse and fuller of explanation than most of his contemporaries. In the General Argument appended to his poems he seeks to elucidate the ideas which shape his apostrophes to those of his fellows—Harry Crosby, Hart Crane, for whom the conflicts of modern life proved intolerable; to his martyred heroes: Sacco and Vanzetti; and to his pet hate: the selfish morality of secularized puritanism. Such work as this presupposes not only a knowledge of economic history and of recent shipwrecks off the coast of Bohemia, but something of the author's interest in logic and theology, and an appreciation of the fact that the man addressing us is in revolt against the cramping aspects of the New England tradition, and shares Blake's revolutionary bent, though not his naïve vision. A more straightforward poet, Cecil Day Lewis, who, like Wheelwright, drives metaphysics and revolution tandem, explains that the theme of his *Transitional Poem* is the pursuit of single-mindedness, and notes that certain lines have reference to such sources as the letters of Spinoza, the *Old Testament*, Dante's *Inferno*, Wyndham Lewis's essay on *The Art of Being Ruled*, the *Ballad of the Twa Brothers*, James's *The Ambassadors*, and the refrain of a music-hall ditty. James Agee, while offering no such guides to his thinking, gives his readers some assistance by dedicating his verse to all who appear to have inspired its author, directly or indirectly, among them, Christ, Dante, Mozart, Swift, Shelley, Van Gogh, James Joyce, Charlie Chaplin, Albert Einstein, Diego Rivera, Yehudi Menuhin, and the Holy Catholic and Apostolic Church.

161

Since poetry is primarily a matter of emotional conviction, verse that needs such explanatory appendices or that, lacking them, puzzles the intelligence, is apt to be rejected as not poetry at all. And in many instances it is not. One can enjoy symbolist verse without at once understanding it, because the melody and the vague associations stir some manner of response. One cannot relish intellectual verse without understanding it, where, as too often, it is wanting in tone-color, deficient in wit, offensively angular, and highly abstract. But delay of communication is a different thing from failure, and a statement of confusion or of dilemma may have the value of making the confusion significant, the dilemma pregnant.

That a certain dryness is in itself valuable is proven more variously by the poets of the present than by those of the past. It is the merit of more than one of the imagists, notably William Carlos Williams, and of those who followed in their train and learned from their practice. As a check upon romantic grandiloquence, it is evident in the early productions of Alfred Kreymborg, as in many of the more ambitious pieces by "Others": the poets who slyly reminded their readers that "the old expressions are with us always, and there are always others." Aridity may be a token of that self-critical intelligence from which the sincere artist has nothing to fear. One finds it in the later poems of Yeats, written when he discovered, having swayed his leaves and flowers in the sun, that he might "wither into truth," and bearing testimony to his reading of that Parisian wit of the fifteenth century: François Villon. Pound is too vigorous to be often less than savage, but he learned from his French exemplars that one may occasionally prefer the light barb to the shattering spear.

Robert Frost is not so close to John Clare and to Wordsworth in his homely eclogues but that he can infuse them with an astringent slyness. His mature work blends wit and a deeper sombreness in a more intimate fashion than his earlier, and tends to be metaphysical both in subject-matter and treatment. In one of these later poems he speaks of himself, awkwardly enough, as "a sensibilitist"—one who makes a virtue of his suffering, as he confesses, from nearly everything that goes on round him:

> Kit Marlowe taught me how to say my prayers:
> 'Why, this is Hell, nor am I out of it.'

But he does not speak Kit Marlowe's tongue. Rhetoric is impossible to this gentle and discerning man. His recent verse shows him to be one "acquainted with the night," if also one who knows how to value even a transient peace. But chiefly it indicates a new-found gift for fusing thought and feeling through some unifying image. His lovely lyric addressed to a tree at his window is typical of this phase of his work:

> Tree at my window, window tree,
> My sash is lowered when night comes on;
> But let there never be curtain drawn
> Between you and me.
>
> Vague dream-head lifted out of the ground,
> And thing next most diffuse to cloud,
> Not all your light tongues talking aloud
> Could be profound.
>
> But tree, I have seen you taken and tossed,
> And if you have seen me when I slept,
> You have seen me when I was taken and swept
> And all but lost.
>
> That day she put our heads together,
> Fate had her imagination about her,
> Your head so much concerned with outer,
> Mine with inner, weather.

Another instance, more nearly in his first manner, is the title-poem of *West-running Brook*, in which one of two speakers likens the brook to existence itself:

163

'The universal cataract of death
That spends itself to nothingness—and unresisted,
Save by some strange resistance in itself,
Not just a swerving, but a throwing back,
As if regret were in it and were sacred . . .

It is this backward motion toward the source,
Against the stream, that most we see ourselves in,
The tribute of the current to the source.
It is from this in nature we are from.
It is most us.'
                              'Today will be the day
You said so.'
                              'No, today will be the day
You said the brook was called West-running Brook.'
'Today will be the day of what we both said.'

Raymond Holden's subdued penetrating verse bears witness to
a sensibility akin to Frost's. Mark Van Doren, among whose
chief admirations are this gentle poet of New England and
the forthright seventeenth-century wit, John Dryden, has shown
in not a few of his lyrics the uses of a light, dry tone. He has
even tried to make one of them the vehicle of his pleasure in it:

> Wit is the only wall
> Between us and the dark.
> Wit is perpetual daybreak
> And skylark
> Springing off the unshaken stone
> Of man's blood and the mind's bone.
>
> Wit is the only breath
> That keeps our eyelids warm,
> Facing the driven ice
> Of an old storm
> That blows as ever it has blown
> Against imperishable stone.
>
> Wit is the lighted house
> Of our triumphant talk,
> Where only weakly comes now
> The slow walk
> Of outer creatures past the stone,
> Moving in a tongueless moan.

164

This temper is one of the charms of Elinor Wylie, whose devotion to Shelley never fooled her into believing that he was her proper model. Indeed, her early lyrics are remarkable for their reminders of William Blake and Emily Dickinson, two mystics who knew when to barter the thunderstone for the tinder-box.

The peculiar character of Mrs. Wylie's work is that it marries a spiritual insight to the wit of a woman of the world, and that the wedding is celebrated with a ceremony and a music of distinction. This combination of elements sets it apart from the verse of such sensitive and thoughtful women as Genevieve Taggard, Louise Bogan, and Eda Lou Walton. Mrs. Wylie could sing of Love the lamblike and the leonine with the simplicity of the *Songs of Innocence,* and she could also embroider upon her attachment to the civilized scene or to the English language in verse as urbane as it is lovely. She was an extraordinarily skillful craftsman, delighting in the chiseling of a phrase, the manipulation of a rhyme, the poising of light and heavy syllables. Words, their grain and color, their shape and weight, the careful balance of vowels, the nice consideration of consonants, were her particular concern. She cherished them as she cherished other man-made things: rich stuffs, fine china, tooled volumes, gardens, jewels. She seemed to love her nouns and adjectives as she did these ornaments and amenities—for the decorative element in them and for whatever reminders they could offer of a sumptuous and gracious life. Hence the smooth immaculateness, the orbed and pointed character of her verse. Its hard lustre is emphasized if one takes certain of her poems, as *The Broken Man:* the exquisite porcelain figure whose fall was less tragic than his being mended by a rivet, or *Miranda's Supper,* the account of a Virginian lady's recovery of the treasures she had buried at the coming of the Northern invader, and contrasts these pieces with those in which Edith Sitwell recalls with an equal tenderness "Echoes of elegances lost and fled." Miss Sitwell, like Mrs. Wylie, is homesick for the dignities and beauties of an irrecoverable world. She, too, has a fine sense of verbal texture. But she works by means of association and suggestion, using what she has called "a new scale of sense values," but one which is actually as old as the Rig-Veda, and as familiar as Baudelaire's theory of the correspondences between the senses:

Comme de longs échos qui de loin se confondent,
Dans une tenebreuse et profonde unité
Vaste comme la nuit et comme la clarté
Les parfums, les couleurs et les sons se répondent.

She confides her meaning to a musical nuance, and her poems stir reveries as fluent as an escaping fragrance. Oppressed by modern vulgarity, she gathers, as from some storeroom of fabulous antiques, a confusion of images which summon up an aristocratic past tinged with retrospective melancholy. But when her poetry is thoughtful, or seeks to incorporate fragments of book-learning, it has a dismal way of turning platitudinous, stiff, and dull. Mrs. Wylie's style, on the contrary, seldom fails to offer the delight of a scrupulously carven and polished intaglio. Her phrases are blunted neither by the grace of her metrics nor by the richness of her rhymes.

But what aligns her with the metaphysicals is chiefly that she displays a mind dispassionately studying its own wounds. The fact that she employed the very vocabulary of Donne has been adduced to prove that she did not fully assimilate what she learned from him. But her frequent self-portraits, showing a woman of fanatical pride and invincible irony, seem to refute that charge. Certainly it is contradicted by the nineteen sonnets which celebrate passion not so much in his language as with his fervor. The introductory one especially recalls the mood and the manner of her great predecessor:

Although these words are false, none shall prevail
To prove them in translation less than true
Or overthrow their dignity, or undo
The faith implicit in a fabulous tale;

166

FILIATIONS WITH METAPHYSICALS

> The ashes of this error shall exhale
> Essential verity, and two by two
> Lovers devout and loyal shall renew
> The legend, and refuse to let it fail.
>
> Even the betrayer and the fond deceived,
> Having put off the body of this death,
> Shall testify with one remaining breath,
> From sepulchres demand to be believed:
> These words are true, although at intervals
> The unfaithful clay contrive to make them false.

Poems like *This Corruptible*, in which the Mind, the Heart, and the Soul discourse upon the dissolution of the body with that fusion of sensuous and intellectual ardor that is essentially metaphysical; *Virtuous Light*, with its desperate acknowledgment of the mystic's danger; and the superb *Birthday Sonnet*, composed most fittingly the day before her death, offer further support to her alliance with that inquisitorial lover and passionate priest.

No less sensitive a craftsman than Mrs. Wylie, but one more inclined to employ the methods of symbolism, is that rare and fastidious poet, Léonie Adams. Her vocabulary and her lyricism seem to derive rather from Yeats than from Donne, although she is a student of the latter. The natural scene, meadow or woodland, and its wild life, the mutable architecture of the clouds, figure in her verse more frequently than such moons as may fill the bowls of silver spoons, or the beauty that

> sets its sandal on a London roof
> And takes polluted Thames to be its mirror.

But her acute response to that spectacle of which man is neither the artificer nor the participant, but merely the beholder, makes her no less a metaphysical poet. Her mind, like Marvell's, is capable of

> Annihilating all that's made
> To a green Thought in a green Shade.

167

Her soul, like his,

> into the boughs does glide,
> There like a Bird it sits, and sings,
> Then whets, and combs its silver Wings;
> And, till prepar'd for longer flight,
> Waves in its Plumes the various Light.

None of her contemporaries has recorded with more delicate precision the motions of the hours and the seasons as sky and earth body them forth. The shadow and the shining of dawn and evening sky, harvest and winter solstice, fill her poetry, not without aching reference to generation and decay, as these touch the human spectator. She is as no other the poet of light, whether it be that of the dawn who "comes wildly up the East," of the moon: "The harrier of clouds, a flame half seen," or of the evening sky:

> How now are we tossed about by a windy heaven,
> The eye that scans it madded to discern
> In a single quarter all the wild ravage of light,
> Amazing light to quiver and suddenly turn
> Before the stormy demon fall of night;
> And yet west spaces saved celestial
> With silver sprinklings of the anointed sun.
> The eye goes up for certitude,
> Driven hither and thither on that shifty scene
> To the dome closing like impenetrable hoar,
> And down from the cold zenith drops abashed;
> O desolation rent by intolerable blue
> Of the living heaven's core,
> Nor death itself at last the heavenly whim.
> For how can an eye sustain
> To watch heaven slain and quickening, or do
> To stretch in its little orbit and contain
> Sky balancing chaos in an inconstant rim?

Although Herbert is one of her acknowledged masters, the reader is reminded rather of Vaughan's imagery:

> I see them walking in Air of glory,
> Whose light doth trample on my days.

168

Filiations with Metaphysicals

There is in God (some say)
A deep, but dazzling darkness.

The unthrift Sunne shot vitall gold
  A thousand peeces,
And heaven its azure did unfold
  Chequer'd with snowie fleeces,
The air was all in spice...

Her senses keyed to the ecstasy and the anguish aroused by the heavenly theatre, she pays due tribute to the unseen dramatist—time. Her preoccupation with this theme, and her manner of handling it, are testimony to her kinship with poets who vexed their hearts over the abstractions of a believing age, and their later fellows. Her lyric, *Time and Spirit*, has the accent, for all its more disciplined music, of the New England mystic who wrote of the long summers of Hesperides. Her poem, *The Mount*, recalls the mood which inspired *The Sunflower*, though it presents time as Blake did not envisage it, under the aspect of eternity:

No, I have tempered haste,
The joyous traveler said,
The steed has passed me now
Whose hurrying hooves I fled.
My spectre rides thereon,
I learned what mount he has,
Upon what summers fed,
And wept to know again,
Beneath the saddle swung,
Treasure for whose great theft
This breast was wrung.
His bridle bells sang out,
I could not tell their chime,
So brilliantly he rings,
But called his name as Time.
His bin was morning light,
Those straws which gild his bed
Are of the fallen West.
Although green lands consume

169

Beneath their burning tread,
In everlasting bright
His hooves have rest.

Her love lyrics are no less ethereal, no less acute, than her
poems on themes not so immediately human. Here, too, her
concern is with the most subtle states of mutual consciousness, the most piercing moments of communion or division
between lovers. Here, too, the scene is furnished by unearthly
elements, the mortal pang quickened or assuaged because it
is endured in sight of

The sky, that's heaven's seat.

However personal the emotion which prompted these poems,
or the symbols chosen for its expression, they are not private
in the sense of being strictly occasional or teasingly obscure.
Their references are too large to admit the first fault, their
imaginative quality too keen to admit the second. This is
not to deny that Miss Adams's scope is limited. Her poetry has
not the richness of T. S. Eliot's, the wit of John Crowe Ransom's, the variety of Elinor Wylie's. But if she does not range
widely, she cuts deep. The same may be said of the work of the
young poet, Elder Olsen, which sometimes delicately recalls
hers. In all her lyrics an ecstatic awareness of the sensual min-
gles with a passionate exploration of supersensual realities.

It is this, as much as her vocabulary and her imagery, which
knits her work so closely to that of William Butler Yeats. By
the same token, it is this which proves Yeats to be no less a
metaphysical, in the literary historian's sense of the word, than
a symbolist. He has told us how he peopled the Irish hills and
streams with those gods and kingly men whose images he
thought must inflame the imagination of his countrymen as
they had kindled his own, and how, tutored by Pater, Mallarmé,
and Villiers de l'Isle Adam, he elaborated the poetry which
was the vehicle of his dream. He has told us, too, that he
eventually abandoned the dream, or changed it out of recogni-

tion. Yet the chief feature of his work, the quality which lets him say,

> There is not a fool can call me friend,
> And I may dine at journey's end
> With Landor and with Donne,

is that the dream does not ever obliterate the actual, but wears indeed its most expressive lineaments.

He understood at the opening of his career that if he wrote sincerely and naturally, out of the deeps of experience, he would, provided his life were an interesting one, be a great poet. It is this fundamental sincerity, this hatred of whatever is facile, casual, unrealized, joined with a fervent sense of powers now beyond our knowledge, if partially within our control, which gives his work its strength. Nor can one discount the fact that his life has been an interesting one. He has known bad luck: the misery of "returned yet unrequited love," the ugliness of the struggles of a small oppressed nation, the bitterness of civil war; and good luck: intimate contact with some of the most powerful personalities of three generations of artists, thinkers, and revolutionaries. But it is not alone the stress of private tragedy and of public life, nor even submission to strict discipline in his art, which has made him the major figure that he is. He has continued to draw sustenance from a native tradition formed to satisfy his ineradicable mysticism, and from a native landscape which has offered to his more active imagination the equivalent of what the Lake landscape offered Wordsworth. In marrying the Irish landscape to Celtic myth he made the two equal, and in all his poetry the physical is nowise shamed before the supernatural.

Perhaps because his fantasy more often chooses pagan and Eastern than Christian symbols, he shows his delight, with a freedom otherwise impossible to him, in the world of sense. Perhaps, too, because he is a passionate man whose life was molded by a desperate love for that "phoenix" of whom he

171

wrote some of his finest poems and by hopeless labor in his country's cause, he can no more deny the body than the spirit. It did not take him long to exchange pre-Raphaelite detail for the more rigorous exactness of Villon and Dante. Even in his earliest lyrics, suffused as they are with the heavy fragrance of the mystic Rose, one finds him pleading for a little space that the rose-breath does not fill, so that he may still be aware of common things and ordinary mortal hopes. The lament of the old pensioner who spits "into the face of Time" that has transfigured him is an anticipation of Yeats's own complaint of decrepit age which has been tied to him, like "a sort of battered kettle" at the heel of a dog. He asks in one of his late poems whether Homer had any theme but original sin. He mocks the shuffling scholars who would be abashed by the presence of the Catullus whom they annotate so learnedly, as he mocks the ghosts railing at Don Juan's sinewy thigh. He will not admit that the body must be bruised to pleasure the soul, or that love can take the one without the other. He knows as well as John Donne that

> Loves mysteries in soules doe grow,
> But yet the body is his booke.

It is a thought which finds the confirmation of the general in the query of a recent popular song: "Have you ever seen a dream walking?" The question is rhetorical. Lover and poet both have their dream: both have seen it in act.

The medievalism which obtrudes itself in so much of his poetry fades before the acuteness and energy of the poet's physical self. When he speaks of sex it is without subterfuge or aggressiveness, but with that complete self-possession that Blake knew:

> Abstinence sows sand all over
> The ruddy limbs & flaming hair,
> But Desire Gratified
> Plants fruits of life & beauty there.

172

FILIATIONS WITH METAPHYSICALS

Yeats is less abstract than Blake, especially in *Words for Music Perhaps*, where Crazy Jane and Tom the Lunatic are the speakers:

> 'Whatever stands in field or flood
> Bird, beast, fish or man,
> Mare or stallion, cock or hen,
> Stands in God's unchanging eye
> In all the vigour of its blood;
> In that faith I live or die.'

The mystic has been defined as one who believes in the spiritual apprehension of truths beyond the understanding. The metaphysical poet may be defined as one who is capable of the sensual apprehension of truths that torment the understanding, and who communicates them with passion. If he is a mystic, as is not seldom the case, his work is the very utterance of the intellectual love of God. If not, it still expresses an intellectual love, but this time a love of all that makes man lament his mortality. Both notes are sounded in the poetry of Yeats, and, if not with the force of his genius, yet clearly, in that of the young poet, Léonie Adams.

Both are sounded, too, though the first more urgently, in the work of Gerard Manley Hopkins, whose tardy recognition and current influence allow one to reckon him as belonging to our own time. It was not until 1918 that his somewhat overweening friend, Robert Bridges, had his poems published, thus drawing them out of the obscurity which had shrouded them during the lifetime of the poet and for twenty-nine years after his early death. There are now several studies of Hopkins's work available, as well as the two magnificent volumes of his letters; but the chief testimony to his power is found in the impress he has made upon the younger generation of English poets. The technique of men like W. H. Auden and C. Day Lewis derives obviously from Hopkins, and this is the more remarkable since their theme is the union of mankind in a new economic set-up, iconoclastic in its assumptions and

173

scientific in its bias, while the Jesuit poet, living in the closed circle of the Catholic tradition, celebrated tirelessly the single, unique individual. The attraction exercised over Hopkins by Duns Scotus, a medieval schoolman not generally admired by the Jesuits, is noteworthy. Scotus was acceptable to him as one who exalted the will above the intellect, declared the individual to be the highest form of reality, and stimulated the rise of secular science on an empirical basis. It has been suggested that it was precisely because he was dedicated to an ordered way of life, a discipline from which there was no dissenting, that Hopkins knew such delight in whatever was "counter, original, spare, strange," be it the "dark-gale skylark" or "the weeds and the wilderness," so that even in his poem lamenting the wreck of the Deutschland one is conscious of his sensuous surrender to "the burl of the fountains of air, buck and the flood of the wave." Certainly his craftsmanship was nothing if not singular—like his corn-shocks at harvest: "barbarous in beauty." It was by his extreme difference from his contemporaries that he enriched English poetry, abandoning the Franco-Italianate foundation upon which Chaucer built so firmly, to explore the neglected vein of Anglo-Saxon verse and to make innovations of his own.

His prosody goes back to *The Vision of Piers Plowman*. Its fundamental principle is the reliance upon the number of stresses rather than upon the number of syllables in a line. It has been called Anglo-Saxon prosody, it has been called stress prosody—Hopkins's phrase for it was "sprung rhythm": by any other name it would be as musical. As in music you may have a measure consisting of one whole note and another measure, directly following it, consisting of a flock of sixteenths, so here you may have a foot of from one to four syllables, any seeming inequality being compensated by pause or emphasis. The important thing is not the metronomic beat, but the melodic phrase, or what Pound calls "thematic invention."

In one of D. H. Lawrence's early letters to Edward Marsh

he discussed the subject of rhythm in a fashion which shows how fully he would have sympathized with Hopkins's experiments. "I think more of a bird with broad wings flying and lapsing through the air, than anything, when I think of metre. . . . I hate an on-foot method of reading. It all depends on the *pause*—the natural *lingering* of the voice according to the feeling—it is the hidden *emotional* pattern that makes poetry, not the obvious form." And, after quarreling with Marsh's admiration of Flecker's correctness, he concludes: "I can't tell you what *pattern* I see in any poetry, save one complete thing. . . . Yet I seem to find about the same number of long lingering notes in each line. I know nothing about it. I only know you aren't right." Lawrence lacked the scholarly concern for technique which made Hopkins careful not merely of his procedure but of the vocabulary he used to describe it, but he got at the heart of the matter. Hopkins's emotion often dictated rapid, hurdling, soaring, suddenly dropping measures, and it was perhaps this rush of feeling which made him so frequently choose the image of a bird, "flying and lapsing through the air." On reading over some lines of his *Loss of the Eurydice*, "as one commonly reads, whether prose or verse, with the eyes, so to say, only," Hopkins wrote: "it struck me aghast with a kind of raw nakedness and unmitigated violence I was unprepared for: but take breath and read it with the ears, as I always wish to be read, and my verse becomes all right." The fact that in reading his verse, one must scan the stanza as a whole, recognizing the pattern, as Lawrence did, to be one complete thing, is final proof of Hopkins's care for the melodic phrase, as distinct from crabbed metrics.

What he took from Anglo-Saxon verse was not merely stress prosody, but the emphatic alliteration, the energy, which characterized it. To this he joined the use of rhyme and of the stanzaic form which have sometimes been considered incompatible with free verse—not that his verse is "free" in the sense that Whitman's is. These tended to soften and sweeten his poetry, and, indeed, he was capable as well of the tenderest as

175

of the most violent tone. He combined extreme vigor with extreme delicacy, his style, as with every consummate poet, being the very body of his thought. His apprehension of experience was intellectual as well as emotional, and his poems are a palpable record of this dual response. In a manuscript note on one of Donne's songs:

> Sweetest love, I do not goe
> For wearinesse of thee,

Coleridge remarked that "in Poems where the Author *thinks*, and expects the reader to do so, the sense must be understood to ascertain the metre," an observation which has been truly said to apply with special force to Hopkins. He could be as liquid as Swinburne, whose "delirium-tremendous imagination" he hated, as gnarled as Browning, with whom he had much in common as regards diction. He was influenced, too, by Welsh poetry, and approximated the consonantal harmonies of *"cynghanedd"* in such phrases as "warm-laid grave of a womb-life grey," or "lush-kept plush-capped," and "now burn, new born."

It is noteworthy that his most difficult verse is so by virtue of his effort to be most direct. His rhythms, as he analyzed them, were those of ordinary speech, and if his syntax was extraordinary to the point of obscurity, it was because in his eagerness to get the thing said with forcefulness and immediacy, he addressed his reader as one intimate speaks to another, compressing phrases, inserting a clause between two parts of a compound word, eliding inessential words (he had, in particular, no patience with the relative pronoun), choosing and ordering his words with a regard to significance which made him careless of grammatical usage.

He had a private vocabulary with which to describe aspects of the physical and spiritual world to which, like Emily Dickinson, and like the German mystic, Rainer Maria Rilke, he was peculiarly sensitive. Thus he used the word "sake" to denote the special quality which distinguishes a thing for its

176

observer: the clarity of a voice, the brightness of a reflected image, the bulk of a body casting shadow, the genius of a man. In a similar fashion he employed "instress," and devised the word "inscape" to mean the effect, in poetry, comparable to that of melody in music and design in painting. In a letter to Bridges, who not seldom complained of his lack of "literary decorum," he observed acutely: "it is the virtue of design, pattern, or inscape to be distinctive and it is the vice of distinctiveness to become queer." But if, as he admitted, he did not escape the vice, he wonderfully exhibited the virtue. He never sought oddity for its own sake. It was merely that he packed his verse so closely with meaning, filled it so full of music, that he had no room for the elaborate forms required by grammatical correctness. The difficulty which readers find in his work is due to the crowded character of his lines, to the strangeness which this imposed on his diction, somewhat to a pleasure in neologisms anticipatory of Joycean usage, and, at bottom, to the complexity of the personality which produced these poems.

Repeatedly they display, as Bridges deprecated, "the naked encounter of sensualism and asceticism." It would be truer to say that the encounter is between the sensual and the intellectual man. And it is as naked as the meeting of wrestlers or of lovers. Here is the very mark of the metaphysical poet. His most obviously metaphysical poem is *The Blessed Virgin Compared To The Air We Breathe,* which opens:

> Wild air, world-mothering air,
> Nestling me everywhere,
> That each eyelash or hair
> Girdles; goes home betwixt
> The fleeciest, frailest-flixed
> Snowflake...
>
> This air, which, by life's law,
> My lung must draw and draw
> Now but to breathe Its praise,
> Minds me in other ways

177

Of her who not only
Gave God's infinity
Dwindled to infancy
Welcome in womb and breast,
Birth, milk, and all the rest
But mothers each new grace
That does now reach our race—

And continuing his extremely subtle comparison between the air:

This needful, never spent,
And nursing element,

and the Virgin, through whom and from whom flows the glory of God, His providence and His mercy, he writes:

If I have understood,
She holds high motherhood
Towards all our ghostly good
And plays in grace her part
About man's beating heart,
Laying, like air's fine flood,
The deathdance in his blood;
Yet no part but what will
Be Christ our Saviour still.

Here Hopkins takes the original conceit and with a gentle, deft penetration which is itself airy, makes, in a poem of one hundred and twenty-six lines, idea and image one living, breathing whole. In his more compact and difficult *Tom's Garland,* there is the same union of perception and thought:

Tom—garlanded with squat and surly steel
Tom; then Tom's fallowbootfellow piles pick
By him and rips out rockfire homeforth—sturdy Dick;
Tom Heart-at-ease, Tom Navvy: he is all for his meal
Sure,'s bed now. Low be it: lustily he his low lot (feel
That ne'er need hunger, Tom; Tom seldom sick,
Seldomer heartsore; that treads through, prickproof, thick
Thousands of thorns, thoughts) swings though. Commonweal

178

Little I reck ho! lacklevel in, if all had bread:
What! Country is honour enough in all us—lordly head,
With heaven's lights high hung round, or, mother-ground
That mammocks, mighty foot. But no way sped,
Nor mind, nor mainstrength; gold go garlanded
With, perilous, O nó; nor yet plod safe shod sound;
   Undenizened, beyond bound
Of earth's glory, earth's ease, all; no one, nowhere,
In wide the earth's weal; rare gold, bold steel, bare
   In both; care, but share care—
This, by Despair, bred Hangdog dull; by Rage,
Manwolf, worse; and their packs infest the age.

Hopkins "laughed outright and often, but very sardonically" when he learned that this sonnet was incomprehensible to his intimates. The explanation which he gave them is so perfect an exposition, not only of this particular piece but of his way of thinking and writing generally, as to bear quoting at some length. "It means then that, as St. Paul and Plato and Hobbes and everybody says, the commonwealth or well-ordered human society is like one man; a body with many members and each its function; some higher, some lower, but all honourable, from the honour which belongs to the whole. The head is the sovereign, who has no superior but God and from heaven receives his or her authority: we must then imagine this head as bare (see St. Paul much on this) and covered, so to say, only with the sun and stars, of which the crown is a symbol, which is an ornament but not a covering; it has an enormous hat or skullcap, the vault of heaven. The foot is the day-labourer, and this is armed with hobnail boots, because it has to wear and be worn by the ground; which again is symbolical; for it is navvies or day-labourers who, on the great scale or in gangs and millions, mainly trench, tunnel, blast, and in other ways disfigure, 'mammock' the earth and, on a small scale, singly, and superficially stamp it with their footprints. And the 'garlands' of nails they wear are therefore the visible badge of the place they fill, the lowest in the commonwealth. But this place still shares the common honour,

179

and if it wants one advantage, glory or public fame, makes up for it by another, ease of mind, absence of care; and these things are symbolised by the gold and the iron garlands. (O, once explained, how clear it all is!) Therefore the scene of the poem is laid at evening, when they are giving over work and one after another pile their picks, with which they earn their living, and swing off home, knocking sparks out of mother earth not now by labour and of choice but by the mere footing, being strongshod and making no hardship of hardness, taking all easy. And so to supper and bed. Here comes a violent but effective hyperbation or suspension, in which the action of the mind mimics that of the labourer—surveys his lot, low but free from care; then by a sudden strong act throws it over the shoulder or tosses it away as a light matter. The witnessing of which lightheartedness makes me indignant with the fools of Radical Levellers. But presently I remember that this is all very well for those who are in, however low in, the Commonwealth and share in any way the common weal; but that the curse of our times is that many do not share it, that they are outcasts from it and have neither security nor splendour; that they share care with the high and obscurity with the low, but wealth or comfort with neither. And this state of things, I say, is the origin of Loafers, Tramps, Cornerboys, Roughs, Socialists and other pests of society. And I think that it is a very pregnant sonnet, and in point of execution very highly wrought, too much so, I am afraid..." One need not be a monarchist to recognize that it is indeed a pregnant sonnet, and whatever Hopkins may have said of "pests of society" one remembers that he called himself a communist in 'seventy-one.

Perhaps his most famous, certainly one of his finest poems, *The Windhover*, further illustrates his capacity for joining sensuous delight with intellectual energy. One may, of course, take this sonnet as merely an appreciation of the kestrel in flight, but one cannot read it repeatedly without feeling that the underlying thought is that beauty is the by-product of all

180

energy, of every truly self-expressive act, and one cannot ignore the dedication: To Christ, our Lord, recalling that to many Catholics and possibly to this Jesuit poet, Christ is the image of intellectual beauty as well as, perhaps therefore, the son of God.

> I caught this morning morning's minion, kingdom of daylight's
>   dauphin, dapple-dawn-drawn Falcon, in his riding
> Of the rolling level underneath him steady air, and striding
> High there, how he rung upon the rein of a wimpling wing
> In his ecstasy! then off, off forth on swing,
>   As a skate's heel sweeps smooth on a bow-bend: the hurl
>   and gliding
> Rebuffed the big wind. My heart in hiding
> Stirred for a bird,—the achieve of, the mastery of the thing!
>
> Brute beauty and valour and act, oh, air, pride, plume, here
>   Buckle! AND the fire that breaks from thee then, a billion
> Times told lovelier, more dangerous, O my chevalier!
>
>   No wonder of it : sheer plod makes plough down sillion
> Shine, and blue-bleak embers, ah my dear,
>   Fall, gall themselves, and gash gold-vermilion.

As a Catholic, Hopkins had assurances in which to rest which are denied the skeptical intelligence. Yet no one can read his "terrible" sonnets without realizing that he struggled not only to reconcile his sensual pleasure in the world with the asceticism demanded by his vows, but that, confronting the forces of evil, he had to fight a despair that only a religious can know.

> Wert thou my enemy, O thou my friend,
> How wouldst thou worse, I wonder, than thou dost
> Defeat, thwart me?

he asks, and again, in a mood of more resigned melancholy:

> My own heart let me more have pity on; let
> Me live to my sad self hereafter kind,
> Charitable; not live this tormented mind
> With this tormented mind tormenting yet.

These are confessions of misery, as indeed the closing lines
of *The Windhover* are acknowledgment of deep distress, but
none so clear as in the darkest sonnet of all:

> I wake and feel the fell of dark, not day.
> What hours, O what black hoürs we have spent
> This night! what sights you, heart, saw; ways you went
> And more must, in yet longer light's delay.
>   With witness I speak this. But where I say
> Hours I mean years, mean life. And my lament
> Is cries countless, cries like dead letters sent
> To dearest him that lives alas! away.
>
>   I am gall, I am heartburn. God's most deep decree
> Bitter would have me taste: my taste was me;
> Bones built in me, flesh filled, blood brimmed the curse.
>   Selfyeast of spirit a dull dough sours. I see
> The lost are like this, and their sweating selves. But worse.

This recalls Donne's

> Batter my heart, three person'd God; for, you
> As yet but knocke, breathe, shine, and seeke to mend;
> That I may rise, and stand, o'erthrow mee'and bend
> Your force, to break, blowe, burn and make me new.
> I, like an usurpt towne, to'another due,
> Labour to'admit you, but Oh, to no end,
> Reason your viceroy in mee, mee should defend,
> But is captiv'd, and proves weake or untrue.

There is the same violent conflict between the skeptical mind
and the believing heart, the same anguished honesty and
sensual alertness in the expression of the struggle, the same
energy of feeling forcing the rhythm out of its natural smoothness, even the hard throb of the alliterative phrasing is the
same:

>   God's most deep decree
> Bitter would have me taste.
>
> Bones built in me... blood brimmed the curse

182

is paralleled by:

Batter my heart ...

bend

Your force, to break, blowe, burn and make me new.

If one turns from Hopkins to those poets of our own time who have learned his packed expressive style, one finds passages which fairly parallel this sonnet. There are lines in the Choruses of Auden's charade, *Paid on Both Sides,* which echo its opening:

> O watcher in the dark, you wake
> Our dream of waking, we feel
> Your finger on the flesh that has been skinned.
> By your bright day
> See clear what we were doing, that we were vile.

Here it is no longer one man's sense of spiritual defeat which is in question, but the shame of a social class which has refused or abused the responsibilities of power. But though the theme widens, it can, plainly, be handled in a like fashion. There are other lines in the same chorus which, for all the difference of imagery, sharply recall Hopkins:

Though heart fears all heart cries for, rebuffs with mortal
    beat
Skyfall, the legs sucked under, adder's bite.

Throughout Auden's work there are stronger reminiscences than Hopkins affords of the rhythm of *Piers Plowman,* a poem which Hopkins cited as warrant for his own practice.

    C. Day Lewis draws more obviously upon this master. He prefaces the fourth section of *The Magnetic Mountain* with a quotation from the curtal sonnet, *Peace:* "He comes with work to do, he does not come to coo"—a gentler version of "I come not to bring peace, but a sword." He employs the image of *The Windhover* both at the opening of the poem:

183

> Now to be with you, elate, unshared
> My kestrel joy, O hoverer in the wind,
> Over the quarry furiously at rest
> Chaired on shoulders of shouting wind,

and in the third part, where the kestrel is envisaged both as the joy of a new era and as the airman who flies in the van of it, who fights for its coming. He pays unambiguous tribute to Hopkins in the phrase, "O hoverer in the wind," which is a pun on the superb *Windhover* poem. Occasionally his language has the muscular quality which is present in the Jesuit's most spiritual lyrics. Indeed, one of the major differences between Hopkins and these late-come pupils of his is that their work is wanting in the testimonies to physical energy, physical sensitiveness in which the priest's poems abound. When they look away from the ruin of the old order toward the glorious commonwealth promised by faith in social revolution, they write almost with the vague fervor of romanticism. They have a nearer kinship with Shelley than with Keats, to whom Hopkins, acutely aware of the actual, was closer than he knew. They are not inclined to question their own torment, as he did in the "terrible" sonnets, or to elaborate a single conceit, as he did in more than one poem about the Blessed Virgin, so that they do not plainly exhibit a metaphysical strain. One must make an exception of Lewis, whose *Magnetic Mountain*, for all its Audenesque paraphernalia, is built on the conceit of the lodestone, Marxian theory, drawing us toward a regenerated society:

> Follow the kestrel, south or north;
> Strict eye, spontaneous wing can tell
> A secret. Where he comes to earth
> Is the heart's treasure. Mark it well.
>
> Here he hovers. You're on the scent;
> Magnetic mountain is not far,
> Across no gulf or continent,
> Not where you think but where you are.

Stake out your claim. Go downwards. Bore
Through the tough crust. Oh learn to feel
A way through darkness to good ore.
You are the magnet and the steel.

Out of that dark a new world flowers.
There in the womb, in the rich veins
Are tools, dynamos, bridges, towers,
Your tractors and your travelling-cranes.

His *Transitional Poem*, which has for its theme the single mind, and utters, not seldom with the voice of Emily Dickinson, the thoughts of Spinoza, is metaphysical in intent rather than in method. On the other hand, *From Feathers To Iron*, a series of poems capable of political interpretation, though actually dealing with the experience of a man awaiting the arrival of his first-born, contains a large proportion of lyrics which answer to the requirements of the school of Donne. Hugh MacDiarmid is another communist poet given to the elaboration of conceits and inclined to pasture his fancy on intellectual uplands.

What Hopkins has in common with the metaphysical school: the probing of his own mind, the wrestling of the intellectual with the sensual imagination—these younger poets do not evidence so clearly. For this and other reasons only a passing reference to their performance is in place here. But it may be noted that in exploiting the prosodic vein which Hopkins reopened they follow, at a little distance, Donne's conversational rhythms; that their vocabulary, being less idiosyncratic than Hopkins's, if sometimes equally obscure, is nearer than his to the simple vocabulary of Donne; while in their delight in paradox, and their use of imagery taken from contemporary ideas, they again resemble the master of the metaphysicals.

English poetry appears now to be turning away from the seventeenth century, to an older and therefore less familiar tradition. The perplexities of the present century in its adolescent years are, for many poets, resolved, and a firmer if not a more mature attitude is evident in the work of the younger

185

generation. Yet however poetry may change, it must always return to refresh itself at the springs which fed the work of men like Donne and Marvell. These poets kept wide the gates of the senses without closing that of the intellect; but if passion made them think, thought did not qualify their passion. It is this dual interpretation of experience by the body and the mind, it is this intense pursuit of its meaning, which make for metaphysical poetry and for good poetry generally.

CHAPTER VII

THE BURDEN OF THE MYSTERY

> Greater glory in the sun,
> An evening chill upon the air,
> Bid imagination run
> Much on the Great Questioner;
> What He can question, what if questioned I
> Can with a fitting confidence reply.
>
> *Yeats.*

THERE ARE several reasons why men write poetry, and obedience to any one of them may produce memorable things. But the reason which has the most significant appeal for the reader is likely to be that most urgent for the poet—the need to find adequate form for the eternal question, and, by giving it shape, temporarily to silence it. There have been those who, serving a serene aristocracy, have produced gay, gracious, elegant verse. But the periods when such allegiance seems possible are rare, and the sensitive man is apt, even in the face of the triumphs of the race, to hear at his back time's hurrying chariot-wheels, to see at his feet that fine and private place where nothing is done, suffered, or enjoyed, or, looking at the evil end of the just, "Call no man fortunate that is not dead." The tragic sense of life which is felt to be basic in *Samson Agonistes,* as in *Lear,* which must be allowed brief utterance even in *Hyperion,* and which exercised a poet as close

187

to us as Hardy, is complicated for later generations by the immediate evils of our present society. It is not strange, then, that those contemporaries who have been most oppressed by

the heavy and the weary weight
Of all this unintelligible world,

have sometimes spoken unintelligibly of their travail. Yet under the spell of a tale not altogether unlike that of the wretched mariner, we are arrested as was the wedding-guest: we cannot choose but hear.

Thus it is that D. H. Lawrence holds us as only those can hold us who have borne, if not the body of the albatross, "the burthen of the mystery." The greater part of Lawrence's verse (omitting consideration of his novels, which have also been estimated as poetry), is flawed by his lack of control over his material. His technique is slipshod: his diction is sometimes inexact, sometimes verbose; his cadences are faulty (witness, for example, *Frohnleichnam,* which stumbles where it should dance). Not seldom his ineptitude is the outward and visible sign of his inward confusion. Good poetry, whether it be emotion recollected in tranquillity, or tranquillity recollected with emotion, always exhibits order. Much of Lawrence's work appears to be merely jottings for poems which he might some day have written, had he imposed on himself the necessary discipline. Some of his verse is no more than the groans and retchings and curses of a sick man. Yet if one examines the whole body of his poetry, one finds in it an attitude toward life which makes him free of the company of a Blake, a Rimbaud, a Whitman.

It is easy enough to hear the voice of Blake in these poems, the voice fulminating against the "dark Satanic mills," framing the *Proverbs of Hell:* "He who desires but acts not, breeds pestilence," the voice of the Bard

The Burden of the Mystery

Calling the lapsèd Soul,
And weeping in the evening dew;
That might controll
The starry pole,
And fallen, fallen light renew.

Even more clearly sounds the voice of Walt, though Lawrence deprecated a barbaric yawp only less than he hated the smooth tones of civility, though the America he saw was no eagle but perhaps a goose laying a golden egg: "Which is just a stone to anyone asking for meat"—an "addled golden egg." Yet here, plain upon page after page, is Whitman's sensual delight in the earth, in the sun and the serpent which it brings forth, in the darkness, and the miracle of the senses which are alive in the dark. Here, stronger than the rage against the arrogant stupidity of the well-born, the fatuous stupidity of the rich, the violent stupidity of the mob (all of which Whitman heavily discounted), is the will to preserve, to consecrate, the integrity of the individual. Here, in the last poems, are echoes of Whitman's *Passage to India*, of *Whispers of Heavenly Death*, of the *Last Invocation:*

At the last, tenderly,
From the walls of the powerful fortress'd house,
From the clasp of the knitted locks, from the keep of the
    well-closed doors.
Let me be wafted.

Let me glide noiselessly forth,
With the key of softness unlock the locks—with a whisper,
Set ope the doors O soul.

Tenderly—be not impatient,
(Strong is your hold O mortal flesh,
Strong is your hold O love.)

Using almost the same images, speaking, perhaps, too much, as a man will who has not much time to speak, Lawrence tells of his *Ship of Death:*

189

I sing of autumn and the falling fruit
and the long journey towards oblivion.

The poem moves on slowly, gathering power as it moves, to
the implacable urgency of the final lines:

Oh lovely last, last lapse of death, into pure oblivion
at the end of the longest journey
peace, complete peace!
But can it be that also it is procreation?

Oh build your ship of death
oh build it!
Oh, nothing matters but the longest journey.

The vision of Blake, who had cleansed "the doors of perception," and looked out upon a universe throbbing with infinite
energy; the summons of Whitman, singing the body electric—
Lawrence's poems are luminous with that insight, resonant
with that call. One may find other influences here: in the early
poems, with their glimpses of Nottinghamshire tragedies, traces
of Hardy; in a few later lyrics, oblique tributes to the imagists,
of whom he was mistakenly accounted one. But what of Rimbaud? Why name in this connection a man who personified
so much of what Lawrence was fighting? Lawrence tolerated
neither the bohemian, nor the revolutionary, nor the trader:
Rimbaud had chosen all three avatars. Lawrence shuddered
back from that "long, immense, deliberate derangement of all
the senses" whereby Rimbaud had sought to become a seer,
a poet in the magical sense of the term. Certainly Lawrence,
although a symbolist beyond question, lacked the interest in
technical precision which belonged to the school; and where
its members would distill into their lyrics the volatile essences
of feeling, he poured into his poems the crude emotion of the
moment, in all its turbidness. True, he, like Rimbaud, had
spent a season in hell. He, too, strove perpetually for an image
great enough to body forth his struggle. Is this sufficient to
make him kindred to that tormented and savage genius? Say,

190

rather, that at the core of Lawrence's poetry pulsed a like flame.

At the close of *Saison en enfer* occurs a line which might be the epigraph for the best of Lawrence's work: "Welcome every influx of true vigor and tenderness." In a letter written to Harriet Monroe two years before his death, speaking of *Lady Chatterley's Lover*, Lawrence repeated what so many of his poems reiterate, his belief in the necessity for restoring what he called "the phallic consciousness" in our lives: "because," he wrote, "it is the source of all real beauty, and all real gentleness. And those are the two things, tenderness and beauty, which will save us from horrors... In my novel I work for them directly, and direct from the phallic consciousness, which, you understand, is not the cerebral sex-consciousness, but something really deeper, and the root of poetry, lived or sung."

Rimbaud had said true vigor and tenderness. Lawrence said, tenderness and beauty. It comes to the same thing. *The Wild Common*, which opens his *Collected Poems*, for all its ineptness of phrase and cadence, utters this conviction:

> The quick sparks on the gorse-bushes are leaping
> Little jets of sunlight texture imitating flame.
>
> Sun, but in substance, yellow water-blobs!
> Wings and feathers on the crying, mysterious ages,
>   peewits wheeling!
> All that is right, all that is good, all that is God takes
>   substance! a rabbit lobs
> In confirmation, I hear sevenfold lark-songs pealing.

Virgin Youth, a hymn to the risen phallus, a cry for pardon for denial of life, sounds the key-note of his major work. There are other early lyrics which are an index of his weakness, his need to retreat from a world which failed to honor his god—witness *From A College Window*, with its

> I sit absolved, assured I am better off
> Beyond a world I never want to join.

191

There are scattered throughout his poems confessions of the bond which held him to a buried past, so that having crossed the threshold of maturity he could still say to his dead mother:

> ...that is not your grave, in England,
> The world is your grave.

And in the very breath with which he would have denied her, cry out:

> I am a naked candle burning on your grave.

Yet his later poems are reiterations of that initial statement in *Wild Common:* "all that is God takes substance,"—are affirmations of life. Even his elaborate fantasies about birds, beasts, and flowers, where he shows a creation distorted under the load of his own anger and scorn, offer signs and tokens of his deep-seated passion for the world in all its fierce strangeness. And in the final poems, after his endlessly renewed battles with abstractions, he asserts the profoundest of sensual experiences to be the sense of truth and the sense of justice, in protest against an anaemic Platonism, in defense of true vigor and tenderness. It is among these lyrics that one finds two short poems which, together with the *Ship of Death,* may be taken as the substance of Lawrence's legacy: *Bavarian Gentians,* wherein he invokes the blue torch of the flower as a symbol of the fructifying dark, and *Flowers And Men,* which is a variant of his demand for

> lovely dangerous life
> And passionate disquality of men...

Here again is the blue gentian, bluer and richer for the memory of the earlier lyric in which he made it Persephone's flower:

> Flowers achieve their own floweriness and it is a miracle.
> Men don't achieve their own manhood, alas, oh alas! alas!

192

THE BURDEN OF THE MYSTERY

All I want of you, men and women,
All I want of you
is that you shall achieve your beauty
as the flowers do.

Oh leave off saying I want you to be savages.
Tell me, is the gentian savage, at the top of its coarse stem?
Oh what in you can answer to this blueness?
. . . as the gentian and the daffodil. . .
Tell me! tell me! is there in you a beauty to compare
to the honeysuckle at evening now
pouring out his breath.

Perhaps because, as the son of a coal-miner, he came to the
cultural tradition of England half a stranger, Lawrence seems
to have as strong filiations with American as with British poets.
Certainly one finds a distrust of the intellect which is apparent
in Whitman, and a need for escape from society felt by a
poet who is in some ways an offshoot of Whitman: Robinson
Jeffers. For Lawrence the principle of evil rests in the egocentric man and the soulless machine; God realizes Himself in
substance, yet life is rooted in profound impalpable darkness;
the promise of oblivion is blessed. For Jeffers, the principle of
evil is introverted man and his self-centered civilization; the
universe is the body of God; the ultimate values are strength
to endure life and the promise of oblivion. The thinking of
both men is more complex and more flexible than such a
summary would imply. Yet it reveals, with due allowance for
simplifications, the kinship between these two poets.

Lawrence, though not intellectually arrogant, had the temer-
ity of the self-taught. Jeffers, who balances a religious and
classical education with the scientific equipment of a medical
student and the special knowledge of a forester, and who spent
much of his youth traveling and studying in Western Europe,
is restrained by his greater learning from Lawrence's brash
pronunciamentos. But he, too, is a poet who writes novels
(though his fictions are in verse) which objectify his feeling

193

about man and the universe; his poetry, too, symbolizes a serious inner conflict not uncommon in our time.

His earliest work wanted the directness and originality of Lawrence's. It was about the time he wrote *Tamar,* the poem which brought him his first fame, and which was produced when he was already in his thirties, that Jeffers seems to have found his style. *Tamar* startled with the violence of its theme: the downfall of an incestuous house—startled particularly because the time of the drama was the present, and the place that unfamiliar portion of the California coast which the poet has made profoundly his own. It surprised, too, with its long rolling rhythms, rising and breaking and rising like the surf which beats on those rocky headlands, and with the challenge of Jeffers's doctrine:

> Humanity is the
> start of the race; I say
> Humanity is the mold to break away from, the crust to break
> through, the coal to break into fire,
> The atom to be split.

It was not *Tamar,* however, nor yet *Roan Stallion,* but Jeffers's version of Orestes' story in *The Tower Beyond Tragedy* which gave this book its dignity. Here, as in no other long poem of his, the slow weight of the syllables, the savage simplicity of the imagery, keep the rhetoric passionate. The high points are the vision of Orestes and the prophecy of Cassandra, crying that where prosperous peoples are, there are her enemies, bidding her spirit

> Curse Athens for the joy and the marble, curse Corinth
> For the wine and the purple, and Syracuse
> For the gold and the ships; but Rome, Rome,
> With many destructions for the corn and the laws and the
> javelins, the insolence, the threefold
> Abominable power: pass the humble
> And the lordships of darkness, but far down
> Smite Spain for the blood on the sunset gold, curse France

For the fields abounding and the running rivers, the lights in
    the cities, the laughter, curse England
For the meat on the tables and the terrible gray ships, for old
    laws, far dominions, there remains
A mightier to be cursed and a higher for malediction
When America has eaten Europe and takes tribute of Asia,
    when the ends of the world grow aware of each other
And are dogs in one kennel...

Cassandra, foreseeing the exploitation of earth and sea and
air, foreseeing at last the coming of the frost which will play
with her enemies as a cat with a crippled bird:

        O clean, clean,
White and most clean, colorless quietness,
Without trace, without trail, without stain in the garment,
    drawn down
From the poles to the girdle...

The mad prophetess, outwearied with lived and imagined
agonies, cries upon death to give her some non-human
shape. Orestes' vision, which brings the poem to a close, is his
veritable escape from humanity into the peace, "fierier than
any passion," of identity with the universe. It is a conscious
divesting of the self of its desires and its hatreds, which frees
it for possession by the inhuman world. Jeffers opposes this
attitude to the doctrine of the Oriental mystics, who would
absorb the world into the self. He contrasts Electra, desiring
incestuous union, with Orestes, who has broken away from
his kind, climbed the tower beyond tragedy, and found release
from that introversion which is to the poet the plague of the
race.

In one narrative after another he is preoccupied with this
theme of incest, a theme recurrent in the poetry of the ancient
Greeks and of the early English romantics, both of whom have
nourished his imagination. In none of his poems is the special
symbolism it has for him as clear as in this powerful work.
Nor, in his modern versions of tragedies which are older than
history, are the characters any more sharply individualized

than they are here. Nearly all his people speak with his voice, use his chosen images, feel with his nerves the torturing remembrance of man's fate, respond with his stoic joy to the natural scene.

The motifs vary little from poem to poem, though the tragedy has different nodes. There are the recurrent themes of an all-too-human love, centered upon the self, and of the peace whose source is contemplation of the impersonal, nonmoral universe. The self-delusion of man's self-importance is corollary to this. Opposed to it is the frequent reminder—instanced by violent action and horrible harvest—of the danger involved in a crude interpretation of Jeffers's a-social thesis. He may fly from what Lawrence called the "insipid, unsalted, rabbity, endlessly hopping" people, so many they nibble the earth to a desert. He may see messianism as mere lust for power, and praise only solitude and withdrawal. Yet a hovering pity for humanity finds expression in another repeated symbol: the injured hawk or eagle. The bird whose blood burns for flight, the wild carnivorous creature maimed and caged, is shown in *Cawdor* (where it is subordinate to the incest motif of a modern Phaedra) as "the archetype body of life," passionate, wounded, and bound. And in the passage in which the eagle image is given significance, the poet, though seeing life as the "scape-goat of the greater world," admires and accepts it:

> A torch to burn in with pride, a necessary
> Ecstasy in the run of the cold substance...

The frustration and horror of energy thrust inward upon itself, the anguish of power blinded or with torn wings, alternates with the theme of love, tender and helpless, as in *The Loving Shepherdess*, or that of love, possessive and distorting, as instanced by Barclay in *The Women At Point Sur*, by the image of Jesus in *Dear Judas*. Whether or not belated revulsion from his early religious training disgusted Jeffers with the anthropocentric view, his disgust is mated to a great com-

196

passion, doubly wounding because it is half-scornful of itself. He cannot find tragedies violent enough, he cannot show physical torture, mental anguish, grinding enough, to satisfy this cruel hatred and this ravaging pity. His plots, mostly woven out of gossip and old tales of the countryside, enlarged by legendary associations, are overwrought, and have roots in racial myth so obscure or so literary that they engage us only superficially. Moreover, the extravagance of horrors heaped on horror is paralleled by a language which does not always escape the perils of rhetoric. Exciting though these narratives are at first reading, one returns to them neither for the interest of the action nor for the delineation of character, but for the flashes of lyricism where some wretched girl or tormented old man becomes suddenly, like Orestes in *The Tower Beyond Tragedy*, the mouthpiece of the poet, the witness to spiritual conflict, spiritual redemption.

The best of Jeffers is to be found less often in his ambitious pieces than in his short poems. Here the thoughts which filled Arnold's verse with pathos, Tennyson's with anxious optimism, Hardy's with desperate courage, are given new reality by association with the American scene and by the use of more colloquial diction. His acquaintance with science has not sapped his imaginative power—his poetry has a dual source of strength in fact and myth. Further, while Jeffers is ignorant of music, his deep-lunged verse, built on a stress prosody, the changing tempo regulated by his feeling for quantity, proves his sensitiveness to rhythm and pitch.

He owns, too, the enormous advantage of having been free to choose where he would live, and having chosen a sea-coast whence he can look across a river valley and beyond, to the hills that go down to the sea, to the cliffs of the peninsula and their wind-beaten cypresses, and over the whole sweep of the western sky. This coast region is striped with scattered fruit farms and cattle ranches, pocked with abandoned works: mills and lumber camps, lime kilns, coal mines. It remembers

the Spaniards, whose priests finished the work their soldiers
began, it remembers the more ancient ways of the Indians
who were there before the Spanish came. This landscape, with
its haunted habitations, above which broods the inhuman
majesty of nature, has given Jeffers's poetry what the Lake
landscape gave to a more placid pantheist, what the Irish
landscape gives to Yeats, who asked himself in his youth
whether all races had not their unity in the beginning "from
a mythology that marries them to rock and hill." Jeffers cares
little for racial unity: he is the solitary, the worshiper of impersonal power, of beauty unstained by man's small busyness:

Still the mind smiles at its own rebellions,
Knowing all the while that civilization and the other evils
That make humanity ridiculous, remain
Beautiful in the whole fabric, excesses that balance each other
Like the paired wings of a flying bird...
In order to value this fretful time
It is necessary to remember our norm, the unaltered passions,
The same-colored wings of imagination,
That the crowd clips, in lonely places new-grown; ...
From here for normal one sees both ways,
And listens to the splendor of God, the exact poet, the sonorous
Antistrophe of desolation to the strophe multitude.

But Jeffers has his mythology, too: the hawk-headed god that
is life, the stone-limbed god that is peace. If he seems to
choose silence and darkness, repeatedly he owns to a pleasure
in its opposite, in *Continent's End* addressing the ocean thus:

The tides are in our veins, we still mirror the stars, life is your
    child, but there is in me
Older and harder than life and more impartial, the eye that
    watched before there was an ocean.

That watched you fill your beds out of the condensation of
    thin vapor and watched you change them,
That saw you soft and violent wear your boundaries down,
    eat rock, shift places with the continents.

The Burden of the Mystery

Mother, though my song's measure is like your surf-beat's
    ancient rhythm I never learned it of you.
Before there was any water there were tides of fire, both our
    tones flow from the older fountain.

And again, praising the fishing-boats off the coast cautiously
trailing each other through the fog, he confesses:

> ...A flight of pelicans
> Is nothing lovelier to look at;
> The flight of planets is nothing nobler; all the arts lose virtue
> Against the essential reality
> Of creatures going about their business among the equally
> Earnest elements of nature.

In his most sombre mood, standing beside the dark cairn of
the ancient lord of Ulster,

> A man of blood who died bloodily
> Four centuries ago,

he asserts:

> ...but death's nothing, and life,
> From a high death-mark on a headland
> Of this dim island of burials, is nothing either.
> How beautiful are both these nothings.

At such moments he is at peace no less with himself than with
the universe to which he would resign himself.

As his extravagant imaginations lead him toward the pitfall
of rhetoric, so his bitter earnestness sometimes traps him into
sententious utterance. There is much in his verse which would
range him with the traditionalists. But in his awareness of
contemporary America, "heavily thickening toward empire,"
in his readiness to deal with the uglier concrete details of
existence, in the freedom of his vocabulary and of his rhythms,
he shows himself a modern. His finest passages achieve a harmony which is acceptable because it is no facile cheerfulness,
but has as its fulcrum a tragic intensity.

199

One cannot use the word "intensity" without summoning up the figure of the poet who, beyond all others in our time, exhibits that quality. It is scarcely necessary to have read Yeats's *Reveries Over Childhood and Youth* and *The Trembling Of The Veil* to perceive that he has always delighted in passionate men and women, at first in the leonine presence of his grandfather, the shipowner and sea-captain, then in the goddess-like image of his beloved. What were his verse, one is tempted to ask, had she not haunted it? It is clear, too, that his poetry has been quickened by the excitements, personal, literary, and political, in which he has lived, that it has been given force by the integrity he has preserved in the most brutalizing as in the most brilliant circumstances.

Yeats was unique in his generation in deliberately rejecting the scientific approach and the stoical skepticism which it fostered. One has but to contrast his attitude with that of Hardy, who was writing his first lyrics when Yeats was an infant, or that of Robinson, who began publishing some half a dozen years after the appearance of Yeats's *Wanderings of Oisin*, to recognize how broad a gulf lies between him and them. Yet the mixture of Celtic legend, Hindu philosophy, and sheer superstition, which seems to make up the religion he created for himself, has served him better than their more honest way of thinking served them.

The reason for this lies not in his curious "system" of beliefs, to which, it seems, he gives but emotional credence, his intellect, like the wicked King John of the nursery rhyme, living its life aloof. The body of his verse suffers more than it gains from his wayward medievalism. His poetry is great because, to employ a distinction as valuable as it is venerable, it is the product not of Fancy, but of Imagination. Both Hardy and Robinson are, of course, imaginative and not fanciful poets, but in Yeats the modifying, unifying energy is more powerful, ranges more easily back and forth between the physical and the ideal world. One finds it in his early love lyrics, overwrought though they are with elaborate symbol and dim with cloudy metaphor. One finds it more clearly at work after the poet, tired of the rich romantic coloring which he had first used, began deliberately, as he tells us, to remodel his style, trying to make verse that should be

> as cold
> And passionate as the dawn.

The poem called *The Fisherman*, in which he describes his altered mood in the changed manner which it effected, is a consummate example of that coldness—as of bare stone, and of that passion—as of a lighted sky.

It may be of some interest to contrast this with the early poem beginning

> I wander by the edge
> Of this desolate lake
> Where the wind cries in the sedge...

The opening lines of the love lyric at once suggest and are enhanced by the memory of that exile from fairyland encountered where the sedge was withered from the lake and no birds sang. The scene here is representative of the lover's desolation partly because of this association, partly because of its inherent greyness, and a little because one feels it to be a scene which he has often explored, as he is now exploring his unhappy destiny. But immediately this image is replaced by another: the axle "that keeps the stars in their round." This figure carries the mind away from the man listening to the cry of the wind in the marsh-grass toward an ideal of order and universal law, uplifting in its grandeur, but all the more terrible to one who feels that it refuses admittance to his desire. The intrusion of the supernatural, with the hands that are to hurl "the banners of East and West" into the deep, makes Nature less awful but not more benign, while the latent suggestion that when the world is consumed at last, the lovers may lie breast to breast, is but a cold kind of comfort. And yet there remains something exalting in the very opposition of the stars,

201

"the banners of East and West," and "the girdle of light," to the small earthly actuality of lake and sedge which is the scene of the lover's dismal contemplation. The impersonal serenity of the sky, ignorantly illumining the path of human suffering, may thus strangely relieve that suffering. The tragic significance of the poem is at once heightened and made endurable by the fantastic imagery of the heavens. And this in turn is shorn of extravagance as the poem drops to the simplicity of its close, which brings it round full circle to the human grief which is its theme. And yet, remembering Yeats's delight in symbol, the reader is haunted by the suspicion that the poem means more than it says; that it speaks not of the defeated love of a man for a woman, but of the impossibility of union between the physical world and that intellectual beauty which is the theme of many of his lyrics of this period. So that the loveliness of the poem is enhanced and clouded by its mystery.

This mystery, and the romanticism which the first lines suggest and which is felt more vividly in the rich metaphors which follow, are more apparent when one sets the lyric beside the austere poem about the fisherman. Here the meaning seems to be all on the surface, something for a man as simple as the fisherman to take in his net. In the plainest possible words the poet states the disappointment of his ambition in choosing to write for his own race, his decision to abandon it, and to write for an ideal audience, represented by the figure of the fisherman. One recalls that Chinese poet of the ninth century, Po Chü-I, who is said to have recited his verses to an old peasant woman, and to have changed any word that she failed to understand. But if Yeats's poem is clear, it offers a subtler interest, too. The vulgar crowd which moves along the street is at the opposite pole from the freckled man in homespun on his solitary height, and from the image of the dawn which is part of his experience and also symbol of an inhuman power enlarging that experience for the reader. The poet's hope and the reality he found seem to change their contours, side by side; the self-seeking mob and the self-sufficient fisherman are likewise defined by juxtaposition; and, toward the close, the real and the ideal qualify one another, since the fisherman, though we can see him plain, is, we are told,

> A man who does not exist,
> A man who is but a dream.

It is for this imaginary audience that the poet would write one

> Poem maybe as cold
> And passionate as the dawn.

This *is* the poem it describes: intelligible to the wise and simple peasant whose presence it calls up, and filled, for the sophisticated reader, with profounder implications. Yeats has here brought image, music, and meaning together in such a way that, just as the cold mountain stream takes warmth from the passion of the coloring sky, and the figure of the fisherman puts on greatness against the wonder of the natural scene, so the ideal is humanized and the real transfigured. Much of the poetry of his middle life and his old age is thus "cold and passionate," a conjunction of attributes which is incredible until one examines the work in which they exist together.

This union of opposites is what makes Yeats a metaphysical poet, in the sense that Donne is such. He has not Donne's curiosity about current ideas. Indeed, one can more readily fancy him in converse with that seventeenth-century divine on topics of interest to the medieval mind than having intellectual intercourse with a modern physicist. But he has Donne's energy and his wit, his intensity and his self-awareness. He is like him, too, in having yoked together two parts of a personality which almost seem two selves: the mystical and the practical, the attentive Platonist and the active patriot. For if the wealth of Celtic mythology and Irish folk-lore consoled Yeats for the bareness and sordidness of modern urban life, he recognized early that his dream of a free and united Ireland would bear no fruit unless it were manured by practical politics. Nor has his keen feeling for an aristocratic tradition withheld him from taking a shovel to the dung-heap: he has been a member of the Irish senate, he has been a censor of moving-pictures. He may have sought escape into fairyland, into the credulous middle ages, and on the peaks of legendary Indian mountains, but his absorption in Irish realities—bewildering as these often are—has kept him from losing his hold on this present world.

The greater part of his work has consisted of lyrics on personal themes, and he has published not a few poems in which the references to his "system" are an obscuring as well as an obscurantist element. Yet one cannot consider Yeats as other than a major poet. This is partly thanks to the fact that one finds traces of his influence in the performance of artists as diversely gifted as Ezra Pound, Léonie Adams, and C. Day Lewis. But it is primarily because the body of his writings springs from "the root of poetry, lived or sung." It is not only in the love lyrics (indeed, less there than elsewhere) that one finds the frank celebration of sex as a thing of beauty and a joy. Moreover, and here is the heart of the matter, that acknowledgment comes always trailing allusions to something more significant than the satisfaction of personal desire. Yeats has been accused of doing little more than attest to his faith in the virtues of aristocracy, and indeed the courtesy and dignity of the well-bred seem to shine for him with a particular brilliance. But he has never lost sight of his dream of bringing together this excellence—so often demeaned by worldliness—together with another virtue which he has found in the poorer, simpler, and coarser members of his people: fanatical devotion to an ideal. His delight in race, his recurrence to a noble tradition, his will to realize it afresh by giving Ireland cultural unity, has fired his poetry with something closely akin to the "idea of the good" that so puzzled the prisoners in the Platonic allegory of the den, and changed wholly the lives of those who escaped into the light.

Only some extraordinary power could keep intact a personality that must reconcile sensualist and idealist, aristocrat and fanatic. That Yeats is gifted with such power, no reader of his mature work can doubt. Like Lawrence, he has had little formal education, and, like him, has allowed himself to fabricate notions about the world with a large indifference to their factual basis. But he has had a far richer education by his association with acute intelligences, and, unlike the younger romantic, he has been a scrupulous craftsman. Whether he is turning a savage epigram, whispering a love song, naming over to himself friends and enemies among political martyrs, or dreaming a waking dream in a haunted tower, he writes a poem utterly self-contained. He is neither sentimentalist nor rhetorician, so that even when one cannot accept his "vision of reality," one is persuaded into a willing suspension of disbelief by the force of his art. His claim to greatness lies both in the vigor and integrity of his personality and in the high skill with which he expresses his response to life. But it is something beyond these—a combination of energy and vision and technical competence that allows him to ply unhampered between the two worlds denoted by Santayana as the realm of matter and the realm of essence.

One may perhaps define the poet's undertaking as the conduct of a traffic between these two worlds. The vast claims made for poetry by the romantics of the nineteenth century and still being made for it by the psychological critics and the communist singers of the twentieth, would seem to be based upon such an interpretation of what its practitioners are about. Shelley rhapsodizing over his art as one which "redeems from decay the visitations of the divinity in man," Keats declaring that "it should strike the reader as a wording of his own highest thoughts, and appear almost as a remembrance," Wordsworth calling it "truth ... carried alive into the heart by passion," all have reference to those values which, like the rivers and mountains of the Chinese lyricist, are "changeless in their glory," and which constitute the happier part of the realm of essence. But, as even the romantics sometimes appeared to understand, and as the materialists like to remind

us, it is through the existence of the physical self, the locus of
our sensations and emotions and thoughts, and the substantial
inhabitant of the realm of matter, that the mind creates and
recognizes a disembodied value. And it is not seldom the
sensual world, as it is apprehended by ear and eye, which
startles and kindles the imagination, so that the work of strings
and wood-winds, or the sound of the sea, the lighted sky or
even a mean street, the motions of a dancer, or the contours
of a face, lend the coloring of reality to ancient myth, and
form stuff whereof the mind may weave the fabric of a vision.
The poet, more sensitive than other men both to the values
in the ideal universe and to the crowding solicitations of the
physical world, bears testimony to both. Moreover, he is dealing with words, which, being things in themselves, to be seen
on the page and sounded with the voice, and being symbols
also, make him more keenly aware of his dual allegiance. So
that one might say that the greatest poet is he who is most
agile in leaping from the sensual plane to the spiritual and
back again. Yeats himself says that there is no meeting of
spirit and sense, "but only change upon the instant." In his
own later work, the change is instantaneous: it is dizzying.
This rapidity of movement, this feeling that he is about to
straddle two universes, adds to the difficulty that work presents.
It is a difficulty which is apt to attend all poetry that is
metaphysical, whether in the strictly literary or the more
general sense of the term.

Any good poem loses by translation, even into words of the
same language. In such a poem as *The Tower*, where the force
of a man's entire life, and in some part the life of his nation,
informs a work, translation becomes almost an impertinence.
What one finds undeniably in all Yeats's later poetry is an
amazing vigor, though nothing could be tenderer than the
prayer for his son, the poems *Upon A Dying Lady*, the terrible
Easter, 1916. And this vigor, since Yeats has come to three-
score and ten, must now reconcile itself with the fact of old
age, with the imminence of death. Nothing can exceed the

passion of those very poems which seeem to express resignation to the passionless existence of the old. If one turns from the wistful meditative music and cloudy imagery of his early verse to these songs, it would appear that he has reversed the usual process, and is drawing upon springs of energy which his youth did not find. There is abstraction here, too—Plato and Plotinus pass and repass, carrying what dim load of meaning! There is symbolism, not always as easy to read as the symbol of the soul in swan or butterfly, of aspiration in the tower, of recurrence in the wheel. But there is always a saving awareness of the concrete, a firm grasp of the breathing actuality, a capacity for response to purely sensual experience, which flushes these abstractions with life.

There is a distinct difference in Yeats's approach to the Great Questioner, as he calls death, from that of Lawrence, or of Jeffers. Lawrence's farewell to the world was reminiscent of Whitman's. "I am not sure," said Whitman, speaking of *Passage To India*, "but the last inclosing sublimation of race or poem is, what it thinks of death. After . . . the pervading fact of visible existence, with the duty it devolves, is rounded and apparently completed, it still remains to be really completed by suffusing through the whole and several, that other pervading invisible fact, so large a part (is it not the largest part?) of life here . . ." Whitman confronted that fact, and gently but firmly made that largest part of life an accepted part, as Lawrence did after him. Jeffers looks upon it with equable eyes, finding it bulk as beautiful as it is enormous. But Yeats is no less the pupil of Pater than of Villiers de l'Isle Adam. One to whom consciousness is exquisitely precious, one for whom the creative imagination of man is a constant theme, must look upon death as an enemy. The fact that Yeats plays seriously with the idea of reincarnation, and that in this play, over which hover the austere presences of Hindu mystics, he thinks of the psyche as betrayed into life, does not change his reluctance to depart.

But if death is an enemy, it is not like old age, a horror:

207

"A sort of battered kettle at the heel"—something to be evaded, or defended from by "monuments of unaging intellect." It is to be met on equal terms. And in preparation for it the poet, testing all he thinks, believes, or makes, declares

> those works extravagance of breath
> That are not suited for such men as come
> Proud, open-eyed and laughing to the tomb.

Nor can all the accumulated misery of these last years, the bitter memory of unrequited love, the defeat of his most cherished dream, the loss of friends, the growth of enmities, the violence of civil war, of mob rule, the distresses of age— sorrows enough to overwhelm a lesser man, chill him into a desire for oblivion. He looks back over his life, its failures, its pains, and casts out remorse, nay, is shaken from head to foot with the sweetness that flows into his breast.

> What matter if I live it all once more?
> Endure that toil of growing up;
> The ignominy of boyhood; the distress
> Of boyhood changing into man;
> The unfinished man and his pain
> Brought face to face with his own clumsiness; ...
>
> I am content to follow to its source,
> Every event in action or in thought;
> Measure the lot; forgive myself the lot!
> When such as I cast out remorse
> So great a sweetness flows into the breast
> We must laugh and we must sing,
> We are blest by everything,
> Everything we look upon is blest.

This is no idle yea-saying, though were it not balanced by a record of tearing grief and savage indignation, it might perhaps be reckoned so. If confirmation of this were needed, one has but to listen to the wild summoning music of his latest songs, where with deliberate obscurity he sings of the ruin that has come upon his land and the land of heart's desire. The demand for a country both economically and culturally sound and whole, horror of the mob which destroys that hope, delight in every excellence, physical, intellectual, spiritual, which is the heritage of the well-born, despair of seeing any excellence survive in a land ridden by fanatic, slave, and clown—all speak through the heartbreaking melody and the fierce coarse words. If he prays to seem "a foolish, passionate man," these bitter lyrics but make plain that his passion is for a discipline which will transform, in Hugo's phrase, the mob into a people, and that his folly is to hope for a union of the natural and the supernatural which only mystics believe they have glimpsed, only visionaries have dared to affirm. Seeking to reconcile mind and body, dream and reality, the delight of philosophical speculation and the practical need for action, he takes an attitude somewhat resembling Vico's, being, as he says proudly, "Blake's disciple, not Hegel's," and asserting: "the spring vegetables may be over, they have not been refuted." The poems of this foolish passionate old man speak of wisdom as a certain fragrance speaks of ripeness. They deal, as great verse must, with ultimate things. Blazing with sensual energy, they acclaim the world of imagination. Suffused with the fact of death, they are the testament of life. This is the very substance and significance of poetry.

CHAPTER VIII

THE POST-WAR SCENE

fortitude as never before

frankness as never before,
disillusions as never told in the old days,
hysterias, trench confessions,
laughter out of dead bellies.

Pound.

DURING THE decade which followed the War the poets had time to explore the ache a man feels in amputated beliefs as well as in amputated hands and legs. Walt Whitman, living through a similar experience, and struck down physically by the suffering he had shared, could maintain his faith in the common man, in the ultimate triumph of the democratic ideal. These young poets had not only seen death wholesale, but they had seen it a machine affair, an international industry. They had "walked eye-deep in hell." They had limped out of it into the purgatory tellingly described by Ernest Walsh in his tribute to his hospital-mate, Kennedy:

Six years of weak lungs and strong guts
Six years of Camp Kearny Hospital number sixty-four
In the long stable-like wards
Six years of paintless-board-walls facing a prairie
Six years of Goodmorning-Kennedy-how-do-you-feel-today
Six years of temperature-taking never below a hundred

And a pulse a grasshopper would think fast
Six years of greasy food cooked by tired underpaid cooks
Six years of cold meals eaten mixed up with the smell of dying
      men
In the beds around you
Six years of this Kennedy
And then meningitis and an American Legion funeral.

Even those who had not been at the front could not escape.
They were like men who had lived through the Plague, and
who must suffer the added horror of survival under the reign
of a plutocracy as dismally vulgar as it was predacious. The
chief weapon left them was irony. Only by becoming grotesque
could poetry mirror so grotesque a world.

With the possible exception of MacLeish, whose poetry
dwells persistently and gravely with the fact of death, and
Hart Crane, who tried to keep faith with the certainties of
Whitman and Emily Dickinson, the poets of this period were
apt to look quizzically at emotion. Thus, E. E. Cummings may
declare that his poetry competes with the eyes of mice, roses,
and locomotives—a variant of MacLeish's:

> A poem should not mean
> But be

yet most of Cummings's verse is not simply one experience
competing with others, it is also comment upon experience.
The comment may be as silent as the flicker of an eyelid or
as seemingly irrelevant as the cartwheel of a vaudeville acrobat,
but it is there. He may protest that he looks at the scene before
him with the virginal, unmoral eyes of a child. But it is noteworthy that just after the armistice the scene before him
included not only the falling snow and the old balloon-man:
it was equally apt to be a speakeasy filled with hard-mouthed
whores and muzzy-eyed drunks. If some of his love lyrics are
as simple as they are poignant, most of his work expresses, in
carefully disrupted diction studded with colloquialisms, the
mordant post-War temper. Possessed by a lust for life, a rage

211

against death, he includes in his attack those spiritual skeletons at the feast: the stuffed shirts, the "famous fatheads," the hollow men.

Cummings's style waylays as often as it startles. His splitting up of words and syllables and the sandwiching of the *membra disjecta* within one another, like his personal punctuation and unexpected capitals, are sometimes effective devices. His more obvious effects remind one of the "tale" of Lewis Carroll's mouse curling down to a dot on the page, or of Herbert's Easter Day poem, printed sidewise in the shape of two angelic pinions. At its best the result is in the nature of an ideograph. His idiosyncratic use of language vividly conveys certain aspects of metropolitan life: the jazz tempo of winking electric signs, the blare of the loud-speaker, the streets where cars which could go sixty miles an hour move through the obstructions of traffic like ox-carts. But often even the attentive and sympathetic reader is disconcerted by tricks which don't quite come off. The difficulty is largely one of training the eye to catch more at a glance than is customary. Indeed, the chief objection to his style is that it is almost exclusively visual in its appeal. Some of his pieces obstinately refuse to be read aloud at all, while others can only be stammered forth. His typographic hesitations and jack-in-the-box celerities jump at the eye, leaving the ear vacant. There are occasions when he is indeed a child, the good child who should be seen and not heard, and like that small creature, silently plotting against our peace.

Cummings is equally maddened by the gaudiness in which death parades the pavements, the insane cheerfulness of the brotherhood of advertisers and high-pressure salesmen, and by those versifiers ("Beauty Hurts Mr. Vinal") who, having no eyes for these things, repeat the old platitudes to the old tunes.

Contrast Cummings's poem about the "flyspecked abdominous female" who hurries "to blow incredible wampum," with Sandburg's pictures of the same civilization, and the difference in method, an index to a more profound difference, is immediately clear.

>   impossibly
>   motivated by midnight
>   the flyspecked abdominous female
>   indubitably tellurian
>   strolls
>   emitting minute grins
>   each an intaglio.
>
>   Nothing
>   has also carved upon her much
>
>   too white forehead a pair of
>   eyes which mutter thickly (as one merely
>   terriculous American an instant doubts
>   the authenticity
>
>   of these antiquities) relaxing
>   hurries
>
>   elsewhere; to blow
>
>   incredible wampum

Sandburg might be capable of the phrase "to blow incredible wampum," though he would be apt to substitute for the last two words: "unbelievable mazuma." Cummings's free use of slang and of advertising slogans is a device which Sandburg employed much earlier. But whereas the latter gave the impression of a plain man conveying the feelings of his companions, Cummings's diction usually mocks the patter of the man in the street, who accepts the go-getter's viewpoint. The fact that he juxtaposes literary and colloquial diction is another instance of their difference. The cheerful Northern offshoot of the good gray poet would certainly not have described the lady in this particular poem as "indubitably tellurian," nor would he have had the subtlety to write

Nothing
had also carved upon her much

too white forehead a pair of
eyes which mutter thickly...

It is not that Sandburg fails to employ synaesthesia, but the introduction of this element of romantic poetry in such a satirical portrait as this makes for bizarrerie of another order. Nor would Lincoln's idolater find the swift mordancy of "Nothing has carved." Both of these poets celebrate the grotesque, both frequently strike a wistful note. But in Sandburg's work the pathetic tone is paramount, in Cummings's the satirical. And the younger man expresses his response to current experience by a technique reflecting a mood his senior does not know.

His most recent work, which satirizes alike American Babbittry and the "kumrads" who would build a fairer world, indicates how little he has changed with the changing years. He has not learned that while he, in his chosen isolation, and the radicals as a group, may not have the same friends—to borrow a phrase from Yeats—they do have the same enemies.

Such poets as Archibald MacLeish, Alan Porter, Horace Gregory, among others, bear witness, however variously, however indirectly, to the fact that they were open to the same literary influences, influences to which the War and its developments made them peculiarly sensitive. They found themselves in a region peopled largely by Eliot's Hollow Men—straw-brained paralytics going around a prickly-pear, discovering that the world ends "Not with a bang but a whimper." The nostalgic lines of Allen Tate, with their Elizabethan rhetoric, their Eliotesque symbols, presenting the contrast between the confusion of our hasty urban culture and an established agrarian order, sing a song of mockery. From a similar elevation, John Peale Bishop surveys the land of his fathers and laughs sardonically at what he sees. Archibald MacLeish, more obviously indebted to Pound than to Eliot, has a firm hold on

214

the evocative image, the thing seen, tasted, handled. But he, too, likes to have a shot at that gross beast, the vulgus, and to feather his shaft with satire. When he writes, in *Corporate Entity:*

> The Oklahoma Ligno and Lithograph Co
> Weeps at a nude by Michael Angelo,

when he makes *Critical Observations On The Great American Novel*, or, in *Verses For a Centennial* and in *Aeterna Poetae Memoria*, refers to his more unpleasant fellow-citizens, he proves himself of this distressed company.

Yet if a distorted civilization is one of MacLeish's frequent themes, he dwells more persistently on another motif recurrent in poetry but emphasized in post-War verse. His work is filled with the horror of death which haunted the Elizabethans, the sense of thieving time which pierced Andrew Marvell and which MacLeish's well-known apostrophe to that seventeenth-century poet expresses with aching intensity. It is characteristic that he sets as an epigraph to *A Pot Of Earth* a passage from *Hamlet:*

"For if the sun breeds maggots in a dead dog, being a god-
    kissing carrion,—Have you a daughter?"

"I have, my lord."

"Let her not walk i' the sun."

The poem is built upon an ancient fertility ritual connected with the figure of Adonis, which, like all such rituals, is enacted under the shadow of mortality. It is natural that a poem with such a theme should contain some echoes of *The Waste Land:*

Seven days I have been waiting for the rain now, ...

There was nothing to do, there was nothing to do but wait,
But wait, but wait, but wait, and the wind whispering
Something I couldn't understand beneath the door. ...

215

This is a variation on *What The Thunder Said:*

> If there were water we should stop and drink
> Amongst the rock one cannot stop or think

and the rest of that tortured passage, as also on the hysteria of the lady in *A Game of Chess:*

> "What is that noise?"
>   The wind under the door.
> "What is that noise now? What is the wind doing?"
>   Nothing again nothing.

His introduction of moments from contemporary life recall similar passages from Eliot's poem, and the tragic sense of waste which dominates it.

The Hamlet of A. MacLeish is another cry of agony, shot through with Shakespearean echoes, concluding on the lines which bear the load of dreadful night:

> Thou wouldst not think
> How ill all's here about my heart!

In half a dozen short lyrics he reiterates a grief which is as old as man, as fresh as the raw clods of an open grave. What gives this poetry power is MacLeish's gift for the significant detail, his feeling for cadence, charging the lines with a halted, andante music. What gives it sharpness is his unhappy awareness of these times. Thus, *The End of the World* offers a picture of the cock-eyed circus that is this world: the armless ambidextrian is lighting a match between his toes, the lion biting the complaisant lady's neck, the monkeys are coughing and swinging in waltz-time, when suddenly the top blows off,

> And there, there, there overhead, there, there, hung over
> Those thousands of white faces, those dazed eyes,
>   ...the black pall
> Of nothing, nothing, nothing—nothing at all.

216

THE POST-WAR SCENE

This poem suggests both the conclusion of *The Hollow Men* and the passage in *Crime and Punishment* where Svidrigailov says quietly: "We always imagine eternity as something beyond our conception, something vast, vast! But why must it be vast? Instead of all that, what if it's one little room, like a bath house in the country, black and grimy and spiders in every corner, and that's all eternity is? I sometimes fancy it like that."

It is the custom of poets to berate death, to quarrel with time, and such writers as Hardy and Housman and Edna Millay have heaped up a cairn of polished lyrics for the doomed. But where Hardy is in the habit of flinging rhetorical questions at the purblind Doomsters, where Housman is apt to make grim gestures of resignation, and Millay to behave with a pretty petulance, MacLeish rejects a noble and graceful attitude as a man would in the actual presence of the dead. His phrases are broken, their cadences those of one who must draw his breath in pain to tell man's story. His language is simple, his imagery biting—he speaks as one constrained to speak, knowing all speech is vain.

He has said that the poet's business is to record the flowing away of the world. His own record is given in such statements as *You, Andrew Marvell; Cinema of a Man; 'Not Marble Nor The Gilded Monuments'; Yacht For Sale*. The acuteness of his response is equally evident in two poems which offer sharply contrasted experiences, the one: *Eleven*, recalls with emotion the more tranquil hours of childhood; the other: *... & Forty-Second Street*, gives the character of the liveliest thoroughfare of the largest city in the modern world. It may be of some interest to set them here, side by side. In the first the child that would seek refuge from the adult world of a summer morning in the tool-shed; where,

>   ... one by one,
> Out of the dazzled shadow in the room
> The shapes would gather, the brown plowshare, spades,
> Mattocks, the polished helves of picks, a scythe

217

Hung from the rafters, shovels, slender tines
Glinting across the curve of sickles—shapes
Older than men were, the wise tools, the iron
Friendly with earth. And sit there quiet, breathing
The harsh dry smell of withered bulbs, the faint
Odor of dung, the silence. And outside
Beyond the half-shut door the blind leaves
And the corn moving...

Until at noon would come the old gardener, smelling of sun and summer, and bending over his baskets, "like a priest, like an interpreter," while the child would sit, saying nothing, happy as though he were a non-human thing, growing. In the other poem, ...& *Forty-Second Street,* which may be quoted in full, one has the impact of a totally different scene upon that child grown into a sensitive man:

Be proud New York of your prize domes
And your docks & the size of your doors & your
                                        dancing
Elegant clean big girls & your
Niggers with narrow heels & the blue on their
Bad mouths & your bars & your automo-
biles in the struck steel light & your
Bright Jews & your sorrow-sweet singing
Tunes & your signs wincing out in the wet
Cool shine & the twinges of
Green against evening...

        When the towns go down there are stains of
Rust on the stone shores and illegible
Coins and a rhyme remembered of
                                swans say
Or birds or leaves or a horse or fabulous
Bullforms or a falling of gold upon
Softness

        Be proud City of Glass of your
Brass roofs & the bright peaks of your
Houses
        Town that stood to your knees in the
Sea water be proud be proud
Of your high gleam on the sea

218

THE POST-WAR SCENE

Do they think

Town

They must rhyme your name with the name of a
Talking beast that the place of your walls be remembered

At its best MacLeish's verse is sharp as the New York sky-line, crisp as the smell of new-cut shavings, troubling as the beat of a pulse. The success of *Conquistador* is largely the success of his imagery, his ability to create atmosphere, to give the special curve and color of the thing seen, the peculiar tang of the thing on the tongue or in the nostrils, that which sets one hour apart from others and comes back, long afterward, like something palpable, to the mind. There are such lines in the Preface of Bernal Diaz, who herein chronicles the conquest of Mexico as he, one of the conquerors, now poor and blind and old, remembers it:

I: poor as I am: I was young in that country:
These words were my life: these letters written

Cold on the page with the spilt ink and the shunt of the
Stubborn thumb: these marks at my fingers:
These are the shape of my own life. . . .

and I hunted the

Unknown birds in the west with their beautiful wings!

Old men should die with their time's span:
The sad thing is not death: the sad thing

Is the life's loss out of earth when the living vanish:
All that was good in the throat: the hard going:
The marching singing in sunshine: the showery land:

The quick loves: the sleep: the waking: the blowing of
Winds over us: all this that we knew:
All this goes out at the end as the flowing of

Water carries the leaves down: and the few—
Three or four there are of us still that remember it—
Perish:

219

Reading MacLeish's lyrics, one feels, as with few poets, that the words are the shape of his own life, not in the sense of being strict autobiography, but in having caught the smells, the sounds, the savors, the quality of experience, that make his life dear to him, and its flowing away scarcely to be borne.

Conquistador is a superb record of a lost world, and technically of interest as a fine example of terza rima in English. The skillful use of assonance and of unexpected feminine endings saves it from monotony. The narrative is fascinating because the poet has so well realized what the conquest meant physically to the men who discovered and ruined that alien civilization. If the poem lacks something, it is a deeper motive than that supplied by the poet-historian: a central theme, a myth.

MacLeish has suggested that the experience of the Spanish conquerors has been paralleled in our own time by "the generation of men who have moved into and explored and conquered and debauched the unknown world of modern technics," but while the idea of this parallel may have helped him to make the poem a living thing, it has not transpired in the work itself, which therefore remains a smaller and less significant performance than it might otherwise be. There is abundant evidence in the body of his work that he feels the lack of the central unifying force that the older poets found in Church or State. He cannot be considered a regionalist, but his evocations of his native background in *American Letter*, no less than his praise of his country in his too much maligned *Frescoes For Mr. Rockefeller's City*, offer testimony to his need for establishing himself in a place ample enough to afford him a spiritual as well as a physical home. He is incapable of the exuberance of that dying veteran, Ernest Walsh, writing in exile, how as he walked down the aisle toward the altar

> ... the gargoyles spat and bit off their hands
> And the birds screeched the angels have gone gone
> And the postcard merchants asked have you any

THE POST-WAR SCENE

> In America like this meaning
> The Duomo and the half-shown postcard depends
> Whether you are male or female I shake
> My head and say America is uptown
> And downtown overhead and underground
> But we can't get it on a postcard yet

On the contrary, MacLeish recognizes sadly that his country, his people, is "neither a land nor a race." As early as in *The Hamlet of A. MacLeish* he asked:

> How shall we learn what it is that our hearts believe in?

Nor is he alone in his asking. The need of a homeland, the lack of a myth, obsesses the poets of the post-War period.

In *Valediction To My Contemporaries*, Horace Gregory cries:

> How shall we find
> the bodies of those unslain, exiled from war
> but now returned, furloughs of exile signed
> from all green ports on earth?

Gregory's apostrophes to such Americans as Emerson, Whitman, Randolph Bourne (all men who had reaped the grim harvest of war), his tireless exploration of the native land in which such spirits as his are in perpetual exile, are a more bitter variant of MacLeish's sad asseveration. Only in mockery could the poets now phrase the question which Robert Frost had put in all seriousness a few years earlier:

> How are we to write
> The Russian novel in America
> As long as life goes so unterribly?

With the signing of the Versailles Treaty, meaning had gone out of the world, and since, for the poet, the world and the word are one, meaning had gone out of language. He had to find a new symbol, a new vocabulary. Hence the difficulty of much modern work: the poet communicates not only his personal response to private experience, by his own unique means: he has first to construct the ideal bases of that experience, and his poetry must realize them also. The repressed anguish of Eliot:

> Consequently I rejoice, having to construct something
> Upon which to rejoice
>
> And pray to God to have mercy upon us

finds an antistrophe in John Peale Bishop's

> The ceremony must be found
>
> Traditional, with all its symbols
> ancient as the metaphors in dreams;
> strange, with never before heard music; continuous
> until the torches deaden at the bedroom door.

In a similar mood the same poet writes:

> Christ is dead. And in a grave
> Dark as a sightless skull He lies
> And of His bones are charnels made.

More dryly, Tate observes:

> Narcissus is vocabulary. Hermes decorates
> A cornice on the Third National Bank. Vocabulary
> Becomes confusion, decoration a blight.

But if these poets inhabit a wasteland, strewn with broken lares and penates, and pocked with treacherous holes, the work done by their immediate predecessors has given them certain technical advantages in exploring it. Pound's insistence on the live detail, on the music that fits the matter; Eliot's gift for loading a phrase with associated meanings, his habit of juxtaposing incongruities, the better to realize our anomalous situation, are so many tools to their hands. And overlaid by these influences, but none the less present, is the effect of Frost, focusing intently on the native, the local, scene, and of Masters, uncovering the

222

shames of older smaller wars, and of Sandburg, using without embarrassment the idiom of the man in the alley.

These younger men have not been accepted by the public as warmly as were their forerunners. Their manner, though founded on the work of earlier craftsmen, is unfamiliar to the general. Moreover, by its very nature, poetry exhibiting the verbal acrobatics of Cummings, the arrogant intellection of Ransom and Tate, the cinematic close-ups and fade-outs of Gregory, who, though belonging to a younger generation, has written many lyrics expressive of the post-War sensibility, is unintelligible to people accustomed to traditional verse or to the more facile and obvious realism of Masters and the familiar populist bias of Lindsay. When the shafts of the ironist go home, he is deprived of his target. Eliot's hollow men, his ape-neck Sweeney and his Bleistein ("Chicago Semite Viennese") continued to provide the target that Babbittry affords the lyrical sharp-shooter long after their creator tired of attacking them. Much post-War verse was an elaborate variant of the observation:

> (The lengthened shadow of a man
>   Is history, said Emerson
> Who had not seen the silhouette
>   Of Sweeney straddled in the sun.)

Eliot had recommended that poets no longer content themselves with looking in their hearts, but that they examine as well the nervous system and the digestive tract. They took his advice, but if they were studying aspects of themselves which the Elizabethan courtier ignored, it should not be forgotten that they were conducting their researches in the light thrown by the anthropologist and the psychologist. Moreover, the objects which agitated the nerves and loosened the reins of the moderns had no counterparts in the rural scene familiar to their predecessors. The commercial development of an Elizabethan age, the disturbances of the French Revolution and its sequel, were of a different order from the processes of twentieth-century capitalistic enterprise with the discrepancies it involves: technological advance and cultural decay, democratic professions and plutocratic rule.

The poetry of this generation attests to the truism, stated a century ago by Wordsworth, that the discoveries of men of science become the material of poetry as soon as those discoveries affect men as enjoying and suffering beings. But the pantheist of Grasmere could not foresee that the changes brought about by laboratory workers and technologists would coincide with economic changes as destructive of the old attitudes as the machine has been of the old culture. What the poets were now forced to work with was not merely the actual scenery of the city—the back-drop of the industrial drama, and this in the novel, abstract language of a scientific age, but they had also to express the complexities of a world in which dinosaur's eggs, the spoils of Egyptian tombs, and the comparatively familiar elements of wars and revolutions, competed for attention with split atoms, schizophrenia, and five-and-ten-cent store princesses, all thrust hot upon ear and eye by radio and cinema. Eliot had been one of the first to formulate in English poetry the reaction of a sensitive nature to the contemporary world. And it is natural that his juniors, responding in a similar way to the same surroundings, should be haunted by the voice of Eliot and Eliot's models.

When Tate writes:

> Heredity
> Proposes love, love exacts language, and we lack
> Language. When shall we speak again? When shall
> The sparrow dusting the gutter sing?

it seems a reminiscence of the hysterical lady's cry in *The Waste Land,* and of Eliot's *Third Prelude:*

> "And when all the world came back
> And the light crept up between the shutters,
> And you heard the sparrows in the gutters,
> You had such a vision of the street
> As the street hardly understands..."

224

That is not simply because both poets are talking of sparrows in gutters. It is rather because both are obsessed by the dinginess of the vulgar life around them, and the helplessness of the poet who must be heard above the nervous cacophony. Tate's first book is thick with such echoes.

> I see you old, trapped in a burly house
> Cold in the angry spitting of a rain
> Come down these sixty years. . .

is a variant of the opening of *Gerontion,* that epitome of decline, and throughout the volume there are further tokens of a sympathetic reading of Eliot. The other poets whose work reflects his are likewise not mere plagiarists (though he would seem to have shed a grace upon plagiarism). To set Ransom's sonnet with the line: "A macaroon absorbed all her emotion" beside *Mr. Apollinax,* which concludes

> Of dowager Mrs. Phlaccus, and Professor and Mrs. Cheetah
> I remember a slice of lemon, and a bitten macaroon,

is to observe that the one piece recalls the other not because a polite tea-party is their common setting, but because both poems are a commentary on civilized futility. Eliot's *Preludes* are reëchoed repeatedly, most clearly perhaps in this fragment from Bishop's poem on *Montmartre:*

> . . . Dawn begins not as a light
> But as the sound of ashmen's feet. . .
>
> If this is day it has
> The complexion of a night-beggar's
> Unshaven and disastrous face. . .
>
> The taxis roll before the Trinity
> The taxis roll about the empty square
> Like billiard balls in a room one has left.
> At the corner of Saint Lazarus
> Workmen lean on coffee cups
> Devouring crescents. Blouses
> Bluer than the sky and as the morning ravenous. . .

225

> Memory wipes away the night
> As a damp rag might smear a dirty glass...

Nor is it alone such whispers as

> And look behind the broken chair.
> And look along the shadow on the
> Wall. Rat turds. Spiders.
>
> There was no one ever there!

which evoke the dry bones, the stale smells, the horror of emptiness which haunt the *Preludes* and their more symbolical companion-piece: *Rhapsody On A Windy Night,* as also Eliot's later work.

The replacement of rural by urban imagery, the obtrusion of science and machine technology, isolated instances of which could be found earlier in the work of verse-makers as various as Maxwell Bodenheim, Louis Untermeyer, and Joseph Auslander, is characteristic of the poetry of this period. Sometimes these elements occur only to be sneered at, as in Cummings's:

> While you and i have lips and voices which
> are for kissing and to sing with
> who cares if some oneyed son of a bitch
> invents an instrument to measure Spring with?

Sometimes they are conceded special treatment, as in MacLeish's *Einstein,* and Tate's less ambitious poem on the subway, or in MacKnight Black's repeated eulogies of the Corliss engine and his passionate invocations to the skyscraper, as in *Structural Iron Workers:*

> What love do these men give their women
> That is like the love they spend
> On this iron harlot
> With the sky between her breasts?
>
> What kisses
> Like the red sting of rivets
> Have they left on any lips?

226

You will not find
The full fruit of their loins
In any daughters, any sons—
But lift your gaze and stare long
Toward the sky's edge.

Often these elements of modern life are part of the accepted environment, as in this metaphor of Tate's:

... a vision flashes
Like the headlong gust from a motor-car.

The rhythms of modern poetry also reflect the tempo of modern life, and the noises peculiar to our civilization begin to make themselves heard in our verse. For centuries poets had sought to imitate the voices of birds and of rivers:

The palm and may make country houses gay,
Lambs frisk and play, the shepherds pipe all day,
And we hear aye birds tune this merry lay—
Cuckoo, jug-jug, pu-we, to-witta-woo!

Sabrina fair
Listen where thou art sitting
Under the glassie, cool, translucent wave,
In twisted braids of Lillies knitting
The loose train of thy amber-dropping hair...

It ceased; yet still the sails made on
A pleasant noise till noon,
A noise like of a hidden brook
In the leafy month of June,
That to the sleepy woods all night
Singeth a quiet tune.

Towery city and branchy between towers;
Cuckoo-echoing, bell swarmèd, lark-charmèd, rook-
racked, river-rounded...

227

The contemporary hears fewer larks, nightingales, and placid streams, and more factory sirens, motor horns, grinding gears, coughing engines. So one finds Eliot, following up the "Twit twit, tereu" of Elizabethan bird-song with the lines:

> At the violet hour, when the eyes and back
> Turn upward from the desk, when the human engine waits
> Like a taxi throbbing waiting. . .

The mention of the "human engine" of course assists the impression, but the blunt movement of the participles in "Like a taxi throbbing waiting" is as near the pulse of a halted taxi as Milton's liquid syllables are like the flow of gentle waters. Similarly, in A. S. J. Tessimond's poem, suggested by a Russian film and suggestive of some Soviet poetry, *La Marche des Machines*, the rhythm has the stiff angular character of mechanical motion:

> This piston's infinite recurrence is
> night morning night and morning night and
> death and birth and death and birth and this
> crank climbs (blind Sisyphus) and see
>
> steel teeth greet
> bow deliberate
> delicately lace
> in lethal kiss
>   God's teeth bite whitely tight
>
> slowly the gigantic oh slowly the steel spine
>   dislocates
>
> wheels grazing (accurately missing) waltz
>
> two cranes do a hundred-ton tango against the sky

Thus, all too obviously, in Louis Aragon's *Red Front*, which E. E. Cummings, in spite of his anti-Soviet animus, made the courteous gesture of translating into English verse, one hears the pistons plunge and the whistle scream:

The Post-War Scene

The red train starts and nothing shall stop it
UR
SS
UR
SS
UR
SS

What particularly distinguishes the work of these men is, however, not that their verse carries the shriek of machinery and the purr of domesticated engines, but that each of them, conveying these noises, could quote the well-known lines:

> But at my back from time to time I hear
> The sound of horns and motors, which shall bring
> Sweeney to Mrs. Porter in the spring.

What disturbs the poets, in fine, is not the horns and motors, but the fact that they are bringing Sweeney to Mrs. Porter— that the season of renewal, of the birth of Christ the Tiger, is to be marked by the union of two creatures vulgar enough to be emblems of the failure of our civilization: poor pieces of a unique mythology. Even Hart Crane, who derived from Rimbaud and Emily Dickinson rather than from Donne and Laforgue, repeatedly staged in his verse the conflict, which eventually brought him to his death, between his transcendental dream and the harsh actualities beating on his nerves. He could mix the sensuous incitements obtained through synaes-thesia with a severe abstract quality, and he tangled syntax in his haste to convey at once the rapidity of his sensations and his mystical interpretation of them. But he also found a plainer metaphor than any of his fellows when disgust gagged him:

> The phonographs of hades in the brain
> Are tunnels that re-wind themselves, and love
> A burnt match skating in a urinal—

The force of this passage is not lessened because it recalls, in its juxtaposition of ugliness and ecstasy, no less than its exact reference, Rimbaud's: "Oh, the little fly, drunk at the tavern urinal, amorous of borage, and which a ray of light dissolves!"

Along with the mood of disgust and scorn was a desire to startle, to *épater* in a more violent manner the increasingly monstrous bourgeoisie. Together with such urban phenomena as motor horns, subway tunnels, sky-signs, and the physical and spiritual malaise these produced, went the radio, the cinema, and the cabaret. These offered not only new material but new techniques. The poets had been willing to attend Laforgue, arguing with the moon above a Paris street, to follow Rimbaud, sailing up the time-stream in his drunken boat. They were all the readier to listen to Guillaume Apollinaire, the god-father of surréalisme, who died on the eve of the Armistice, and to delight in Jean Cocteau, the acrobatic dreamer who glided like a tightrope-dancer on roller-skates across the giddy nihilism of Dada into the arms of the Catholic Church. Not that the poets writing in English quite paralleled the performance of their foreign confrères. But the War, with its speeding-up of sensation and emotion, and the difficult adjustment to the post-War world, were much the same for poets in all the western countries, and furthermore, not a few of those writing in English took refuge from peace-time realities at home in literary conflicts abroad.

These conflicts, at first quasi-philosophical, more recently quasi-political, were not entirely by-products of the War, though the extravagant gaiety with which they were conducted may well have been so. The investigation of the subconscious reflected in surréalisme, which developed poetry not about things, but about the imagery of dream-life, derived from psychological studies of a much earlier period. The interest in the stream of consciousness was another aspect of the Bergsonian philosophy of flux, and was assisted by the prose of Bergson's cousin, Marcel Proust. The attraction of the perverse and the fantastic was natural in an art which was holding the mirror up to science. Inventions were annihilating space, reversing time. Airplanes fly over an ocean, over the

230

peaks of the Andes, over the jungle, frightening a herd of elephants into a mad gallop. The cinema studio creates a looking-glass universe where, without bottles labeled "Drink me" or cakes labeled "Eat me" or keys to impossible gardens, creatures are elongated or telescoped, movements accelerated or slowed up, in a fashion suggesting that the world is made of india-rubber or collapsible tin. The ghost of the future glimmers through the immediate scene, the present dissolves into the past. Sound waves travel like light across continents. Mariners singing Christmas carols at the South Pole are answered by a jazz band on Broadway.

The poet who most clearly shows the influence of these fantastic realities is perhaps inevitably a symbolist. A method which seeks to register the motions of the mind under the pressure and the friction of modern life is peculiarly able to render back the image of that life, as does the poetry of Hart Crane and Horace Gregory. Although suffering noticeably from the obscurity inherent in the symbolist technique, Gregory's work communicates with energy and sincerity the emotions of a man alive to his times. Hammered by all the obscene forces which sent Eliot to find questionable solace in the fold of Anglo-Catholicism and rallied some of the Fugitives around the banner of a local patriotism, which drove Hart Crane to seek refuge in sex and drink and finally in suicide, which made Lawrence writhe and spit like a fretful invalid, Gregory, with his back to the wall, pleads quietly for power "to stay in no retreat and not to die."

He shows us a man walking, without armor, into the blaring streets and dingy cemeteries, into the rich orchards and beside the gracious rivers, and then back into the nervous rooms of this America, where men and women, maddened by the complexities and tragic absurdities of their existence, chatter, brood, make love, dance, get drunk, and sometimes, with a markedly deliberate gesture, put out the light. He shows us this man plunging into subways, climbing skyscrapers, scanning head-lines, answering the telephone—this man beaten upon by the

231

city lights, the city noises, reaching out to answer the solicitations of the countryside, seeking to satisfy the hungry intellect,
the starved spirit—this man, watching, listening, with quivering nerves and shaken heart, remembering, pitying, and loving.

Give Cerberus a non-employment wage, the dog is hungry.
This head served in the war, Cassandra, it lost an eye;
that head spits fire, for it lost its tongue licking the paws
of lions caged in Wall Street and their claws
were merciless.

> Follow, O follow him, loam-limbed Apollo, crumbling before
> Tiffany's window; he must buy
> himself earrings for he meets his love tonight,
> (Blossoming Juliet
> emptied her love into her true love's lap)
> dies in his arms.
> He is a poet,
> kiss him, Socrates.

They say the red arm of the Proletariat swings,
Hammer and Sickle, a quarter moon in the sky,
the dogstar comets leap . . .
They say Macbeth embezzled funds, the market
fell too soon, too soon the hands of Christ
withered on the cross.
His wife was barren
(her eyes are flowers
blowing in the field down where the Lackawanna railroad runs:
flow softly rivers of coal and steam)
His life insurance went to the banks.

There are five limousines, unbought, rotting behind plate glass,
delicate worms in leather and sharp April grass
piercing steel joints . . .
Talk to the guns, Cassandra, tell them this is peace,
not war, not war,
peace,
PEACE.

This fragment from the opening poem of *No Retreat: New
York, Cassandra*, gives an indication of the effectiveness of his

method. The fluent images, the sudden close-ups, the shifting angle of vision, suggest the technique of the cinema. His changing music—reminiscent of Spenser and Tom Moore and Catullus, abruptly broken by a shrill modern note—suggests the swift transitions of the radio. He acknowledges chaos with a candor which cannot evade fear, but he seeks refuge neither in an irrecoverable way of life nor in oblivion.

Gregory's later work is the product rather of a pre-War than a post-War sensibility. Both directly and indirectly, *Chorus For Survival* bears the mark of his sojourn in England and Ireland. The sharp imagery and wild tune of at least one lyric shows the influence of Yeats's political songs, as the body of the book attests that he has Yeats's essential integrity.

> *Through streets where crooked Wicklow flows*
> *I saw a man with broken nose:*
> *His venomous eyes turned full on me*
> *And cursed the ancient poverty*
> *That scarred his limbs and mired his clothes.*
>
> O cursed, wind-driven poverty
> That breaks the man and mires his clothes.
>
> *Beyond the street, beyond the town,*
> *Rose hill and tree and sea and down:*
> *O drear and shadowy green ash-tree,*
> *O hills that neither sleep nor rest*
> *But are like waves in that dark sea*
> *That rides the wind, nor-east, nor-west,*
>
> O cursed, wind-driven poverty!
>
> *Below the hill, below the town,*
> *Deep, whispering voices everywhere*
> *Break quiet in the morning air*
> *And mount the skies to pierce the sun.*
>
> *I saw the naked, cowering man*
> *Shrink in the midnight of his eye,*
> *There, to eat bitterness within,*
> *And close the door and hide the sin*

233

That made his withering heart run dry.
O venomous, dark, unceasing eye
That turned on street and town and me,
Between the waves of hill and sea
Until the eyelid closed the sky.

      The rain-rilled, shaken, green ash-tree
      Spread roots to gather him and me
      In downward pull of earth that drains
      The blood that empties through men's veins
      Under the churchyard, under stone
      Until the body lies alone
      And will not wake: nor wind, nor sky
      Bring sunlight into morning air
      And breathe disquiet everywhere
      Into the heart of hill and town.

O heart whose heart is like my own
And not to rest or sleep but climb
Wearily out of earth again
To feed again that venomous eye
That is the manhood of my time,
Whether at home or Wicklow town.

This is my street to walk again,
O cursed, wind-driven poverty,
        I hear the coming of the rain.

The poems in this book are less elegiac, more summoning, but no less bitter.

As the map changes, through the cold sky,
Lean from the cockpit, read
The flower of prairie grass in seed
(Though here is war
          my hand points where the body
Leaps its dead, the million poor.
Steel-staved and broken
          and no grave shall hold them
Either in stone or sea; nor urn nor sand,
Skyline of city walls, their monument,

234

And on this field, lockstep in millions joined,
New world in fire opens where they stand.)

Gregory realizes, as sensitive members of his generation must, that a new conflict is in preparation, and that its issue is doubtful. Nor can he forget the boom that was the last war's Greek gift to the victors, and the death that crept by night out of its belly. But he does not despair. His recent poetry proves that he can still draw courage from the American past. It shows him, above this mad, stricken era, leaning forward to hail a new Atlantis. Nor is he alone in this brave hope.

Poets are turning away from the personal problem, the private vision, to a more inclusive if not a more profound theme. Maxwell Bodenheim surrenders his deliberate bohemianism, Alfred Kreymborg his sly whimsical dialogues, Isidor Schneider his virile eroticism, to the celebration of a new freedom, a new debate, a new love. With varying success but with remarkable unanimity those post-War poets who have not retired to a remote plantation or a sea-coast fastness, seek to convey the tremors of this pregnant time. It is perhaps not surprising that the younger men should be the most alert. Not yet bound by any accepted tradition, sharply aware of their misshapen world, they are better able than their seniors to respond vigorously and immediately to the needs of the moment. Muriel Rukeyser, while indebted to Gregory and also to the younger British poets, seems to be developing a strong authentic voice. The work of Kenneth Fearing admirably exemplifies the new element in American verse. His *American Rhapsodies*, with their shocking substitutions of raw fact for the happy commonplaces of the child's game, his satiric use of current slogans, his evocations of cold, hunger, pain, the day to day horrors, the endless anonymous casualties in the war of poverty, are a cry, a blow, a challenge. His very titles are significant: *Winner Take All, Dividends, Dear Beatrice Fairfax, What If Mr. Jesse James Should Some Day Die? $2.50, 20th Century Blues*, and *X minus X*:

Even when your friend, the radio, is still; even when her
  dream, the magazine, is finished; even when his life,
  the ticker, is silent; even when their destiny, the boule-
  vard, is bare,
  and after that paradise, the dancehall, is closed; after that
  theatre, the clinic, is dark,

Still there will be your desire, and her desire, and his desire,
  and their desire,
  your laughter, their laughter,
  your curse and his curse, her reward and their reward, their
  dismay and his dismay and her dismay and yours—

Even when your enemy, the collector, is dead; even when your
  counsellor, the salesman, is sleeping; even when your
  sweetheart, the movie queen, has spoken; even when
  your friend, the magnate, is gone.

Dirge is a lament for something other than a human cipher;
it is a demand, no less vehement because it is not articulate,
that a system which produces and enthrones the nonentity be
wiped out:

And wow he died as wow he lived,
  going whop to the office and blooie home to sleep and biff
    got married and bam had children and oof got fired,
  zowie did he live and zowie did he die,

With who the hell are you at the corner of his casket, and
  where the hell we going on the right-hand silver knob,
  and who the hell cares walking second from the end
  with an American Beauty wreath from why the hell not,

Very much missed by the circulation staff of the New York
  Evening Post; deeply, deeply mourned by the B.M.T.,

Wham, Mr. Roosevelt; pow, Sears Roebuck; awk, big dipper;
  bop, summer rain;
  bong, Mr., bong, Mr., bong, Mr., bong.

Written between the quiet lines of *Lullaby* are the words of
Debs: "While there is a soul in prison, I am not free":

236

THE POST-WAR SCENE

Wide as this night, old as this night is old and young as it
   is young, still as this, strange as this,
filled as this night is filled with the light of a moon as grey;
dark as these trees, heavy as this scented air from the fields,
   warm as this hand,
as warm, as strong,

Is the night that wraps all the huts of the south and folds the
   empty barns of the west;
is the wind that fans the roadside fire;
are the trees that line the country estates, tall as the lynch
   trees, as straight, as black;
is the moon that lights the mining towns, dim as the light
   upon tenement roofs, grey upon the hands at the bars
   of Moabit, cold as the bars of the Tombs.

The depression did not suddenly breed a new race of poets,
speaking a strange tongue, beating their drums to a novel
rhythm. The impress of Pound and Eliot has not been erased.
But a new temper is evident in current verse; a fresh impulse
is at work. Some years ago a devotee of psychoanalysis
exclaimed: "The muse of Darwin! Next, the muse of Freud!"
Had this sonneteer been gifted with prescience, he might have
anticipated the advent of the muse of Marx. The march of the
muses is not quite so deliberate, but one can perceive in the
poetry of the last quarter of a century the influence of these
thinkers dominating successive periods to a remarkable degree.
The younger poets manage to pay their devoirs to all three,
analyzing a sick society with the weapons of psychopathology,
looking forward toward economic and spiritual as well as
biological evolution, and justifying alike their diagnosis and
their prognostication by the Communist Manifesto. Fortunately
for poets, as for other men, the fatigue, the bitterness, the
nausea of the post-War years could not go on indefinitely. A
new generation is looking at life with the aggressive eyes of
the young.

237

CHAPTER IX

POETRY AND POLITICS

A' men's institutions and maist men's thochts
Are tryin' for aye to bring to an end
The insatiable thocht, the beautiful violent will,
The restless Spirit of Man, the theme o' my sang
Or to the theme o't what Man's spirit and thocht
Micht be if men were as muckle concerned
Wi' them as they are wi't fitba' or wimmen,
Poets' words as the neist door neighbours' . . .

Hugh MacDiarmid.

NOT DOGGED courage, but a bold note of challenge is heard in poetry today, sounding most thrillingly from across the water. The bitterness of the War poets, Sassoon, Graves, Wilfred Owen, is foreign to these young Englishmen, though they are well aware of living under the shadow of war. They have come to grips only vicariously with the evils of poverty, the agony of industrial slavery, the horrors of class warfare, that such writers as Arturo Giovannitti, Michael Gold, Carl Sandburg, recorded with some vigor and much earnestness twenty years ago. Happy in their faith in a not too distant millenium, they chant the refrain of Rex Warner's *Hymn:*

Come then, companions. This is the spring of the blood,
Heart's hey-day, movement of masses, beginning of good.

Among the less cheerful of them, sardonic laughter has found

238

a new object—their own inadequacy. The plea for strength is seldom uttered. These young men are acutely conscious of the age in which they are maturing: not the horns and motors at their back, but the airplane engine humming overhead, the drill grinding at their feet to make a cave for refuge from the gas-bombs of the next war, are what occupy them. And always, beyond the horizon, lies new country, defying the old order whose collapse they would hasten. Sometimes one seems to hear under their shouts of enthusiasm a murmured paraphrase of one of Kipling's old imperialist songs:

> If th' Union were what th' Union seems:
> Not the Soviet Union of our dreams,
> But only Stalin, brass, and paint,
> 'Ow quick we'd chuck 'er,—but she ain't!

But though they have been stimulated and supported in their faith by the Russian experiment, they appear to be realistic enough to insist that if they are to build the new Jerusalem in England's green and pleasant land, the task must be done by British workmen, if not with English bricks and English mortar.

They are revolutionaries both technically and politically, a fact which makes them almost unique in literary history. For while the poet is often in advance of his time and in opposition to the governing power, those concerned for the niceties of their art are apt to ignore the social question, as the more earnest propagandists are apt to let esthetic considerations go by the board. C. Day Lewis, however, with his colleagues, W. H. Auden and Stephen Spender, have gone to school to Eliot, to Wilfred Owen, and more particularly to Hopkins. They have learned as much from Hopkins's theory as from his inimitable practice, returning to the simplicities of the nursery rhyme, to the easy lilt of the ballad, rather than exploiting "sprung rhythm" with the fastidiousness of its Victorian godfather. They accept the conversational tone and to some extent the free associations of Eliot, though their transitions from the style

239

of one period to that of another are perhaps not as swift as his, if possibly more various. They do not frequently follow Elizabethan practice, and, not having had to revolt from free verse, they do not often employ the tight stanza of Gautier. They are not averse to internal rhyme, which, unlike end-rhyme, fails to accentuate the metre, but they incline more to the assonances employed by Wilfred Owen. Since they do not share his fondness for Keats, they avoid the lush quality which is sometimes at variance with what Owen has to say. They feel his passionate desire to uproot the forces of evil which make our world what it is, but not having known the actual horrors of the front, and so less appalled by the anguish war entails than belligerent in their advocacy of a new social order, their poetry inclines, unlike his, to drama and didacticism.

In one important respect they differ from all of these "ancestors," as they like to call those men on whose spiritual powers they are able to draw. Their imagery refers largely to the machine age, and their symbolism, derived from this urban and industrialized society, as well as from the study of geology, biology, and the findings of Freud and Koffka, is almost allegorical in its definiteness. The vocabulary of industrial warfare: the spy, the bully (or thug), the abandoned works, the ruined farm, and the social parasite seen as a menace to the healthy organism, the effects of a dominating money power seen as manifestations of disease—these recur in their work with hammering persistency. And alike in their concrete details and in their frequent puns they are more anti-poetic than their predecessors. Two quotations from Lewis will illustrate both their exactitude of phrase and the spirit which animates their poetry. He dismisses one division of the enemy—the comfortable, unimaginative bourgeois—thus:

> Counters of spoons and content with cushions
> They pray for peace, they hand down disaster.

240

And thus simply he states what he and his companions demand:

Men shall be glad of company, love shall be more than a guest
And the bond no more of paper.

Contrast this with Alfred Prufrock's despairing symbolism:

I have measured out my life with coffee spoons;

and with his creator's stricken prayer in *Ash Wednesday*:

Terminate torment
Of love unsatisfied
The greater torment
Of love satisfied. . .

Grace to the Mother
For the Garden
Where all love ends.

The difference in method and attitude is at once apparent.

Technically, their debt is to the poets of their own country, rather than, as their predecessors' was, to the poets of France. Indeed, as was noted above, they travel back some six centuries to take lessons from Langland, and find in his homely Anglo-Saxon verse a suitable form for their address to the plowman's modern counterpart. Not that the English laborer would understand the idiom of Lewis or Auden, but the vigorous rhythm and marked alliteration of *Piers Plowman* appeals to these poets for its summoning qualities. Like Hopkins, they are in too great haste to get the thing said to wait upon grammatical usage; like him, they constantly play upon words, revel in puns and knottier ambiguities. This clipped manner of speech, with its elisions and compressions, may signify, as in Hopkins's case, passionate conviction, or, as in the case of Eliot, an assumption that one is addressing intimates only. Indeed, nothing is stranger—until one has analyzed it—than the contrast between the tone of these poets and their ultimate intention. They proclaim the dear love of comrades, they announce the imminent

241

birth of a new world of real brotherhood, in phrases charged with paradox, in music often harsh with mockery. Auden, the most obscure, in some respects the most stimulating, nicely illustrates this divergence and its meaning.

His poems are scarcely intelligible until one has read them in their entirety. Not only is nearly every poem an inseparable entity, but, furthermore, most of the pieces are supported by the body of his work. The whole here is greater than its parts. One becomes accustomed to the abrupt syntax:

> In his day-thinking and in his night-thinking
> Is wareness and is fear of other,
> Alone in flesh, himself no friend.

One comes to understand that when he speaks of "a memory of fish" he is referring not to the pond or the dinner-table, but to a remote period in evolutionary history. One learns to think quickly, although what happens in the mind of the attentive reader is perhaps not thought, driving the staples of logic for a bridge across the gaps, but intuition flinging hasty planks or flying over at the tail of a balloon. But one must beware of being waylaid by references too new to assimilate in passing. Here is none of the delight in machinery which allowed MacKnight Black to talk about turbines and dynamos as though they were bursting buds, none of the disgust for it that made the Fugitives long for the peace of the plantation. Here, moreover, is not that intense realization of war which fills the verse of Sassoon and Wilfred Owen with appalling pain. Auden takes both machinery and war for granted in a fashion impossible to his seniors. He expresses neither praise nor dispraise. It is all part of the landscape, or as Hopkins might say, the "inscape" of the modern world to which he belongs, the world which he sees crashing toward destruction and rebirth. Foreseeing the destruction, he speaks of "Equipment rusting in unweeded lanes." Accepting the struggle as inevitable, he commands:

242

Cover in time with beams those in retreat
That, spotted, they turn though the reverse were great.

In the course of a poem sung to a jazzed tune which gives it an effectiveness it would otherwise lack, a poem filled with peacetime imagery, he observes:

> In my spine there was a base;
> And I knew the general's face:
> But they've severed all the wires,
> And I can't tell what the general desires.

The acceptance of the machine, and more especially of machine warfare, which allows him not merely to introduce it casually and frequently, but actually to convert it into metaphor, is one of the distinguishing marks of Auden's verse. But more significant than this are the unexpected gaps and reversals which make it difficult to know where to have him next.

It is plain enough that he is satirizing capitalist society. The Announcer in his *Dance of Death* describes a good deal more of Auden than is contained in that sharp little comedy with his opening speech: "We present to you this evening a picture of the decline of a class, of how its members dream of a new life, but secretly desire the old, for there is death inside them. We show you that death as a dancer." From behind the curtain the Chorus responds: " 'Our Death.' " This is but an echo of the passage in one of his poems where the poet cries out that love

> Needs more than the admiring excitement of union,
> More than the abrupt self-confident farewell,
> The heel on the finishing blade of grass,
> The self-confidence of the falling root,
> Needs death, death of the grain, our death,
> Death of the old gang...

Here is the reason for the sudden air-pockets that Auden's poems seem to strike in their bold flight. How shall a man, in himself or as representative of his class, consent to death?

243

Here is the explanation of the severed wires, the ignorance of the general's wishes in the lines quoted above. How in this crisis shall the general—the will—be understood? How, knowing the need for the extinction of the old gang, and naturally reluctant to go down, shall a keenly conscious member of it avoid satirizing not merely society, but the enemy within?

If one is to understand Auden's poetry one must recognize that he is attacking the Old Gang, the declining class, and therewith attacking everything in himself which clings to that sick part of society. The attack—since he is a gay as well as an angry young man—takes the form of buffoonery. And the obscurity of his verse comes from sources over and above the expressive novelty of his technique, the abrupt syntax, the urban and mechanical imagery, the puns. It is due in part to the fact that he turns without warning from mocking the social order he would defeat to mock himself and mock his friends who, because of their breeding and background, are interfering with that defeat.

There are passages in Auden's work that the blind could read, as when he considers the older generation:

These ordered light
But had no right,
And handed on
War and a son

Wishing no harm.
But to be warm
These went to sleep
On the burning heap.

Or again, when he addresses his contemporaries or those elders in whom the blood still runs:

Shut up talking, charming in the best suits to be had in town,
Lecturing on navigation while the ship is going down.

Drop those priggish ways for ever, stop behaving like a stone:
Throw the bath-chairs right away, and learn to leave ourselves
    alone.

POETRY AND POLITICS

If we really want to live, we'd better start at once to try;
If we don't, it doesn't matter, but we'd better start to die.

This poem is richer for one who hears under it the ironic echo:

For I dipt into the future, far as human eye could see,
Saw the Vision of the world, and all the wonder that would be;

Saw the heavens fill with commerce, argosies of magic sails,
Pilots of the purple twilight, dropping down with costly bales;

Heard the heavens fill with shouting, and there rain'd a ghastly dew
From the nations' airy navies grappling in the central blue;

Far along the world-wide whisper of the south-wind rushing warm,
With the standards of the peoples plunging through the thunder-storm;

Till the war-drum throbb'd no longer, and the battle-flags were furl'd
In the Parliament of man, the Federation of the world.

Similarly, when, in the *Journal of an Airman*, Auden writes:

His collar was spotless; he talked very well,
He spoke of our homes and duty and we fell,

those who remember the verses in which the poets of antiquity praised the patriots who died for their country will savor the satire more keenly. Which brings up another point in regard to Auden's obscurity in particular and the obscurity of contemporary poetry in general.

It is an ironic commentary on popular education that one of its results has been to make it impossible for the poet to communicate except to a narrowly limited circle. Where every one has a minimum of information, every one pretends to be educated, but only the fewest attain more than a shallow learning. The necessity for specialization, with the advance of

245

science and technology, is also somewhat to blame for this situation. The result is that the poet, knowing more of the past than his fellows, more sensitive than they to the present to which that past is tributary, and speaking out of that richer awareness, can be intelligible to the merest handful of people. Moreover, even within this civilized circle, there are bound to be smaller circles: what is comprehensible to people, however cultivated, living in a given quarter of London, will not be equally comprehensible to people, however alert, who live in a very different quarter of New York, or Charleston, or Chicago, and vice versa. When Auden speaks of air-dromes, of music-halls, of the unemployed, one can translate the British scene into American terms. But when he assumes—as he generally does—familiarity with the life that goes on in English country-houses, familiarity with the College Quad and the Cathedral Close, even the traveled American, instructed by generations of British novelists, supplemented by Henry James, T. S. Eliot, and the creator of Jeeves, will have but superficial or second-hand knowledge of the substance of that life, the object of Auden's attack. Add to this that the poet, appreciating the multiple barriers to communication, decides to abandon all pretense of talking to outsiders, however intelligent, and addresses the small group of his intimates. The difficulty would seem to be insurmountable.

It is not. Hopkins, whom these young men have good reason to imitate, made, in a letter to Bridges, an observation which they might underscore. Speaking of the obscurity his friend found in his own verse, he wrote: "Granted that it needs study and is obscure, ... you might, without the effort that to make it all out would seem to have required, have nevertheless read it so that lines and stanzas should be left in the memory and superficial impressions deepened, and have liked some without exhausting all." Elsewhere he said that a poem should have one of two kinds of clearness: "either the meaning to be felt without effort as fast as one reads or else, if dark at first reading, when once made out, *to explode*." Auden is, in more senses than one, explosive. The best of his verse, like that of many of the predecessors against whom he is taking arms, offers superficial impressions which are deepened with re-reading. Because he depends less on connotative effects than do those poets who went to school to the symbolists, these impressions are themselves somewhat foreign. But surrender to the alien element, not unlike that of the child who flings himself into the sea without water-wings, offers the most rapid and exhilarating mode of learning. Thus Charles Madge instructs his audience:

> This poem will be you if you will. So let it.
> I do not want you to stand still to get it.
> You will have it if you go high-speed; it slides in
> Between velocities; you will not need to begin
> But to have begun and to be going; to have started. . .

Another possible analogy is that of children learning to read and write. They can understand words and phrases that they do not themselves employ, use in conversation words that they cannot read, and grasp the meaning of words on the printed page that they are unable to write. Similarly, the amateur of contemporary verse may understand in a poem more meanings than he can formulate or restate, even with some necessary loss, in his own words, and he must exercise some ingenuity to enjoy what he sees.

The key to Auden's position may be found in a sentence from the opening section of *The Orators:* "What do you think of England, this country of ours where nobody is well?" and in his thirtieth poem, in which he prays for power (not sweetness) and light. In this poem he addresses God as one who forgives all but "will his negative inversion"; forgives all, that is, save the will toward death. Among Auden's spiritual forebears not the least important is the one most ignored—Samuel Butler. Like that mid-Victorian modern, he would put the sick in jail and the criminal in hospital: though for Auden it is not the individual, but a social class that is diseased. Like Butler, he

247

would throw off the dead hand of the past, but keep faith with his real ancestors, those whose strength and sanity he can still praise and seek to emulate. Like Butler, the young poet recognizes the force of the unconscious, the seat of racial memory, the keeper of the secrets of desire and fear. Above all, he is with the historian of *Erewhon* in his faith that man is an unfinished creature who has learned how to give himself a swifter foot, a louder voice, and a longer hand by virtue of the machine, but who seems to be the victim of his own ingenuity, and who must become cleverer than fish or bird if, with all his accomplishments, he is not to go the way of the giant saurian. *The Orators*, a refreshing if difficult medley of prose and verse, attacking his perennial enemies, offers in its Epilogue a succinct example of his technique and his temper:

'O where are you going?' said reader to rider,
'That valley is fatal when furnaces burn,
Yonder's the midden whose odours will madden,
That gap is the grave where the tall return.'

'O do you imagine,' said fearer to farer,
'That dusk will delay on your path to the pass,
Your diligent looking discover the lacking
Your footsteps feel from granite to grass?'

'O what was that bird,' said horror to hearer,
'Did you see that shape in the twisted trees?
Behind you swiftly the figure comes softly,
The spot on your skin is a shocking disease?'

'Out of this house'—said rider to reader
'Yours never will'—said farer to fearer
'They're looking for you'—said hearer to horror
As he left them there, as he left them there.

His comrade, Stephen Spender, is more comprehensible because closer to the older poetry. Where Auden is primarily the satirist, Spender is the romantic. He differs from most romantic poets, however, in that the locus of his vision of felicity is not a remote past but what seems to him, as it seemed to Shelley, a compassable future. His revulsion from his own comfortable background is akin to Shelley's. He, too, has remarked, after more than a century, that "Hell is a city much like London." He, too, is torn with pity for the insulted and injured who are its denizens:

—There is no consolation, no, none
In the curving beauty of that line
Traced on our graphs through history, where the oppressor
Starves and deprives the poor.

He, too, is stung with rage at the exploiters, militantly against organized religion: "the church blocking the sun," quickened by a dream of earthly justice:

Oh comrades, step beautifully from the solid wall
advance to rebuild and sleep with friend on hill
advance to rebel and remember what you have
no ghost ever had, immured in his hall.

His imagination, like Shelley's, takes fire from the spark of personal love. But he has a concreteness which his great predecessor exhibited almost nowhere outside of the *Epistle to Maria Gisborne*. Further, Spender is able to incorporate into his poetry the materials of our industrialized and electrified civilization, so that his glittering dreams come closer to contemporary experience than that romantic Platonist's ever could. He has keen pleasure in the beauty of machinery: the singing speed and brightness of the express-train, the prophetic splendor of pylons, the moth-soft motion of the air-liner gliding with shut-off engines through the dusk. But he goes beyond this. He concludes a personal lyric, innocent of any political implication, with the thought that, if certain responses to his beloved were "tricklings through a dam," he must have sufficient love to run a factory, to drive a tram, or to give a city power. This is the usage of Donne, with his maps and compasses, rather than that of Shelley, with his violets and night-ingales.

But if Spender's poetry reflects the industrialized age in which it is being written, he is less fearful than his fellows of images taken from nature. He may stand on street corners, watching the unemployed with unquenchable bitterness, he may walk through streets where "road-drills explore new areas of pain," or, in solitude, ask what, living under so heavy a shadow, he can do that matters. But the grief and the fatigue and the despair bred by a war remembered and a war fore-seen, by the boom and the slump and the insanity of those in power, yield to another mood. In his will to change, he bids his comrades:

> Drink from here energy and only energy,
> As from the electric charge of a battery...

When an older and a sadder poet might do no more than look to the hills whence help cometh, he can refresh his spirit by climbing a mountain. The sun pours through his pages, the actual sun, as well as the symbol which again recalls Shelley:

> Radiant Sister of the Day,
> Awake! arise! and come away!...
> Where...
>   all things seem only one
> In the universal sun.

It recalls, too, the voice of prophesying:

> "...Prometheus shall arise
> Henceforth the sun of this rejoicing world:
> When shall the destined hour arrive?"

This assurance that the rebel Titan will triumph over the tyrant in power, an assurance strengthened by sympathy with that revolutionary mystic of the eighteenth century, William Blake, flows through Spender's poems, and points the differ-ence between him and his companion.

250

Auden has little to say of the soul of man under communism. He is engaged chiefly in painting sardonic pictures of the progress of the rake, capitalism. If he looks ahead, it is only a little way, to the anomalous position of his own class while the social order undergoes a more serious breakdown. The elements of modern life which recur most frequently in his verse are foundries, airdromes, and tottering country houses. He peoples it with spies, aviators, machine-gunners, and a sprinkling of "nice people," the most insidious of the Enemy's cohorts. And his ebullient style, with its sudden jazzed effects, its retreat into nursery rhyme, its sallies into wicked parody of Eliot from whom it has taken not a little, has the curtness proper to satire. Both Auden and Spender are skillful in the use of assonance and alliteration, but the slow, grave movement of Spender's verse contrasts strongly with Auden's quick witty line, his ribald assault. If Spender's poetry expresses a less vivid personality, it seems to tap deeper levels of feeling, so that where Auden is rousing and provocative, his friend stirs a stronger emotion.

Certain poets tend to be hunted, if not to hunt, in couples. One groups naturally Dryden and Pope, Wordsworth and Coleridge, Keats and Shelley; in our own day, Pound and Eliot—more recently, Spender and Auden. With the two last-named is associated a third: Cecil Day Lewis. Indeed, Lewis is so close to Spender in his attitude and so like Auden in his technique as to be sometimes indistinguishable from them. Tutored by Hopkins and Owen, he shares Spender's hope for a "sun returned to power," but above a changed world, and in the final chorus of *The Magnetic Mountain* he sings out: "O sun be soon!" Accepting Auden's vocabulary, he takes the kestrel for the aviator who flies forward undazzled into the sunlit future which will not copy the past; speaks of his generation's inheritance from the old order as marshland to be reclaimed; uses for the forward movement of society the imagery of the railway: the terminus, the express, possible derailment; dramatizes the conflict between the revolutionaries

251

and the conservatives, reactionaries, liberals, as a war between the healthy and the sick. He, too, finds pleasure in the old ballad metres, and recalls Eliot's echoes by wittily parodying an old Christmas carol or a song from *As You Like It*.

But along with the Shelleyan dream and the post-post-War lustiness, is another element. Lewis is more of a metaphysician than his friends, and his references to such American writers as Herman Melville, Walt Whitman, and Emily Dickinson, no less than his epigraphs from Hopkins and Blake, and primarily, of course, his poetry itself, show him to be more jealous than his companions of his individual identity, and more willing to dwell upon traditional themes. His *Transitional Poem*, the title of which suggests the passage from one social order or one allegiance to another, is actually concerned with the theme of the single mind, is suffused with ideas taken from Spinoza, and is technically reminiscent both of Emily Dickinson and of Yeats. Some of his happiest achievements are the purely personal lyrics in *Feathers to Iron*, written during the anxious, hopeful months of attendance on the arrival of his first-born. Here, too, he employs the mechanic imagery of his time, but makes it serve for the sensitive recording of his own feelings in a situation which, while common to multitudes, in this instance touches him more nearly than it can touch any other man.

> But think of passion and pain.
> Those absolute dictators will enchain
> The low, exile the princely parts:
> They close a door between the closest hearts:
> Their verdict stands in steel,
> From whose blank rigour kings may not appeal.

> When in love's airs we'd lie,
> Like elms we leaned together with a sigh
> And sighing severed, and no rest
> Had till that wind was past:
> Then drooped in a green sickness over the plain
> Wanting our wind again.

252

Now pain will come for you,
Take you into a desert without dew,
Labouring through the unshadowed day
To blast sharp scarps, open up a way
There for the future line.
But I shall wait at the railhead alone...

These poems explore a region which the poetry of the past has ignored or merely glanced at, and although not without some flaws, are full of beautiful insights and clean vigor.

There are passages here in which the contemporary imagery is not only without social significance but so obtrusive as to seem false:

Today crowds quicken in a street,
The fish leaps in the flood:
Look there, gasometer rises,
And here bough swells to bud.

On the other hand, in *The Magnetic Mountain* Lewis has produced a poem of nearly fifty pages in which the imagery, partly magical but chiefly deriving from modern technics, is a dynamic expression of the poet's faith in social revolution.

Let us be off! Our steam
Is deafening the dome.
The needle in the gauge
Points to a long-banked rage,
And trembles there to show
What a pressure's below.
Valve cannot vent the strain
Nor iron ribs refrain
That furnace in the heart.

In its more successful parts—for Lewis is an uneven writer—this poem has what he would himself call both "natural" and "adventitious energy." He distinguishes, without precisely defining, these two kinds of energy in the course of his penetrating essay, *A Hope For Poetry*, in which he examines the elements which go to the making of the poetry of his own genera-

253

tion. "Natural energy" might perhaps be described as power native to the poet, which exhibits itself in the felicity of his performance. "Adventitious energy" is rather power derived from the significant use of imagery taken from contemporary life. Lewis points out that such imagery may be used ineffectively by a would-be fashionable versifier, or, if handled objectively by a competent poet, may be innocent of social implications; but where an accomplished technician employs it so as to realize more fully the structure and functioning of the social organism, his poem draws on two sources of power: the intrinsic and the external. In such instances, he observes, "very often a moral judgment results."

If one contrasts the work of Lewis, Auden, Spender, and the revolutionary Scots poet, Hugh MacDiarmid, with Eliot's quiet animadversions against Sweeney or Yeats's mad songs against the mob, the difference in attitude becomes plain at once. Neither *taedium vitae* nor savage indignation is often present here. Instead, plain statement of opposition, or ribald laughter—a frequent weapon against the "Enemy": the good bourgeois, the good European, the good paterfamilias, the decent clergyman, the gentle dreamer of opium-dreams, along with the pander of the press and the swollen exploiter.

A typical example of the post-War poets' reaction to their situation is offered in Eliot's *Sweeney Agonistes*. These "fragments of an Aristophanic melodrama" present a heart-sickening picture of a civilization dead from the waist up. The characters go through the familiar Eliotesque motions: telling fortunes with cards, singing music-hall ditties in the same mechanical fashion in which they make love, do business, and swap lurid stories. The melodrama is punctuated by a

KNOCK KNOCK KNOCK
KNOCK
KNOCK
KNOCK

254

which sounds in this context like a sordid parody of Beethoven's
Fifth Symphony, and there is a variation on the main theme
of *The Waste Land* in the duet about the cannibal isle, where,
Sweeney tells Doris:

> There's no telephones
> There's no gramophones
> There's no motor cars
> No two-seaters, no six-seaters,
> No Citroën, no Rolls-Royce,
> Nothing to eat but the fruit as it grows.
> Nothing to see but the palm-trees one way
> And the sea the other way,
> Nothing to hear but the sound of the surf.
> Nothing at all but three things

Doris: What things?
Sweeney: Birth, and copulation, and death.
> That's all, that's all, that's all, that's all,
> Birth, and copulation, and death.
Doris: I'd be bored.
Sweeney: You'd be bored.
> Birth, and copulation, and death.

In Part Three of *The Magnetic Mountain*, which bears as
epigraph Lawrence's admonition: "Never yield before the barren," Lewis introduces as the First Enemy the barren lover
of love-making. Each stanza concludes with a trite phrase from
stale romances, beginning with "I do like doing things with
you" and concluding: "I suppose you hate me, now." But
although this sounds dimly like Eliot, its effect is entirely
altered by the passages which precede and follow it, in which
the poet advises his fellows that they need "a change of air,"
and in strict didactic strophes bids his lovers remember that the
time for play is past.

It is plain that something over and above the generally
acknowledged elements of poetry is involved here. The problem of belief thrusts up its belligerent head. These poets are
fellow-travelers of the communists; they note the signs of decay

in the established order and anticipate its fall; they hail the new day. Lewis asks:

> You that love England, who have an ear for her music, ...
> Listen. Can you not hear the entrance of a new theme?

Auden asserts:

> This is the season of the change of heart,
> The final keeping of the ever-broken vow.

Obviously their expectation that after necessary conflict and its attendant agony—no worse than the miseries of the present confusion—a new and glorious society will arise upon the rubble of the old, gives vitality to their poetry.

The question which presents itself is whether any sufficiently inclusive, deep-rooted attitude toward the world, be it of acquiescence or rejection, is not equally invalidating? Might not a Catholic find in the poetry of Gerard Manley Hopkins, S.J., an "adventitious energy" deriving from the poet's adherence to the Holy Catholic and Apostolic Church, and from the larger implications of that devotion? And is not the very fact of Hopkins's religious certainty, crossed though it was, as the "terrible sonnets" show, by anguishing doubts, but informing his work with a centrifugal power, one secret of his influence over these young defenders of the communist faith?

The communist will answer that no attitude is based on as complete and profound an insight as his own. What he shares with Hopkins is his love of the world, his love of man, every man being, like himself,

> ... What Christ is, since he was what I am, and
> This Jack, joke, poor potsherd, patch, matchwood, immortal
> diamond,
> Is immortal diamond.

Did not the Jesuit priest admit that he knew in his heart Walt Whitman's mind to be more like his own "than any other man's living"? Did he not, indeed, confess, in a letter only recently published: "Horrible to say, I am in a manner a Communist. Their ideal barring some things is nobler than that professed by any secular statesman I know of... Besides it is just." Guessing this sympathy, the revolutionary poet accepts Hopkins's technique for expressing it, not his dogma or his doubts. The communist, too, has his dogmas—and no doubts —but it should be remembered that his major premise has been granted by poets as remote from one another in time and circumstance as Blake and Whitman and Hopkins and Shelley and Spender. That premise is the perfectibility of man.

The religious would say that man is vile and only God is good. The revolutionary—speaking with the mouth of the Chorus in Auden's charade, *Paid On Both Sides*—declares:

> O watcher in the dark, you wake
> Our dream of waking...
> By your bright day
> See clear what we were doing, that we were vile.

The vileness is plain to both, but for the latter God is not so far away. The ancestor-worship in which these poets indulge is their tribute to those great men who anticipated their vision, as their demand for a new order is a tribute to the greatness they hope for from their successors. They would say with Blake:

> Thou art a Man, God is no more,
> Thy own humanity learn to adore.

These young poets do not take the high road of reason traveled by the heirs of the Enlightenment, nor share the dream of progress indulged in by the nineteenth-century optimists. They have been taught to distrust reason and to analyze dreams. But if they are not so naïve as their great-grandfathers, neither are they so desperate as their elder brothers, the returned veterans. In exchange for a sardonic irony, indicative of hopeless fatigue, they offer the challenge of satire, the summons to action. And therewith they pose the question as to how far the poet may be a propagandist.

One cannot ask this question without recalling the words of Yeats:

> The rhetorician would deceive his neighbours,
> The sentimentalist himself; while art
> Is but a vision of reality.

If the social struggle enters into that vision, it will enlarge the poetry, but there must be no deception about the matter. Whatever social values a poem may have, its roots are in the personal response to a given object, an event, an idea, or some complex of these. It is a reënacting of a fragment of experience, and so it partakes of the nature of dream, or, where the experience approaches totality, of the nature of vision. As the dream repeats and renews the past in symbols, and through symbols enters the future, the poem repeats and renews the past in images, and by images thrusts forward. The difficulty with much propagandist verse is that it has the drive of prose rather than the tension of its sister art. Its imagery is weak. It does not suggest. It does not state. It commands. Granted that poetry, even when it is satiric, can be an incitement to action. It may discover to the poet, and equally to his reader, the significance of a political, an economic, or more probably, a religious issue, and may even make him feel the necessity for fighting on one side of the barricades or the other. But the discovery will come, not as the end of a logical series, rather as a conviction suddenly made manifest. Even though it should mature in the womb of reason, it was begotten by emotion.

The things of the poet are done to a man alone
As the things of love are done—or of death when he hears the
Step withdraw on the stair and the clock tick only...

258

When the revolutionary struggle works on a man like the things of love or of death, when it affects him as an enjoying and suffering being, when it makes him feel the world in a new way, he will inevitably, if he is a good craftsman, write revolutionary poetry of a high order. But until it works on him in this way, he can do nothing with it.

It is, however, the exceptional poet who in a society that is out of joint fails to hear the bones crying to be set right. And if, hearing, he offers them a living language, he need not fear the judgment of posterity. Even in a more satisfactory world than this, great poetry dealing with the social conflict would have the validity that the *Divine Comedy* retains for those who reject Dante's theology, that *De Rerum Natura* retains for those who reject Lucretius's physics. A poem is larger than its logical superstructure, as a man is more than his conscious mental processes.

For this very reason the poet cannot afford to submit himself unquestioningly to the rule of a group, and continue to practice his art. His work is of value not merely because his pulse is timed to the march of the generations and his eye fixed on a radiant future, but because his pulse is more sensitive, his eye keener than the rest. His sympathy with his fellows makes communication possible and necessary, but it is not his likeness to them, it is precisely his difference from them that gives his work significance. If all poets wrote equally well, or if all poets wrote alike, poetry would die. The artist who sacrifices his identity to his church or his class or his nation is lost as an artist, though church or class or nation may be the main root of his art. When Milton took up the sword he wisely, and sadly, and temporarily, laid down the pen.

This does not mean that great poetry necessarily involves for reader or writer the willing suspension of disbelief. That poetry which satisfies our intellects as well as our emotions gives us the greatest emotional satisfaction. But poetry cannot satisfy either our hearts or our minds unless it issues from the deepest self. If the passion for revolution is alive *there*,

259

this age will have found its voice. Poets are not, unfortunately, as they have been said to be, the unacknowledged legislators of the world. But they have always been propagandists. They have always spoken, however ambiguously, however indirectly, for values with which economists do not reckon—for justice, for truth, for love. Even M. Brémond, who desires "pure poetry," a kind of immaculate conception of the spirit, unravaged by the intellect, speaks of poetry as akin to prayer, and therefore a claim upon, a longing for, those values. There are indeed certain lyrics, the songs of Shakespeare, for example, which seem to be unstained by thought. There are certain lines:

Brightness falls from the air

or

Ripeness is all,

which appear to carry a weight of emotion beyond their discernible meaning. Poetry is the result of the interplay between the conscious and the subconscious mind, and in this game the subconscious is not the least important. Even in words seemingly innocent of logic lies hidden a thought too deep for prose, and all the more eloquent of profound conviction. The poet who speaks out of the deepest instincts of man will be heard. The poet who creates a myth beyond the power of man to realize is gagged at the peril of the group that binds him. He is the true revolutionary: he builds a new world.

CHAPTER X

POETIC VALUES

What is now proved was once only imagin'd.
Blake.

THE QUARREL recently revived with some heat, between the poet and the citizen who would build an ideal republic, goes back nearly twenty-five centuries. It was in a time beyond the memory of Plato that poetry could lay unquestioned claim to being one of the useful arts. The mnemonic values of strongly marked rhythm and alliteration, the hypnotic effect of these and other devices, made it the fit vehicle for tellers of tales and weavers of spells. For primitive peoples, as for unlettered groups to-day, it was the record of their past, and, where it was bound up with magic ritual, the safeguard of their future.

A once enormous dominion has shrunk to a small, if intensely cultivated region, subject of late years to frequent raids by dramatist and novelist. Prose of sorts—works of science, histories, fiction, newspapers—supplemented by the theatre, the concert-hall, the cinema, and the radio, have replaced the epic, the ballad, and the incantation. The line which divides poetry from prose has never been satisfactorily drawn, and is perhaps more equivocal to-day than it has ever been. The problem is complicated by the fact that rhythm, diction, and subject-matter—elements which might be thought to help us discriminate between the two modes—are now recognized to offer no such clews.

Rhythm is not only evident in verse, but may be distinguished in all good prose, be it a passage from a seventeenth-century sermon or from a twentieth-century novel. And, similarly, modern verse employs the cadences as well as the diction of common speech. To-day the free verse controversy reads like a story of not unhappy but certainly far-off things and battles long ago. But if, even before the victory of the vers librists, such leaders as Pound and Eliot, in revolt against their slavish followers, revived the strictly patterned style of Gautier, their conversational rhythms and language remain elements of contemporary work.

If, then, the modern poet, like M. Jourdain, talks prose, but with the difference that he knows it and does so deliberately, certainly his subject-matter is apt to be prosaic, too. Only the peasant poet can continue to write naïve nature poetry, and, with the exception of that redundant if sincere sonneteer, Jesse Stuart, where is there a peasant poet to-day? The proletarian versifiers are few, and their comrades among the intellectuals, who seem to be growing in numbers and in power, often burden their verse with abstractions like any theologian. Even where they are not trying to set Marx to music, they treat of such prosy matters as the factory, the slum, the bleak details of the wage-slave's existence. Others, lacking the postulates on which the older poets shaped a world recognizable to all literate men, build upon the doctrines of some school of psychology or metaphysics.

The explanatory prefaces and appendices which they feel it necessary to attach to their work indicate that many of them quarry the same mines, pore over the same sources: the Bhagavad Gita, the Old Testament, the *Greek Anthology*, Dante, and Henry James. These are the heritage of any cultivated person, but since the *Greek Anthology* often and the Bhagavad Gita nearly always are used in an English version, only Dante and the Old Testament (now too much a part of the language to be regarded as a translation) may be considered to have significance *qua* poetry for the writer studying them; and here, too, the poet frequently employs a text as a preacher would, careless of its peculiar lyric values. What goes into this modern work, then, along with the accepted stuff of poetry, is a complex of Indian, Hebrew, Greek, and medieval Christian thought—thought tempered by the reflections of a sensitive nineteenth-century observer who was concerned for the differences between the English, American, and continental civilizations, and the revenge these take upon the individual who seeks to ignore their specific character. What goes into the poems of our more anxious contemporaries is nothing less than the modern European mind, colored by its Asiatic past, and changing its shape, immigrant fashion, when it finds itself in an American environment.

How then, one may ask, do the pleasures such poetry affords differ from those of prose? Does a narrative poem like *Conquistador* differ from a lyrical novel by Virginia Woolf? Does Wyndham Lewis's provocative *One-Way Song*, driving against the romantics on the one hand and the communists on the other, differ in brilliance, sound and fury from the prose fireworks which he delights to set off? Does an objective statement by William Carlos Williams about a suburban servant-girl or the New York skyline differ from a good prose paragraph on the same topics? Is modern verse generally distinguished from prose by more marked rhythm, the occasional use of rhyme, finer verbal texture, richer metaphors, greater concision, or by a more profound quality, of which the form is the index?

It is a quality difficult to hunt down, but one that, with some patience, may be scented, and glimpsed in flight, if not captured. It has been said that the opposite of poetry is not prose, but science (which does not mean that science is its enemy), and that insofar as prose has the intention of science, it divorces itself from its sister art. The scientist erects hypotheses which enable man to weigh and measure the physical universe and to abstract laws which will prosper him in his conflicts with his environment, his fellows, and himself. Poetry

263

communicates the emotions of men in these conflicts and in their resolution. It is, however, no less than science, purposive, practical, and precise. The purpose of the scientist is to decrease the evils with which an indifferent and frequently hostile nature has beset our lives, and to develop the goods it offers. The purpose of the poet is to give the quality of living, and so to help man to realize the world, both inner and outer, more fully. Like virtue, it is its own reward, but not always its sole reward for being.

The psychological critic, concerned with the way in which poetry changes men's attitudes, the energetic younger school, reacting against Eliot's wasting weariness, and instituting a revival of satire, have raised a doubt as to whether poetry is indeed a joy forever, or merely a goad to action. The critic on the other side rifles the armory of his opponent to defend the view that poetry arrests activity; that it partakes of the nature of any experience which is an end in itself. On one point, however, the two seem to be in agreement. Poetry, they admit, has value, the first holding that it is a stimulus to the good life, the second that it is an element of the good life. As a matter of fact, it is both. It is that fiery phoenix whose means are as excellent as its end; whose end is a new birth. Only indirectly, only gradually, can a great poem work on a growing audience to create new ways of feeling and thinking and changed modes of behavior. But without effecting any change, it still pleases by its intrinsic felicity. It is like the sun, whose quickening powers are no less active because they may be ignored by the man whose body it warms and whose eye it kindles.

Rarely, however, is the poet in the position of a more fortunate Faust, perpetually crying out to the moment as it passes: *"Verweile doch, du bist so schön!"* The ethical impulse has found vent in the work of poets as different as Langland and Blake, Milton and Byron, Shelley and Vachel Lindsay, Ezra Pound and Hugh MacDiarmid. Satirical verse, be it Pope's or Auden's, has always some moral bias. The impatience of the

264

contemporary with the moralizing verse of the Victorians is not due to any lack of sympathy with virtue; it is because of the Victorians' too narrow view of it, their too-confident belief in their picture of the universe, the foggy notions of reality which blocked their understanding of what they should desire. For reality is the poet's quarry, and never can he come close enough to it.

In speaking of the purpose of poetry, one must, of course, draw a distinction between the attitude of the poet and that of the reader. The concern of the latter is not with the cause of a work of art, but with its effectiveness, with what has been communicated. For the most part the poet is engaged in expression, in ridding himself of some distress by externalizing it, or of the overplus of some joy by pouring it into the mold of verse. Yet there are instances—the war poetry of Sassoon and Owen, the mocking verse of Auden and Lewis—where he has a conscious motive beyond the desire to set down what he has endured: he wants to communicate the anguish and the horror so that other men, knowing what he has known, feel his rage to stop it.

The man who hopes to inspire a distaste for mean and tawdry living, a disgust with war, is not, however, explicit about it: he is the best missionary who moralizes least. When Mrs. Barbauld said to Coleridge that *The Ancient Mariner* had two faults: it was improbable, and it had no moral, he cheerfully admitted the first count, and added, as to the second, that in his judgment the poem had too much. Owen's war poems are neither improbable nor unmoral, but in the fragmentary notes which preface them he said something relevant to this: "Above all," he wrote, "this book is not concerned with Poetry. The subject of it is War, and the pity of War. The poetry is in the pity. All the poet can do today is to warn. That is why the true Poets must be truthful." Do not, said the great fantast, reviving one of the oldest myths, obtrude the moral sentiment upon the reader. Do not, said the ravaged soldier, battling against one of the firmest instincts—do not be

265

poetic: be truthful. Whether the experience that the writer seeks to express is actual or imaginary, whether it is lovely or horrible, its essence must be precisely conveyed, or its meaning will be lost. It will not work upon the reader for his delight or pain, and so will not have served the poem's purpose. That is the significance, so often misunderstood, of Keats's identification of beauty and truth. Here ethics and esthetics appear to spring from a single root.

There are, of course, more sorts of poetry than critics of opposing schools, in the heat of argument, are prepared to admit. That type which is closest to prose, the satirical, is frankly belligerent, aiming to destroy the thing it mocks. But even this kind of poetry, if it is good work, may win the enemy's admiration, as major feats of aviation in war-time were applauded by both sides, and may continue to delight an audience long after the conflict is over. The larger part of poetry, however, is not satirical, nor is it dramatic. Recent attempts at verse drama incline to be *tours de force* verging on farce. They are either unwarrantedly prosy, like Eliot's *Sweeney Agonistes* and Auden's *Paid on Both Sides,* or tend toward incongruous rhetoric, like MacLeish's *Panic.* It is noteworthy, moreover, that even those who see clearly the need for satire as a weapon against the money power refuse to limit themselves to a narrow view of their office. Lewis writes of the single mind; Hugh MacDiarmid on the restless spirit of man: the energy of thought which transforms the world.

We do not quarrel with Cellini because he is not Michael Angelo, and, similarly, we may take pleasure in the well-wrought lyric, however slight. But a major poem has something more than the elegance which lies in the gift alike of the skillful goldsmith and the clever mathematician. It addresses itself to the whole mind. The themes which repeat themselves in poetry: the theme of the sacrificed god, of the underworld journey, of incest, of rebirth, are related to the most ancient recorded myths and seem to draw, like the dream, upon a kind of racial memory and to express fears and desires inherited with our other instincts from a savage past. It is where the details of the legend fail to tally with experience, or where we seek to rationalize it, that its significance becomes questionable. Myth is of the substance of poetry, not because poetry belongs to the childhood of the race, but because those early imaginative formulations continue to have emotional validity for us. Poetry is rooted in emotion, though it is fed upon fact, and shaped by imagination.

Herein lies the kinship between poetry and religion, which has led some critics to transfer the quarrel between religion and science to a quarrel between science and poetry. It would be truer to say that in the major poem these two ancient enemies meet and are at peace. A skillful verse-man is as conscious of measure and design as any mathematician, and may produce work having the pragmatic value of a scientific hypothesis. But like the religious, he will be guided by emotional conviction, and the result of his nicest calculations may afford the satisfactions that prayer gives the devout. Science seeks to improve the conditions of living, and insofar as religion would reconcile man and nature, and reconcile the needs of the individual with those of the group, it is aiming at like ends. But the chief end of religion is to justify life, and to exalt its integrity by a pious concern for its continuity. Poetry, too, justifies life, and like all the arts helps to unite man with his fellows. Unlike religion, however, its appeal, except in the instance of drama, which seems to begin and end in the church, is primarily to the individual rather than to the group. It may cause him to identify himself more fully with the group. But it becomes the property of the group only when it *is* dramatic, or when it has the simple, direct summons of the ballad, or when, as in the nursery rhyme, its musical values are so strong that its other meanings go by the board. With the vulgarization of learning, the intensification of national feeling, and the sharpening of the class struggle, it is doubtful whether any but the crudest verse can have general currency to-day. But poetry, which speaks to the quickest understanding with the authority

267

of the deepest self, is still, as it has always been, the delight of heroic minds.

Contemporary verse is not greater than the verse of the past. In a charming piece on the theme of poets' relative merits, Robert Graves asks if Shakespeare could lessen Chaucer's goodliness, and denies that the poets of old had any need for fighting, though one might see

> Shelley take Shelley down,
> Blake snatch at his own crown.

Each has his own peculiar virtues and special beauties. Each, in developing, becomes the rival of himself. It is more difficult to produce a Shakespeare to-day than it ever was, because the man of genius has a larger and more complex world to comprehend than he ever had. Modern verse, while it may not be better than the old, is better *for us*, because it interprets, in a living language, a living world, and from that vantage point looks into the dark abysm of the uncreated.

Something more significant than fashion is at work in the shift from one kind of verse to another. The contemporary has no wish to cultivate a form which has been explored to its apparent limits. He is in reaction against his predecessors, but he is also eager to capitalize the gains made by previous craftsmen. Above all, he tries to develop a technique appropriate to his own peculiar circumstances. One may read something of the change recent decades have witnessed by glancing briefly at poems by several moderns all dealing with the general theme expressed in Wordsworth's familiar lines to *Lucy:*

> A slumber did my spirit seal;
> I had no human fears:
> She seem'd a thing that could not feel
> The touch of earthly years
>
> No motion has she now, no force;
> She neither hears nor sees;
> Roll'd round in earth's diurnal course,
> With rocks, and stones, and trees.

Housman, a finer melodist than Wordsworth, and more sensitive than the author of the *Lyrical Ballads* to the language of common speech, uses for the same idea an image the homeliness of which is typical of modern realism and adds distinctly to the poetry:

> The night is freezing fast,
>   Tomorrow comes December;
>   And winterfalls of old
> Are with me from the past;
>   And chiefly I remember
>   How Dick would hate the cold.
>
> Fall, winter, fall; for he,
>   Prompt hand and headpiece clever,
>   Has woven a winter robe,
> And made of earth and sea
>   His overcoat forever,
>   And wears the turning globe.

In one of the less characteristic and less effective pieces of *The New Spoon River*, Edgar Lee Masters has the ghost of one of its inhabitants, Howard Lamson, speak of mortality with less of grimness than of resignation:

> ...Tongues that are dumb report no loss;
> Hands stiffened, well may idle be;
> No sigh is from the breathless breast...
> The rolling earth rolls on and on
> With trees and stones and winding streams—
> My dream is what the hill-side dreams!

Housman is more modern in this particular instance than Masters, but both offer a contrast to Archibald MacLeish, who brings to his treatment of the old motif the impersonal despair fostered alike by modern science and the War:

> Hereunder Jacob Schmidt who, man and bones,
> Has been his hundred times around the sun

269

His chronicle is endless—the great curve
Inscribed in nothing by a point upon
The spinning surface of a circling sphere.

Dead bones roll on.

MacLeish wears the Wordsworthian rue with less of a difference, however, than his friend, John Peale Bishop. In a poem
the title of which adumbrates the learned, derisive melancholy of the post-War period: *This Dim and Ptolemaic Man,*
Bishop exhibits the condensed imagery, the combination of
anti-poetic and lyrical vocabulary, of wit and feeling, which
characterized the verse of those years. The person in the poem
is not a dead but a living (and therefore a dying) man, and
the subject is not so much that man's fate as his obliviousness
of it, yet in spite of these differences, the piece nicely illustrates a contemporary handling of the theme:

> For forty years, for forty-one,
> Sparing the profits of the sun,
> This farmer piled his meagre hoard
> To buy at last a rattly Ford.
>
> Now crouched on a scared smile he feels
> Motions spurt beneath his heels,
> Rheumatically intent shifts gears
> Unloosens joints of rustic years.
>
> Morning light obscures the stars,
> He swerves avoiding other cars,
> Wheels with the road, does not discern
> He eastward goes at every turn,
>
> Nor how his aged limbs are hurled
> Through all the motions of the world
> How wild past farms, past ricks, past trees,
> He perishes toward Hercules.

It is a totally different note which is struck by Hugh Mac-
Diarmid in his long metaphysical poem: *To Circumjack*

Poetic Values

Cencrastus, or The Curly Snake. This hymn to energy and intelligence is written in synthetic Scots, which includes Scots words having no English equivalents, as well as Gaelic and foreign phrases, and so may present verbal as well as intellectual difficulties to the average reader. MacDiarmid is not concerned with the average reader, though he is as much at home with the plain man as with his own peers: it is the half-educated pompous dullard with whom he refuses commerce. The eternal evil to him, as he states in the same poem, is not tragedy, but its absence, not the extreme but "the sordid mean," and like some other modern thinkers he sees anti-Christ in the person of the man in the street:

> O the Devil is neathing strange.
> His face is the crood's or oor ain
> When we cease to be oorsel's
> And become 'like abody' again...

MacDiarmid, too, recalls Wordsworth's *Lucy,* but neither to lament, with Housman, the death of one well-loved; nor to resign himself, with Masters, to the fact of mortality, which wipes out pain along with joy and makes the aching human at one with nature; nor to stand aghast, with MacLeish, before the horror of man's nullity; nor yet, with Bishop, to consider the peasant's ignorance of the universe of which he is so negligible a part. On the contrary, MacDiarmid, who is a hot Scottish nationalist and a communist to boot, makes Lucy his point of departure for an exaltation of the Logos, the mind of man which is the germ of the wisdom of God.

> When Wordsworth saw Lucy row'd
> In Earth's diurnal course
> Wi' rocks and stanes and trees
> He saw by science perforce,
> And contrair to human sense;
> We gang mair contrair still
> Wi' ideas we canna express
> Except by a miracle.

271

The trouble is that words
Are a' but useless noo
To span the gulf atween
The human and "highbrow" view
—Victims at ilka point
O' optical illusions,
Brute Nature's limitations,
And inherited confusions.

Silence is the only way,
Speech squares aye less wi' fact.
Silence—like Chaos ere the Word
That gar'd the Play enact
That sune to conscious thocht
Maun seem a foolish dream.
Nae word has yet been said,
Nae Licht's begun to gleam.

For MacDiarmid, and for not a few of his fellows, it is not
the moral law which, as Kant had it, equals the stars in their
glory, but that movement of the mind which expresses itself
in poetry. It is a claim for the art which only the greatest and
most daring practitioners of it have made, and but a small
fraction of the verse considered in these pages rises to that
height. Yet the progress of poetry from the harsh realism of
Masefield, Masters, Sandburg, through the sardonic symbolism of Eliot and the cruel imagism of Pound to the ecstatic
symbolism of Hart Crane and the revolutionary idealism of
Stephen Spender and C. Day Lewis is proof of Synge's affirma-
tion that if verse learned to be brutal, it would become human
again, and the tenderness and exaltation of the highest verse,
which is "not made by feeble blood," might rekindle English
poetry. With a new and deeper significance the contemporary,
seeking no escape, repeats the words of a forgotten poet of
ancient Egypt:

I have seen violence, I have seen violence—
Give thy heart after letters.

POETIC VALUES

In the poem, sound and picture, emotion and idea, work together to satisfy a hunger which sets man apart from the other beasts. The emotion is as old as his physical inheritance, but the music and the images and the ideas have altered with his changed circumstances, and poetry which takes account of these changes will speak most eloquently to the contemporary mind. Philosophers have applied various terms to humanity in an attempt to distinguish it from the rest of creation, but if man is a talking animal, so is the parrot, and if he is a political animal, so, in a truer sense, is the ant. Man is an imaginative animal. That is what gives meaning to his speech and may yet give meaning to his politics. That is why lovers are so often makers of verses. The physical delight of the lover finds its ideal counterpart in the imagination of the poet. The impulse toward union, be it of minds or bodies, from which, as the ancient legend runs, shall spring the seed of Helen and Achilles, perfect beauty joined with perfect power, is the hope of the race while life on earth persists. In this time, as in any other, the imagination of the major poet enacts that union, without ceasing to love reality.

BIBLIOGRAPHY

I: ANTHOLOGIES AND REVIEWS

Since even a selected bibliography of the works of the poets considered would prove too long for inclusion here, some anthologies containing modern poetry are listed below, together with a few periodicals that specialize in verse.

Active Anthology, ed. by Ezra Pound. 1933.

The American Caravan, a year-book of American literature. 1927-1931, 4 v.

Dynamo, a journal of revolutionary poetry. New York, 1924 to date.

The European Caravan, an anthology of the new spirit in European literature, ed. by Samuel Putnam. 1931.

Fifty Poets, an American auto-anthology, ed. by William Rose Benét. 1933.

Fugitives, an anthology of verse. 1928.

Georgian Poetry, ed. by Harold Monro. 1914—1922, 5 v.

Imagist Anthology: 1930; new poetry by imagists. 1930.

Des Imagistes. London, 1914.

Modern American Poetry, ed. by Louis Untermeyer.

Modern British Poetry, ed. by Louis Untermeyer.

New Country. Prose and Poetry by the authors of New Signatures, ed. by Michael Roberts. 1933.

The New Poetry, an anthology of twentieth century verse in English, ed. by Harriet Monroe and Alice C. Henderson, new ed. 1932.

New Signatures, poems by several hands, collected by Michael Roberts. 1932.

New Verse. London, 1933 to date.

Others for 1919, an anthology of new verse, ed. by Alfred Kreymborg, 1920.

Poetry: A Magazine of Verse, ed. by Harriet Monroe. Chicago, 1912 to date.

Profile, an anthology collected in MCMXXXI by Ezra Pound. Milan.

Some Imagist Poets, 1915; 1916; 1917; 3 v.

transition, ed. by Eugene Jolas. Paris, 1927 to date.

Twentieth Century Poetry, an anthology ed. by Harold Monro. 1930.

We Gather Strength, by Herman Spector, Joseph Kalar, Edwin Rolfe. 1933.

II: WORKS, MAINLY CRITICAL

Some volumes of poetry are listed for the sake of the critical or biographical matter included therein. Roman numerals in parentheses following a title refer to the chapters upon which the item has a special bearing.

Allen, Hervey. *Israfel, the Life and Times of Edgar Allen Poe*, 2 v. 1926. (I, V.)

Are Artists People? Some answers to the *New Masses* questionnaire, in *New Masses*, New York, Jan. 1927. (IX.)

Bazalgette, Léon. *Walt Whitman, the man and his work*. 1920. (I, II, V.)

Bianchi, Martha Dickinson. *The Life and Letters of Emily Dickinson*. 1924. (I, V, VI, X.)

Bodkin, Maud. *Archetypal Patterns in Poetry*. 1934. (VII, X.)

Brémond, Henri. *La Poésie Pure*. 1926. (IX, X.)

Bridges, Robert. *Humdrum and Harum-Scarum*, a lecture on free verse; Collected Essays, Papers, etc., II. 1928. (III.)

Brion, Marcel. "The Idea of Time in the Work of James Joyce," in *transition*, March 1928. (V.)

Brooke, Rupert. *Collected Poems*, with a Memoir by E. H. Marsh. London, 1918. (IV.)

Burke, Kenneth. *Counter-Statement*. 1931. (X.)

Calverton, V. F. *The Liberation of American Literature*. 1932. (I, II, IV.)

Carré, Jean-Marie. *A Season in Hell*, the life of Arthur Rimbaud. 1931. (V, VIII, X.)

BIBLIOGRAPHY

Coleridge, S. T. *Select Poetry and Prose*, ed. by Stephen Potter. 1933. (II, III, IV, V, VII, IX, X.)

Crane, Hart. Two Letters on The Bridge, in *Hound and Horn*, New York, July-Sept. 1934. (V.)

Cummings, E. E. *Is 5*. 1926. (VIII.)

De Gourmont, Rémy. *Book of Masks*. 1921. (III, V, VI.)

————, Decadence and other essays on the culture of ideas. 1921. (III.)

Dickinson, Emily. Letters, ed. by Mabel Loomis Tod. 1931. (I, VI, X.)

Eastman, Max. *The Literary Mind*. 1933. (V, VI, VIII.)

Eliot, T. S. Critical Introduction to *Collected Poems of Harold Monro*, ed. by Alida Monro, with a biographical sketch by F. S. Flint. 1933 (IV.)

————, Introduction to *Selected Poems by Ezra Pound*, 1928. (III, VI, VIII.)

————, Introduction to *Selected Poems of Marianne Moore*. 1935. (III, VI.)

————, *Selected Essays*, 1917-1932. 1932. (VI, VIII, IX, X.)

————, *The Use of Poetry and the Use of Criticism*. 1933. (II, III, IV, VI, IX, X.)

Empson, William. *Seven Types of Ambiguity*. 1930. (V, VI, VIII, IX.)

Ezra Pound, His Metric and His Poetry. New York, Knopf, 1917. (III.)

Fenollosa, Ernest and Ezra Pound. *Noh, a Study of the Classical Stage of Japan*. 1917. (III, V.)

Frank, Waldo. Introduction to *Collected Poems of Hart Crane*. 1933. (I, V, VIII.)

Gregory, Horace. *Pilgrim of the Apocalypse, a critical study of D. H. Lawrence*. 1933. (V, VII, VIII.)

Grierson, H. J. C. *Metaphysical Lyrics and Poems of the Seventeenth Century*. (VI, VII, VIII.)

Hardy, Thomas. *Collected Poems*. 1925. (I, II, IV.)

Hopkins, Gerard Manley, *Correspondence* of, and Richard Watson Dixon, ed. by Claude Colleer Abbott. 1935. (I, VI, VII, X.)

————, *Letters to Robert Bridges*, ed. by Claude Colleer Abbott. 1935. (I, VI, VII, IX, X.)

————, *Poems*, ed. with notes by Robert Bridges; second ed. with an Appendix of Additional Poems and a Critical Introd. by Charles Williams. 1930. (I, VI, X.)

Housman, A. E. *The Name and Nature of Poetry*. 1933. (IV.)

277

Hughes, Glenn. *Imagism and the Imagists*. 1931. (III, V.)

Hulme, T. E. *Speculations,*... ed. by Herbert Read. 1924. (III.)

I'll Take My Stand, the South and the Agrarian Tradition, by Twelve Southerners. 1930. (VI, VIII, IX.)

The Jade Mountain, a Chinese anthology, being 300 poems of the T'ang Dynasty, 619-906, tr. by Witter Bynner from the texts of Kang-hu. 1929. (III.)

Jespersen, Otto. *Language, its nature and development*. 1922. (V, VIII, X.)

Johnson, Samuel. "Life of Cowley," in *Lives of the Poets*. (VI.)

Jolas, Eugene. "The revolution of language and James Joyce," in *transition*, Paris, Feb. 1928. (V.)

Joyce, James. *Tales Told of Shem and Shaun*, three fragments from *Work in Progress*, with a preface by C. K. Ogden. 1929. (V.)

Keats, John. *Letters*. 2 v. (VII, X.)

Lahey, G. E. *Gerard Manley Hopkins*. 1928. (I, VI, IX.)

Landor, Water Savage. *Imaginary Conversations*, XXVIII: Milton and Marvell. (III, VI.)

Lawrence, D. H. *Letters*, ed. with an introd. by Aldous Huxley. 1932. (II, V, VI, VII.)

Leavis, F. R. *New Bearings in English Poetry*. 1932. (IV, V, VI.)

Lewis, C. Day. *A Hope For Poetry, Collected Poems*. 1935. (I, VI, VII, VIII, IX, X.)

Lewis, D. Bevan Wyndham. *François Villon*. 1928. (II, III.)

Lewis, Wyndham. *Time and Western Man*. 1927. (III, V.)

Lindsay, Nicholas Vachel. *Adventures While Preaching the Gospel of Beauty*. 1914. (II, IV.)

———, *Rhymes To Be Traded For Bread*. 1912. (II.)

Lowell, Amy. *Six French Poets*. 1915. (III, V.)

Lowes, John Livingston. *Convention and Revolt in Poetry*. 1919. (III, V.)

———, *The Road to Xanadu, a study in the way of the imagination*. 1927. (V.)

MacDiarmid, Hugh (pseud.). *At The Sign of the Thistle*. 1934. (V, VIII, IX.)

———, *To Circumjack Cencrastus or The Curly Snake*. Edinburgh. 1930. (IX, X.)

Masefield, John. Introduction to *Collected Poems*. 1928. (II, IV.)

BIBLIOGRAPHY

Masters, Edgar Lee. The Genesis of Spoon River Anthology, in *The American Mercury*, New York, Jan. 1933. (II.)

Moore, George. Introduction to *An Anthology of Pure Poetry*, 1925. (IX.)

Mumford, Lewis. *The Golden Day*. 1926. (I, IV.)

Owen, Wilfred. *Poems*, a new ed., including many pieces now first published and notices of his life and work by Edmund Blunden. 1931. (IV, IX.)

Parrington, Vernon Louis. *Main Currents in American Thought*. 1927-1930, 3 v. (I, II, IV.)

Pater, Walter. *Wordsworth*. (II.)

Phare, E. E. *Gerard Manley Hopkins*. 1933. (VI.)

Poe, Edgar Allen. Introd. to *Poems*. 1831. (I, V.)

———, *The Poetic Principle*. (I, V.)

Pound, Ezra. *ABC of Reading*. 1934. (III.)

———, *Instigations*. 1920. (II, III, V, VI, IX.)

———, *Make It New*. 1935. (III, V, VI, VIII.)

———, *Pavannes and Divisions*. 1918. (III, IX.)

Powell, Lawrence Clark. *An Introduction to Robinson Jeffers*, with a portrait and a map. Dijon, 1932. (VII.)

Read, Herbert. *Form in Modern Poetry*. 1933. (IX, X.)

Richards, I. A. *On Imagination*. 1935. (II, V, X.)

———, *Principles of Literary Criticism*. 1924. (III, V, X.)

———, *Science and Poetry*. 1926. (V, VI, VII, VIII, X.)

Riding, Laura, and Robert Graves. *A Survey of Modernist Poetry*. 1927. (V, VI, VIII.)

Rylands, George H. W. *Words and Poetry*. 1928. (I, IV, V.)

Sandburg, Carl. *The American Songbag*. 1927. (II.)

Santayana, George. *Reason in Art*. 1913 (X.)

———, *Three Philosophical Poets*. 1910. (I, VII, X.)

Schneider, Isidor. *Comrade: Mister*. 1934. (IX.)

Shelley, Percy B., Preface to *Prometheus Unbound*. (IX.)

Sitwell, Edith. *Alexander Pope*. 1930. (I, III, V.)

———, *Poetry and Criticism*. 1926. (V.)

Skinner, B. F. "Has Gertrude Stein a Secret?" in *Atlantic Monthly*, Boston, Jan. 1934. (V.)

Spencer, Theodore, ed. *A Garland for John Donne*. 1931. (VI, VIII.)

Stevens, Wallace. Preface to *Collected Poems of William Carlos Williams*, 1921-1931. 1934. (III.)

Stillman, Clara G. *Samuel Butler: A Mid-Victorian Modern.* 1932. (IX.)

Stuart, Gilbert. A Footnote to "Work in Progress," in *Contempo*, Feb. 15, 1934. (V.)

Symons, Arthur. The Symbolist Movement in Literature. 1919. (V.)

Synge, John M. Preface to *The Playboy of the Western World.* 1911. (II.)

————, Preface to *Poems and Translations.* 1911. (II.)

Taggard, Genevieve. *The Life and Mind of Emily Dickinson.* 1930. (I, IV, VI.)

Tate, Allen. Introd. to *White Buildings* by Hart Crane. 1926. (V, VIII.)

Taupin, René. *L'Influence du symbolisme français sur la poésie américaine.* 1929. (III, V, VIII.)

Toklas, Alice B. *The Biography of Gertrude Stein.* 1933 (V.)

transition, Paris, March 1932: James Joyce issue. (V, VIII.)

Trotzky, Leon. *Literature and Revolution.* 1925. (IX.)

Waley, Arthur, tr. *A Hundred and Seventy Chinese Poems.* 1918. (III.)

————, *More Translations from the Chinese.* 1919. (III.)

————, *Japanese Poetry.* 1919. (III.)

Weston, Jessie L. *From Ritual to Romance.* 1920. (V.)

Whitehead, A. N. *Science and the Modern World.* 1925. (I, X.)

Williams, Charles. *The English Poetic Mind.* 1932. (IX.)

Williamson, H. R. *The Poetry of T. S. Eliot.* 1932. (V, VI, VIII.)

Wilson, Edmund. "Art, the Proletariat and Marx," in *The New Republic*, New York, Aug. 23, 1933. (IX.)

————, *Axel's Castle.* 1932. (I, V, VIII.)

Wordsworth, William. Preface to the *Lyrical Ballads,* 2nd ed. (I. II.)

Yeats, W. B. *Autobiographies.* 1927. (V, VII.)

————, *Essays.* 1924. (V, VII.)

————, "Initiation Upon A Mountain," in *The Criterion*, London, July 1934. (VII.)

————, *The King of the Great Clock Tower*, Commentaries and Poems. 1935. (VII, IX.)

————, *Letters to the New Island*, ed. with an introd. by Horace Reynolds. 1934. (I, II, VII.)

————, *A Packet for Ezra Pound.* Dublin, 1929. (III, V, VII).

————, *Wheels and Butterflies.* 1935. (VII, IX.)

INDEX

281